(Il)liberal Europe: Islamophobia, Modernity and Radicalization

Europe sees itself as embodying the ideals of modernity, especially in relation to democracy and the respect for human rights. Faced on the one hand with the need for public recognition of a new population of Muslim identity, and the threat of violent radicalization on the other, Europe is falling prey to the politics of fear and is tempted to compromise on its professed ideals.

Reflecting on the manifestations and causes of the contemporary fear of Islam gaining ground in contemporary Europe, as well as on the factors contributing to the radicalization of some Muslims, *(Il)liberal Europe: Islamophobia, Modernity and Radicalization* offers a diversity of perspectives on both the challenges to social cohesion, and the danger of Islamophobia encouraging a spiral of co-radicalization. Combining empirical studies of several European countries with a comparative account of India and Europe, the book analyzes vital issues such as secularity, domophilia, de-politicization, neo-nationalism, the European unification project and more. Spanning a variety of disciplinary approaches, the volume offers novel insights into the complex landscape of identity politics in contemporary Europe to widen the scope of intellectual inquiry.

This book was originally published as a special issue of *Politics, Religion & Ideology*.

Natalie J. Doyle is Deputy Director of the Monash European and EU Centre, Monash University, Melbourne, Australia, and part of the editorial collective for the journal *Social Imaginaries*. She has researched European social and political thought, classical and contemporary, with particular reference to interpretations of modernity. She is particularly interested in the place of religion in modernity.

Irfan Ahmad is an anthropologist and Senior Research Fellow at the Max Planck Institute for the Study of Religious and Ethnic Studies in Gottingen, Germany. He is the author, most recently, of *Religion As Critique: Islamic Critical Thinking From Mecca to the Marketplace* and founding co-editor of the *Journal of Religious and Political Practice*.

(Il)liberal Europe: Islamophobia, Modernity and Radicalization

Edited by
Natalie J. Doyle and Irfan Ahmad

LONDON AND NEW YORK

First published 2018
by Routledge
2 Park Square, Milton Park, Abingdon, Oxon, OX14 4RN, UK

and by Routledge
711 Third Avenue, New York, NY 10017, USA

Routledge is an imprint of the Taylor & Francis Group, an informa business

© 2018 Taylor & Francis

All rights reserved. No part of this book may be reprinted or reproduced or utilised in any form or by any electronic, mechanical, or other means, now known or hereafter invented, including photocopying and recording, or in any information storage or retrieval system, without permission in writing from the publishers.

Trademark notice: Product or corporate names may be trademarks or registered trademarks, and are used only for identification and explanation without intent to infringe.

British Library Cataloguing in Publication Data
A catalogue record for this book is available from the British Library

ISBN 13: 978-0-415-78672-0

Typeset in Minion Pro
by RefineCatch Limited, Bungay, Suffolk

Publisher's Note
The publisher accepts responsibility for any inconsistencies that may have arisen during the conversion of this book from journal articles to book chapters, namely the possible inclusion of journal terminology.

Disclaimer
Every effort has been made to contact copyright holders for their permission to reprint material in this book. The publishers would be grateful to hear from any copyright holder who is not here acknowledged and will undertake to rectify any errors or omissions in future editions of this book.

Contents

Citation Information vii
Notes on Contributors ix

Introduction: Islamophobia, European Modernity and Contemporary Illiberalism 1
Natalie J. Doyle and Irfan Ahmad

1. 'Alien Religiosity' in Three Liberal European States 6
   Robert Gould

2. Swiss Shock: Minaret Rejection, European Values, and the Challenge of Tolerant Neutrality 26
   Douglas Pratt

3. Something Varied in the State of Denmark: Neo-nationalism, Anti-Islamic Activism, and Street-level Thuggery 41
   Mark Sedgwick

4. In Defense of Ho(s)tels: Islamophobia, Domophilia, Liberalism 67
   Irfan Ahmad

5. Islam and the Quest for a European Secular Identity: From Sovereignty through Solidarity to Immunity 85
   Armando Salvatore

6. Islam, Depoliticization and the European Crisis of Democratic Legitimacy 97
   Natalie J. Doyle

7. Radicalization in Prison: The French Case 116
   Farhad Khosrokhavar

8. Mohamed Merah: From Petty Criminal to Neojihadist 139
   Virginie Andre and Shandon Harris-Hogan

Index 153

Citation Information

The chapters in this book were originally published in *Politics, Religion & Ideology*, volume 14, issue 2 (June 2013). When citing this material, please use the original page numbering for each article, as follows:

Introduction
Islamophobia, European Modernity and Contemporary Illiberalism
Natalie J. Doyle and Irfan Ahmad
Politics, Religion & Ideology, volume 14, issue 2 (June 2013), pp. 167–172

Chapter 1
'Alien Religiosity' in Three Liberal European States
Robert Gould
Politics, Religion & Ideology, volume 14, issue 2 (June 2013), pp. 173–192

Chapter 2
Swiss Shock: Minaret Rejection, European Values, and the Challenge of Tolerant Neutrality
Douglas Pratt
Politics, Religion & Ideology, volume 14, issue 2 (June 2013), pp. 193–207

Chapter 3
Something Varied in the State of Denmark: Neo-nationalism, Anti-Islamic Activism, and Street-level Thuggery
Mark Sedgwick
Politics, Religion & Ideology, volume 14, issue 2 (June 2013), pp. 208–233

Chapter 4
In Defence of Ho(s)tels: Islamophobia, Domophilia, Liberalism
Irfan Ahmad
Politics, Religion & Ideology, volume 14, issue 2 (June 2013), pp. 234–252

Chapter 5
Islam and the Quest for a European Secular Identity: From Sovereignty through Solidarity to Immunity
Armando Salvatore
Politics, Religion & Ideology, volume 14, issue 2 (June 2013), pp. 253–264

CITATION INFORMATION

Chapter 6
Islam, Depoliticization and the European Crisis of Democratic Legitimacy
Natalie J. Doyle
Politics, Religion & Ideology, volume 14, issue 2 (June 2013), pp. 265–283

Chapter 7
Radicalization in Prison: The French Case
Farhad Khosrokhavar
Politics, Religion & Ideology, volume 14, issue 2 (June 2013), pp. 284–306

Chapter 8
Mohamed Merah: From Petty Criminal to Neojihadist
Virginie Andre and Shandon Harris-Hogan
Politics, Religion & Ideology, volume 14, issue 2 (June 2013), pp. 307–319

For any permission-related enquiries please visit:
http://www.tandfonline.com/page/help/permissions

Notes on Contributors

Irfan Ahmad is an anthropologist and Senior Research Fellow at the Max Planck Institute for the Study of Religious and Ethnic Studies in Gottingen, Germany. He is the author, most recently, of *Religion As Critique: Islamic Critical Thinking From Mecca to the Marketplace* and founding co-editor of the *Journal of Religious and Political Practice*.

Virginie Andre is a Research Fellow at the Alfred Deakin Institute, Faculty of Arts and Education, Deakin University, Melbourne, Australia.

Natalie J. Doyle is Deputy Director of the Monash European and EU Centre, Monash University, Melbourne, Australia, and part of the editorial collective for the journal *Social Imaginaries*. She has researched European social and political thought, classical and contemporary, with particular reference to interpretations of modernity. She is particularly interested in the place of religion in modernity.

Robert Gould is Adjunct Research Professor in Applied Linguistics and Discourse Studies at the School of Linguistics and Language Studies, Carleton University, Ottawa, Canada.

Shandon Harris-Hogan is an independent counter-extremism consultant, with experience working for both university and government organizations. He is a former Researcher at the Global Terrorism Research Centre, Monash University, Melbourne, Australia.

Farhad Khosrokhavar is Professor at the Ecole des Hautes Etudes en Sciences Sociales (EHESS), Paris, France. His research interests include political sociology, sociology of religion, contemporary Islam and Iran.

Douglas Pratt is Professor of Religion at the School of Social Sciences, University of Waikato, Hamilton, Waikato, New Zealand. He is also an Adjunct Professor of Theology and Interreligious Studies at the University of Bern, Switzerland, and Adjunct Associate Professor at the School of Social Sciences, Monash University, Melbourne, Australia.

Armando Salvatore is Professor of Global Religious Studies at the School of Religious Studies, McGill University, Montreal, Canada.

Mark Sedgwick is Professor of Arabic and Islam Studies at the School of Culture and Society, Aarhus University, Denmark.

INTRODUCTION

Islamophobia, European Modernity and Contemporary Illiberalism

NATALIE J. DOYLE and IRFAN AHMAD

Monash University

The term 'Islamophobia' has been gaining quite a prominence over recent years.[1] It has been used increasingly to refer to the rejection and discrimination from which the Muslim population in European societies has been suffering over two decades or so. The phenomenon in itself is far from new; but it was aggravated by the terrorist attacks of September 11, 2001 and the discourse of securitization these encouraged and consolidated. Consequently, the politics of fear came to dominate all public discussions. Since the onset of the global financial crisis, these politics seem to have acquired greater magnitude. A conservative British politician, Baroness Warsi, famously stated in 2011 that hostility to Islam had passed 'the dinner table test'.[2] Yet, the notion of Islamophobia (as well as those of liberalism and secularism connected to it; see below) is considerably elusive. Those who favour its employment find it analytically useful whereas those who don't regard it as no more than polemical.[3] Among those who find it particularly helpful are scholars who use it in the diverse contexts of race relations, working class experience, postcoloniality, intellectual and media discourses as well as past and contemporary politics, such as the volumes by Junaid Rana,[4] Esposito and Kalin,[5] and Gottschalk and Greenberg.[6]

This special issue of *Politics, Religion and Ideology* seeks to contribute to the academic debate on European Islamophobia by focusing on the paradox that characterizes the discourses used today to discuss the 'Muslim Question' in Europe: European identity presumably defined by its liberalism is invoked to justify *illiberal* attitudes. In some countries such attitudes have led to the introduction of juridical initiatives that curtail the religious rights

---

[1] On the history of this term and its contemporary usage, see Chris Allen, *Islamophobia* (Farnham: Ashgate, 2010); also see Marwan Muhammad, 'Islamophobia: A Deep-rooted Phenomenon', *Arches Quarterly*, 4:7 (Winter 2010), pp. 96–101.
[2] Jon Kelly, 'What is Baroness Warsi's "Dinner Table Test"?', *BBC*, 20 January 2011, http://www.bbc.co.uk/news/magazine-12240315 (accessed 20 February 2013).
[3] Salman Sayyid, 'Thinking Through Islamophobia' in Salman Sayyid and Abdool Karim Vakil (eds) *Thinking Through Islamophobia: Global Perspectives* (New York: Columbia University Press, 2010), p. 1.
[4] Junaid Rana, *Terrifying Muslims: Race and Labor in the South Asian Diaspora* (Durham and London: Duke University Press, 2011).
[5] John Espositio and Ibrahim Kalin (eds) *Islamophobia: The Challenge of Pluralism in the Twenty-first Century* (Oxford: Oxford University Press, 2011).
[6] Peter Gottschalk and Gabriel Greenberg, *Islamophobia: Making Muslims the Enemy* (Lanham: Rowman and Littlefield, 2007).

of Muslims in Europe. The contributions put together in this issue offer a diversity of perspectives on the trajectories of this paradox, illustrating the complexity of the very concept of Islamophobia and its multiple manifestations.

In most writings and public pronouncements, the term Islamophobia is taken to be a contemporary neologism; it is often traced back to the 1997 British report of the Runnymede Trust. However, some scholars chart a different genealogy of this term going as far back as nearly a century to the French imperial order.[7] One account shows it to have been most prominently used in its modern meaning first in French (*islamophobie*) toward the penultimate days of World War I. Using it in 1918 in their book *The Life of Muhammad – the Prophet of Allah*, Etienne Dinet (who embraced Islam in 1913 and took the name Naser-ed-din) and Sliman Ben Ibrahim consistently employed it for nearly two decades in their many works. What is at stake here, however, is not only a temporal or chronological issue but also a conceptual one. The efficacy or otherwise of a term is not predicated solely upon *when* it was used first, but also *how* it was and is used. That is, whether or not it has the analytical capacity and heuristic strength to explain and describe that which it names. Dinet and Ibrahim used it to underline Europe's hostility to Islam discussing as they did the roles of Islamophobes such as 'Gladstone, Cromer, Balfour, the Archbishop of Canterbury, and missionaries of all stripes'.[8] They critiqued what they called 'the pseudo-scientific Islamophobia' of the orientalists and the 'clerical Islamophobia' of the missionaries. Significantly, their book on the life of the Prophet was dedicated 'to the memory of Muslims who died for France'. Whilst pledging their loyalty to the French state, they also critiqued France's failure to recognize the sacrifice of Muslims and to acknowledge the right of all Algerians to partake of full French citizenship. Recognising the hegemonic political formation which Dinet and Ibrahim named as Islamophobia has an important bearing in contemporary times as well. Is the recent (January 2013) French military intervention in Mali to fight 'terrorism' totally unhooked from Islamophobia? Clearly, it is not. Precisely at the same time the military intervention was decided, the French president François Hollande ordered national security to be brought to its highest level, something that was not without effect on his popularity levels.[9] This would tend to suggest that the west's ceaseless search for culturally 'good' Muslims and its crackdown on politically 'bad' Muslims, as Mamdani noted early on, needs serious re-examination.[10]

Many contributions in this issue touch upon the contradictions of French Republicanism, contradictions anchored in history and the decisions made by the state elites at the end of the nineteenth century to pursue colonial expansion whilst proclaiming fidelity to the tryptich of 'liberty, equality, fraternity'. The early twentieth century saw traditional Christian missionary attitudes being put at the service of colonial domination and these attitudes are still evident in contemporary European forms of hostility towards Muslims, as is apparent in the case of Denmark discussed here by Mark Sedgwick. The early twentieth century, however, also saw in France the emergence of a particularly strong form of political secularism whose presumed cultural uniqueness is conveyed through the use of the French term *laïcité*. The laws defining the place of religion in French society are touched upon in a

---

[7] Abdool Karim Vakil 'When is it Islamophobia Time' in Salman Sayyid and Abdool Karim Vakil (eds) *Thinking Through Islamophobia: Global Perspectives* (New York: Columbia University Press, 2010), pp. 33–41.
[8] Abdool Karim Vakil, op. cit., pp. 39–40.
[9] France 24 International News, 'France Orders Tighter Security in the Wake of Mali Intervention', 13 January 2013, http://www.france24.com/en/20130112-france-hollande-orders-tighter-security-mali-operation; Bloomberg, 'Hollande Popularity Gains After Mali Intervention, Poll Shows', 29 January 2012, http://www.bloomberg.com/news/2013-01-29/hollande-popularity-gains-after-mali-intervention-poll-shows.html.
[10] Mahmood Mamdani, *Good Muslim, Bad Muslim: America, the Cold War, and the Roots of Terror* (New York: Pantheon Book, 2004).

number of articles to highlight the way anti-Muslim illiberalism also draws on the self-perception and imaginary of the secular character of European societies, imaginary that has become associated with the notion of European identity in a way that subsumes their national identities. New forms of legislations have been debated and introduced across Belgium, France and Germany – Robert Gould's contribution discusses them at length in a comparative framework – with a view to preserving national cultures presumably threatened by Muslim experiences of religious faith. Interestingly, Gould observes that whereas in the case of Germany and France it is the state which supposedly stands threatened by the Muslims' presence, in the case of Belgium the stress is put less on the state and more on society and its values. This can perhaps be related to the contemporary weakness of the Belgian nation state threatened by Flemish secession. The articles in this issue thus engage with the political form that unfolded in Europe and came to dominate the world: the nation state.

Whilst all contributions engage with the diversity of political cultures engendered by the various European states and characterized by different modes of secularity, many also stress the existence of a common cultural logic behind European Islamophobia or what Sedgwick prefers to call anti-Muslim activism. Armando Salvatore and Irfan Ahmad seek to explain this common mechanism and logic that stresses the *longue durée* of European modernization and asserts that Islamophobia was a constitutive element of liberalism. Whilst Salvatore stresses the process of cultural immunization that concealed the survival of the Christian tradition in the self-definition of a new, secular form of society, Ahmad coins the expression *domophilia* – love for home identified with a cultural-territorial nation state – to examine the reconfiguration of the religious quest for a spiritual home into nationalist devotion to the secular nation state and highlights the violence implicit in European liberalism.

Other contributions place emphasis on the recent transformation of the European nation states as a result of both the European project of integration and globalization. Whilst Sedgwick highlights the role played by neo-nationalist politics in the spread of anti-Muslim attitudes, Doyle shifts the analytical gaze to the vital role played by elites in promoting a definition of European identity that has accentuated the de-politicization of European national societies and inspired initiatives to find a political purpose through a fetishist attachment to liberal values. This quest for a political project on the basis of an ideological reading of European history has re-activated hostility towards Islam through the illusion that the defence of liberal values can alone recreate a social cohesion lost over previous decades. Douglas Pratt's paper focuses on the success of the Swiss referendum banning the construction of minarets. The peculiarities of the Swiss political system enabled minority anti-Islamic activism to seize the initiative simply because it activated people to vote. Notwithstanding the negative image of Islam in the Swiss media and politics, Pratt optimistically predicts that the law banning minarets might be changed – through legal initiative, or under pressure from international public opinion – in future because such precedence exists in relation to the ban on the rights of Catholics to establish new dioceses.

In this special issue we have collected contributions which make a fine, productive balance between empirically grounded studies on the one hand and theoretical reflections on the other. These two sets of contributions shed light on one another. As a whole, the issue draws attention to the fact that the phenomenon of Islamophobia is inextricably bound up with the limited, skewed understanding that Europeans have of their own historical formations, and of their related cultural coordinates and political matrix. Their understanding of Islam is likewise limited and skewed, as pointed out by Jacques Derrida who, shortly before his death, underlined 'the need to deconstruct the European intellectual construct of Islam'.[11] While Salvatore and Doyle share a similar understanding of the history of secularity, they offer different assessments of its place in the history of European modernity up to the present. Whereas Salvatore's approach inscribes itself in the tradition of Foucault with its specific interpretation of secularity as an epistemic category central to the advent of modern governmentality, Doyle stresses the limitations of the very notion of governmentality and instead highlights the importance or the contemporary sociocultural context which has enabled Islamophobia. In particular, she discusses how the demotic forms of politics manifest, among others, in the labour movement was gradually eroded from above under the banner of the project of European unification, giving rise to new politics of populism. She gainfully connects this transformation in European politics – which she analyses as part of a de-politicisation also induced by new forms of individualism – with the acceleration of the processes of globalization. Mapping the simultaneous catalogues of nation and civilization, Ahmad reads Islamophobia differently. Comparing Islamophobia in India and Europe, he maintains that while in India Muslims for over two centuries have been made to serve as both historical symbolic and empirical 'Other' of the nation, in the west Muslims also became an empirical, non-distant 'Other', but only after World War II, with their migration as cheap, docile labour from the colonies. Analysing the long-term transformation of the world though colonization and associated forms of nationalism, he suggests that the anxiety about the putative lack of integration by Muslims in Europe is possibly reminiscent of the chosen segregation Europeans themselves practised in their vast colonies.

That the fear which Islam inspires among Europeans is that of Europe's own past of illiberal violence and religious fanaticism has forcefully been made by Werbner.[12] This fear reactivated by the so-called 'Islamic terrorism' became that of those 'enemies' hiding within European societies and bent on destroying the permissive liberal society. As various media reports and government documents show, many terrorists linked to various attacks were born or educated in Europe. In his sociologically rich contribution based on extensive fieldwork in various prisons of France, Farhad Khosrokhavar shows how the imprisoned radical Muslims – the percentage of Muslims in jail is unusually higher than their national percentage – lead their lives in jails. With great skills, he details how a combination of factors such as infrastructural inadequacies, the prejudices of the prison authorities as perceived by the jailed radicals, their enhanced sense of religiosity during confinement and the relations they forge with one another may strengthen their radicalization and provide them with a context in which they can bring others to espouse their violent interpretation of Islam, a phenomenon noted in the article by Virginie Andre and Shandon Harris-Hogan devoted to the recent terrorist attacks committed by Mohamed Merah.

Andre and Harris-Hogan examine the changing face of violent radicalization in France from the perspective of the biographical trajectory of Merah, his relationships to his parents and siblings, as well as his transnational connections. This focus on the microcosm of family is very important. It must however also be situated within the macrocosm of geo-political objectives: the rise of Algerian terrorism followed the cancellation by the military of the 1992 elections, cancellation approved, *inter alia*, by the French government. The article highlights the role of family as the locus within which the complex interaction of socio-economic marginalization and cultural alienation has bred feelings of victimization that provide a fertile ground for the Jihadist ideology. It ends on the

---

[11] Mustpha Cherif, *Islam and the West: A Conversation with Jacques Derrida* (Chicago: Chicago University Press, 2008), p. 38.
[12] P. Werbner 'Islamophobia: Incitement to Religious Hatred – Legislating for a New Fear?', *Anthropology Today*, 21:1 (2005), pp. 5–9.

central paradox characterizing Merah's destiny: he was both a son of the French Republic and its enemy.

In this respect, his trajectory manifested the same aspirations to subjective autonomy shared by all French Muslim youth, aspirations which contributed to the revival of Muslim piety apparent in French society. Andre and Harris-Hogan's article thus connects with the point made in different ways by Khosrokhavar and Doyle regarding the incapacity of French society to understand the significance of the new forms of piety embraced by many young French Muslims in the form of non-violent Salafism. This form of Salafism, discussed by Khosrokhavar as *Sheikhi* Salafism as opposed to Jihadi Salafits, functions today in France very much like forms of puritanical Christian evangelism, creating self-sufficient communities that cut themselves off deliberately from the rest of society. Here lies another paradox: this purist version of Islam, which has been taken by French authorities to be totally synonymous with violent radicalization, has in fact changed the face of Muslim faith, in a way that has contained the potential for the legitimate grievances of Muslims to translate into support for the Jihadist cause. The novelty of Salafism in French society, however, has fuelled the politics of fear that have added to the wounded subjective aspirations of many French young Muslims.

The question of subjective autonomy is central to the discussion of Islamophobia. All the articles in this issue share a common awareness of the way contemporary European Islamophobia reveals the failure of European liberal modernity to live up to its promises when it comes to affording Muslims the conditions of subjective autonomy. Whilst they offer different interpretations of the causes behind this failure they exhibit a similar concern for the consequences of the ideological understanding of liberalism now gaining prominence across Europe. As John Gray reminds us, European liberal values were first and foremost the historical *modus vivendi* within which European religious differences were reconciled.[13] Treating them as a superior source of truth defining a single best way of life can only engender the reappearance of violence in a continent that praised itself on having transcended it.

Acknowledgments

This issue is the outcome of a conference held on 16 and 17 June 2011 at the Prato centre of Monash University, Italy: 'Globalization, Illiberalism and Islam: Perspectives from Europe and Australia'. The conference was supported by the Monash European and EU Centre, a joint undertaking by the European Commission of the European Union (EU) and Monash University. The participation of Robert Gould was funded from the grant from the European Commission to the Centre for European Studies of Carleton University, Ottawa. As co-editors we wish to thank Derya Dilara for her valuable help in organizing the conference and Virginie Andre for all the practical support given during the preparation of this journal issue. We also wish to acknowledge the intellectual support of Greg Barton, Acting Director, Centre for Islam and the Modern World, Monash University. Finally, we thank the participants to the conference and all Australian, European and American academics who found the time to act as anonymous referees. Their feedback was most valuable.

---

[13]John Gray, *Two Faces of Liberalism* (Cambridge: Polity Press, 2000).

'Alien Religiosity' in Three Liberal European States

ROBERT GOULD

Carleton University

ABSTRACT *Starting from an indication of the problematic nature of the relationship between religion and the state, this paper examines political debates on the headscarf and face veil in three liberal states – Germany, France, and Belgium – between 2003 and 2011. It shows the significant commonalities – despite both the different arrangements between religion and the state and also despite the radically different political, social, and linguistic situations in these countries. The political debates are hostile and assert that fundamental values closely related to national identity, societal values, and human rights are threatened by what the headscarf or face veil represents. The similarity of argumentation shows that, whether the country has a doctrine of* laïcité *or is more overt about the links between religion and the state, the liberalism of each has reached the limits of the 'alien religiosity' which politicians say their country can bear.*

> How much alien religiosity can our society bear? (Winfried Hassemer, Chief Justice, Second Chamber of the Federal Constitutional Court, Germany)[1]
>
> The de-facto existence of a multicultural society represents one of the fundamental challenges in any consideration of the relationship between religion and politics, particularly in those parts of the world in which this question was previously considered settled. (Michael Minkenberg and Ulrich Willems)[2]
>
> At a time when globalisation is blurring certain markers, it is incumbent on us to ensure the protection of the values and principles on which our social compact is built. (Michèle Alliot-Marie, Minister of Justice and Freedoms, France)[3]

---

[1] 'Wieviel fremde Religiosität verträgt unsere Gesellschaft?' Widely reported in the media, e.g., 'Eine Lehrerin mit Kopftuch oder die Frage des wahren Islams', *Frankfurter Allgemeine Zeitung für Deutschland*, 3 June 2003. The court's decision on this fundamental German headscarf case – BVerfG, 2 BvR 1436/02 vom 3.6.2003 – is to be found at http://www.bverfg.de/entscheidungen/rs20030924_2bvr143602.htm. All translations of statements, speeches, documents, reports and scholarly writing originally in Dutch, French or German are by the author.

[2] U. Willems and M. Minkenberg, 'Politik und Religion im Übergang – Tendenzen und Forschungsfragen am Beginn des 21. Jahrhunderts' in U. Minkenberg and M. Willems (eds) *Politik und Religion* (Wiesbaden: Westdeutscher Verlag, 2003), pp. 13–44: p. 33.

[3] Jean-Paul Garraud, *Rapport fait au nom de la Commission des lois constitutionnelles, de la législation et de l'administration générale de la République sur le projet de loi (n° 2520), interdisant la dissimulation du visage dans l'espace public* (Paris: Assemblée Nationale, 23 June 2010), p. 29, http://www.assemblee-nationale.fr/13/rapports/r2648.asp.

(IL)LIBERAL EUROPE: ISLAMOPHOBIA, MODERNITY AND RADICALIZATION

Introduction

While in Belgium, France, and Germany there is no broad public policy of 'multiculturalism', it is quite clear that each of them contains a multicultural society in the important sense that each has received over the past 50 or even 60 years a significant number of newcomers from parts of Europe, North Africa and the Middle East where Islam is the prevailing religion. These newcomers and their descendants are disparate in their languages, origins, religious practices, and degrees of observance. This paper will consider the arguments made in connection with the legal process of prohibiting the wearing of certain women's garments which hide the hair or face. But behind this there are much broader questions pertaining to national identity in the changing circumstances of the early twenty-first century, questions summarised in the title and introduction of the special number of the *Journal of Ethnic and Migration Studies*, 'Limits of the Liberal State: Migration, Identity and Belonging in Europe'.[4] At the same time there are equally difficult questions concerning the governance of Islam in European countries where, to speak with the opening words of Maussen's *The Governance of Islam in Western Europe: A State of the Art Report*,[5] 'Islam has become a part of the landscape of European societies'. However, in these societies the existing structures of relations between the state and institutions of religion: (a) have developed over a long period of time; (b) are related to the organisational structures of Christian denominations; and (c) were frequently achieved only after significant friction. But with Islam the situation is new, the organisational structures are different, the friction also very evident. Maussen's overview of topics which require attention includes headscarves, but without details on the German debates. Because of its publication date (2007) his paper does not address face veils, which entered the legislative arena only later. Court decisions on Muslim dress, which form a background to the debates in France and Belgium, are explored in Shadid and Koningsveld (2005).[6] After consideration of some of the difficulties encountered in attempts to regulate religion in a modern liberal society, and against the background of the German Federal Constitutional Court's decision on headscarves worn by public servants, this article addresses the parliamentary debates in Belgium and France concerning bills to outlaw other items of female Muslim dress in public places.

The German headscarf case of 2003 initially centred on the desire of a civil servant to wear a headscarf in the performance of her duties. Some of the issues which were raised in this connection are related to the particular position of civil servants in Germany. Some, however, are much wider in their implications: gender equality, the relationship between religion and the state, personal liberties, individual development, the reconciliation of private and public interests, and challenges even to the state itself. All these were of direct relevance for the parliamentary debates in France and Belgium in 2010 and 2011 preceding the enactment of laws to ban face veils in all public places. All of them go to the heart of the question posed by Justice Hassemer, of the 'challenges' noted by Minkenberg and Willems, and of the impact of globalisation on national social norms, about which the French Minister of Justice and Individual Freedoms expressed concern.

One of the 'challenges' as defined by Minkenberg and Willems lies in the fact that in the cases of Belgium and France the arguments are based on the implicit or explicit premise that the absolute norm in society and human development is, as Bramadat says, 'an

---

[4] 37:6 (2011). See particularly F. Adamson, T. Triadafilopoulos and A. Zolberg, 'The Limits of the Liberal State: Migration, Identity and Belonging in Europe', pp. 843–859.
[5] M. Maussen, Imiscoe Working Paper 16 (Amsterdam: IMES/University of Amsterdam, 2007).
[6] W. Shadid and P. van Koningsveld, 'Muslim Dress in Europe: Debates on the Headscarf', *Journal of Islamic Studies*, 16:1 (2005), pp. 35–61.

ineluctable drive to individual autonomy and reason'.[7] This autonomy implies also freedom from particular religious prescriptions. There is also the (implicit) view that religion is, or should be, private and benevolent. German, French, and Belgian politicians consistently make the argument that the Muslim religious practices in question are malevolent to both private – in the sense of personal – and public well-being, where 'public' refers to one or both society and state. The arguments represent, equally, a total disconnect with the conception of religion held sincerely by many believers: that it is religion which gives an over-arching meaning to both individual and group life, and that this meaning is manifest in the subordination to certain divinely-ordained precepts which reduce or even remove individual choice and autonomy.

A further dimension of the potential and real tensions between religion and the state is outlined by Nikola Tietze.[8] Speaking of Europe and its institutions and referring to semantic fields, she defined the overall contours of religion in Europe in the following way: at one and the same time religion forms part of Europe and is also Europe's 'Other'. It is a fundamental defining feature in the sense of European cultural heritage, as a component of identity and origin, and also an ethical contribution to social life. In its institutionalised form and as belief, religion is the 'Other' to which, in certain circumstances, European politics has to ensure protection, whereas, as a political force, it represents the 'Other' which must be excluded.

The principal arguments for placing restrictions on clothing relating to Muslim beliefs are (on the surface) rational arguments attempting to deal with what is fundamentally not rational – belief and its manifestations. In connection with state discourses on religion, Koenig has spoken of 'adherents of secular public reason'.[9] However, the appeal to the non-rational is fundamental to political discourse and is evident in what I shall be considering. There, behind the quasi-rational arguments, is a significant rhetorical appeal to emotion; it is also prominent in the dissenting opinion of the Federal Constitutional Court in Germany, which played an important role in the political process following the decision. And also at the heart of all the debates are questions of national identity in the face of immigration and the 'alien' religion it has brought with it.

Here lies the particular difficulty immediately perceptible in the statement by Justice Hassemer. He speaks of *alien* religiosity and *our* society, thus immediately creating a dichotomy, and a problem, through the way that he presents the situation. It should be noted that the social and religious situation cannot be characterised in this dichotomous manner without distorting the position of Islam in Germany in 2003 (and in France and Belgium in 2010 and 2011). At the time of the utterance, Muslims had been present in Germany in ever-growing numbers for 40 years, with the result that in 2003 it was the religion of the native-born second and even third generations. Hassemer's statement denies this fact and can be characterised as stigmatising it. This stigmatisation is heightened by the use of the verb *vertragen*, which has the sense of 'endure', 'bear'. The 'alien religiosity' is thus not only 'foreign', 'external' or 'other', but it is painful, debilitating, and even harmful. As will be shown, the rhetoric of harm is absolutely fundamental to the parliamentary debates in all three countries considered in this study and reflects a widespread popular

---

[7] P. Bramadat, 'Religious Diversity and International Migration: National and Global Dimensions' in Paul Bramadat and Matthias Koenig (eds) *International Migration and the Governance of Religious Diversity* (Montreal: McGill-Queen's UP, 2009), pp. 1–26.

[8] N. Tietze, 'Religionssemantiken in europäischen Institutionen – politische Dynamiken einer semantischen Topographie' in Matthias Koenig and Jean-Paul Willaime (eds) *Religionskontroversen in Frankreich und Deutschland* (Hamburg: Hamburger Edition, 2008), pp. 400–443.

[9] M. Koenig, 'How Nation-States Respond to Religious Diversity', in Bramadat and Koenig, op. cit., pp. 293–322: p. 317.

discourse. In the German case it is surveyed, for example, by Patrick Bahners in his book with the title (translated) *The Fearmongers: The German Fear of Islam. A Polemic*,[10] which was meant as a response to Thilo Sarrazin's bestseller (approximately 1.5 million copies sold by the spring of 2013) with the title (in translation) *Germany's Road to Ruin. How We Are Putting Our Nation At Risk*.[11] For the neighbouring country of Denmark, Sedgwick's article in this issue provides relevant information on the development of neo-nationalism and Islamophobia, while Pratt analyses similar developments in Switzerland.

One important factor in relation to national (and European) identity is the position of Christianity.[12] In Germany the link between religion and identity has been explicit from the inception of the Federal Republic. In his first statement of fundamental policies to the *Bundestag* on 20 September 1949 Konrad Adenauer said 'our whole labours will be carried forward by the spirit of Christian-Occidental culture and respect for law and human dignity'.[13] Berghahn et al. mention that five states have included a clause which defines 'Christian-Occidental values' as fully compatible with state neutrality in their legislation banning headscarves.[14] And in a headscarf case in 2007, and referring to a Federal Constitutional Court case of 1975, the Hessian Supreme Court made the following statement:

> [Christian] means, notwithstanding its religious origin, a core set of values separate from the religious beliefs themselves but originating in Christian-Occidental culture; this set of values also clearly forms the basis of the Federal Constitution, and due regard should be given to it quite independently of its religious foundation.[15]

At the same time, the urging from different quarters to include references to Christianity in the European Constitutional Treaty of 2004 may be considered testimony to the continuing power of the argument that Christianity is inseparable from Europe and its identity, including even France with its doctrine of *laïcité* (separation of religion and state guaranteeing the free exercise of the former within the limits of public policy).[16]

Against this background, and across diverse political arrangements between religion and the state in the three countries, what I wish to demonstrate are the commonalities between the German case of 2003–2005 on the one hand, and the French and Belgian cases of 2010 and 2011. Some of these can be ascribed to thinking on individual rights, some to shared

---

[10]*Die Panikmacher: Die deutsche Angst vor dem Islam: Eine Streitschrift* (Munich: C.H. Beck: 2011); see particularly chapters 3 and 5.

[11]*Deutschland schafft sich ab: Wie wir unser Land aufs Spiel setzen* (Berlin: dva, 2010).

[12]In this connection, see also Sedgwick on Denmark in this issue.

[13]Konrad Adenauer to the first *Bundestag*: *Deutscher Bundestag. Stenographisches Protokoll der 5. Sitzung*, Bonn, Dienstag, den 20. September 1949, pp. 22–30.

[14]Sabine Berghahn, Gül Çorbacioglu, Petra Rostock and Maria Eleonora Sanna, 'In the Name of Laicité and Neutrality: Prohibitive Regulations of the Veil in France, Germany and Turkey' in Sieglinde Rosenberger and Birgit Sauer (eds) *Politics, Religion and Gender: Framing and Regulating the Veil* (Routledge: London and New York, 2012), pp. 150–168.

[15]*Staatsgerichtshof des Landes Hessen*, 10 December 2007: P.St. 2016; see also *Bayerischer Verfassungsgerichtshof* [Bavarian Constitutional Court], 15 January 2007: Vf. 11-VII-05.

[16]G. Delanty, 'Dilemmas of Secularism: Europe, Religion and the Problem of Pluralism' in Gerard Delanty, Ruth Wodak and Paul Jones (eds) *Identity, Belonging and Migration* (Liverpool: Liverpool University Press, 2008), pp. 78–100: 87; M. de Leeuw and S. van Wichelen 'Transformation of "Dutchness": From Happy Multiculturalism to the Crisis of Dutch Liberalism', ibid., pp. 261–278: pp. 269–270. Jean-Paul Willaime, *Europe et religions: Les enjeux du XXI siècle* (Paris: Fayard, 2004), pp. 100 and 106. Robert Gould, 'Rejection by Implication: Christian Parties on German Identity in 2001–2002', *Seminar: A Journal of Germanic Studies*, 48:3 (2012), pp. 397–412.

views of Islam as the political and cultural 'Other', some to a community of language providing easy access to certain thought patterns despite different political cultures, and many to awareness of what functions well rhetorically and politically. The common element is that they are, in fact, arguments of rejection tailored to fit the particular political and constitutional circumstances of each country.

Secondly, what is also common to both the debates and the legislation in all three countries is the fact that the simple act of wearing the garment in question is sufficient to place the wearer beyond the law. Whatever her political and social views, the woman who wishes to wear a headscarf during working hours may not become a civil servant in the German states which have legislated against the garment. In France and Belgium a woman covering her face is banned entirely from all public places, including all *legal* activities. In no case is loyalty to the state and its principles a defence. And in all cases the argument of gender equality and women's rights trumps that of personal autonomy and free choice. In other words, as Bahners points out, the legal principle that no impediment should be placed in the way of women has been reinterpreted and solidified in a statutory form whereby the state *enforces* a particular view of equality[17] – even against the wishes of independent and strong-willed women in particular segments of the employment market. Furthermore it is a view of equality whereby the state discriminates against, and in Belgium and France criminalises, a visible manifestation of religiosity.

Next, there is the position of language in the formation and expression of national identity. In her seminal work on Austrian identity, Wodak wrote, 'as a special form of social practice, discourse occupies a central position both in the formation and the articulation of national identity'. And specifically, as I shall be referring to language at the centre of political debates, 'part of discursive practice becomes solidified as law. As institutionalised discursive practice, laws create a binding framework for the social practices of political inclusion and exclusion',[18] and, one must add, *social* inclusion and exclusion.

It is important to demarcate just what types of dress are under discussion: sometimes the terminology is unclear, and sometimes it is deliberately made unclear. As mentioned, in the case of Germany the matter before the court turned around the wearing of a headscarf by a civil servant. However, in their emotionally-charged minority opinion the three dissenting justices sought to obfuscate the issue by using the term *Verschleierung* (veiling, §118) – with the primary meaning of something obscuring the face – and repeatedly *Verhüllung* (enveloping and hiding the contours of the whole body),[19] and even *Verhüllung des Gesichts* (hiding the face) (§123). In France and Belgium politicians very frequently use the term *burqa*, though the text of the legislation in both countries prohibits only covering the face and does not use any term such as *niqab*, *burqa*, *chador*, etc. Similarly they use *le voile intégral*, and in Belgium also the synonymous *de allesbedekkende sluier* (the veil covering everything).[20]

---

[17]Bahners, op. cit., p.116. A similar view is expressed by Cesari in connection with the French prohibition of headscarves in publicly-financed schools: 'Islam, Immigration and France', Bramadat and Koenig, op. cit., pp. 195–224.

[18]Ruth Wodak, Rudolf de Cillia, Martin Reisigl, Karin Liebhart, Klaus Hofstätte and Maria Kargl, *Zur diskursiven Konstruktion nationaler Identität* (Frankfurt/Main: Suhrkamp, 1998), p. 70.

[19] Birgit Sauer's claim that some German states have prohibited 'all forms of Muslim body coverings in public institutions' is contrary to fact and obfuscates the issue: 'Headscarf Regimes in Europe: Diversity Policies at the Intersection of Gender, Culture and Religion', *Comparative European Politics*, 7:1 (2009), pp. 75–94. In fact, only headscarves on public servants on duty have been outlawed in those states.

[20]It is important to note that the French term *le voile intégral* [literally: complete veil] is sufficiently vague as to refer to the face veil *and* to the *burqa* or *niqab*. Because it can mean so much more than 'face veil' (as the politicians well knew) the original term will be used throughout, and not translated.

Germany

In their attempt to deal constructively with the new phenomenon of headscarves worn by civil servants, the Federal Constitutional Court decided (a) that civil servants may wear a headscarf on duty, but (b) that the practice could be banned if states wished – though only on the basis of a clear law treating all religions and denominations equally.

What is important to emphasise is that the majority justices avoid any conceptualisations or arguments which present either the appellant, or her values, or the value system possibly represented by the headscarf, in a way which would construct a fundamental opposition between German constitutional, social, and political values on the one hand and non-German value and cultural systems on the other. In stating that the headscarf *is* admissible in the public service, the majority justices are admitting it to what Koopmans has called a 'position of high symbolic value and public visibility' which has 'a positive political and cultural connotation'.[21] For them, this manifestation of 'alien religiosity' can be reconciled with the liberal democratic state. Subsequently if a state does wish to ban it, then it must put Islam on an absolutely equal footing with all other religions and ban their symbols, too. The justices are arguing for a significant shift in German identity, including a reorganisation of private and public religiosity. They are, in fact, suggesting a policy of very broad liberal social engineering: a change on the part of the whole of the population, reflected in the acceptance of a visible sign of Islam in the public administration. However, as Wiese shows, the subsequent legislation did not provide for this acceptance of Islam.[22] It reflects the hostility perceptible, for example, in Kelek[23] and Sarrazin.[24] (A scholarly discussion of this hostility and the position of Muslims in Germany is found in Spielhaus.)[25] The fundamental question 'How much consensus on values does our society need?' was addressed by Schiffauer in his book *Parallelgesellschaften* (*Parallel Societies*), in which he pleaded for 'avoidance of the one-sided stylisation which so dominates the debates'.[26] Although he was writing about Germany in the period before 2007, it will be shown that this unbalanced approach also characterised the subsequent debates in Belgium and France.

The dissenting opinion in the case was very different, and can be summarised by the following points:

---

[21]R. Koopmans, 'Germany and its Immigrants: An Ambivalent Relationship', *Journal of Ethnic and Migration Studies*, 25:4 (1999), pp. 627–647.

[22]K. Wiese, 'Grenzen der Religionsfreiheit ausloten: Zur Diskussion über Kopftuch- und Burkaverbote in Deutschland und Europa' in E. Ariens, H. König and M. Sicking (eds) *Glaubensfragen in Europa: Religion und Politik im Konflikt* (Bielefeld: transcript, 2011), pp. 87–126.

[23]N. Kelek, *Die fremde Braut: Ein Bericht aus dem Inneren des türkischen Lebens in Deutschland* (Cologne: Kiepenheuer & Witsch, 2007). Her view is that Turkish social and family customs and practices are archaic and that 'Turkish religiosity does not mean just membership in a religious community, it means also submission to a whole set of social restrictions which are rooted in the past and which, despite the influence of modernity, are passed on from generation to generation' (p. 243).

[24]T. Sarrazin, *Deutschland schafft sich ab: Wie wir unser Land aufs Spiel setzen* (Berlin: dva, 2010). His fundamental objections are: the low participation of Muslims in the labour market, below-average educational levels, above-average delinquency levels, the dominant theology of Islam is hostile to the whole of Enlightenment thinking and consequently remains pre-modern; Islam in general has a difficult relationship with modernity (esp. pp. 276–280). In his view the presence of Islam in Germany is a threat to German cultural and European identity (p. 308).

[25]R. Spielhaus, *Wer ist hier Muslim? Die Entwicklung eines islamischen Bewusstseins in Deutschland zwischen Selbstidentifikation und Fremdzuschreibung* (Würzburg: Ergon-Verlag, 2011).

[26]W. Schiffauer, *Parallelgesellschaften: Wie viel Wertekonsens braucht unsere Gesellschaft? Für eine kluge Politik der Differenz* (Bielefeld: transcript verlag, 2008).

- The argumentation in the dissenting opinion is based on the related concepts of danger and conflict.
- The headscarf, face veil, and body covering are contrary to human dignity (a very powerful argument as Article 1 of the Federal Constitution specifies 'Human dignity shall be inviolable. To respect and protect it shall be the duty of all state authority').
- It is contrary to the equal rights provision of Article 3 of the Federal Constitution, which is fundamental to society and state.
- It is in contradiction with a 'modern, open-minded and principled public servant'.
- It is a symbol of an intolerant culture, with an implied association with Nazism.
- It is a symbol of Islamic political fundamentalism, and therefore cannot be neutral.
- It is incompatible with the liberal democratic state.
- It has already been a source of conflict in the school and with parents, and represents a dangerous source of future conflict.
- In Germany there exists 'a social environment which strongly rejects the headscarf'.

The final point incorporates a whole extra-legal and non-theoretical dimension into the judicial argument, effectively legitimising en-bloc prejudice against a very varied group. To summarise: the basic position of the dissenting justices is that they are convinced of the irreconcilable opposition of what Busse has called *das Eigene und das Fremde* (native and alien).[27] They are thinking in terms of fundamental evaluative criteria which are subject to a tendency towards the creation of sharp contrasts and which, as we shall see for the debates, consequently lead to the creation of contrasting and irreconcilable clichés.[28] On the basis of its terminology, vehemence, and the nature of its argumentation chains, particularly the repeated use of the native/alien dichotomy, and of the threat topos, the minority opinion is in my view a highly political text, repeating also significant points of the popular street-level anti-headscarf discourse.[29] One might hypothesise that it was deliberately written in such a way in order to contribute to the series of political debates which the justices knew would immediately follow.

That the minority judges' arguments were used politically is quite clear. The consistent position which came to dominate the political debates in the states where anti-headscarf bills were introduced by the Christian Democratic Union and the Christian Social Union, and which was even adopted by the Social Democrats in Bremen and the Sarre, can be summarised by reference to statements in the bill in Baden-Wurtemberg introduced on 14 January 2004. It is later used verbatim or nearly verbatim in the rationale for bills presented by the Christian Democrats to a number of state parliaments. Wearing a headscarf is not permissible:

> ... because at least some of those who support [it] associate it with both a subordinate position of women in society, state, and family that is incompatible with Articles 1 and Paragraphs 2 and 3 of Article 3 of the Federal Constitution, and also with an aggressive fundamentalist position in favour of a theocratic state in

---

[27] D. Busse, 'Das Eigene und das Fremde: Annotationen zu Funktion und Wirkung einer diskurssemantischen Grundfigur' in Matthias Jung, Martin Wengeler and Karin Böke (eds) *Die Sprache des Migrationsdiskurses: Das Reden über 'Ausländer' in Medien, Politik und Alltag* (Opladen: Westdeutscher Verlag, 1997), pp. 17–35.
[28] Gerd-Klaus Kaltenbrunner, *Sprache und Herrschaft: Die umfunktionierten Wörter* (Munich: Herder, 1975), pp. 44–54.
[29] Examples in Siegfried Jäger et al., *Brandsätze: Rassismus im Alltag* (Duisburg: DISS, 1996); Alexander Häusler (ed.) *Rechtspopulismus als 'Bürgerbewegung': Kampagnen gegen Islam und Moscheebau und kommunale Gegenstrategien* (Wiesbaden: VS Verlag für Sozialwissenschaften, 2008).

contradiction of the fundamental values of Article 20 of the Federal Constitution.[30]

Article 20 guarantees that Germany shall be a democratic federal state with separation of powers, based on the concept of popular sovereignty. Consequently the statement is also a group-condemnation which implies that wearers may be guilty of subversion of the very foundations of the state. Similar arguments will be seen as having been used also in both Belgium and France.

The rationales presented with the bills include the following emphases on the position of Christianity in society and state:[31]

- The mention of Christianity in Constitutions and Education Acts of some states.
- The implication that the 'Christian-Occidental' (*christlich-abendländisch*) values in the Education Acts are all totally absent from the Islamic world (implying that they are alien to Muslims in Germany).
- Such 'Christian-Occidental' values are stated to be essential to 'carry out the tasks of the state' (e.g., state of Hesse).
- All Christian denominations and Jewish congregations support constitutional values.
- The headscarf is a political symbol.
- The insistence on community standards for judging the headscarf: i.e., public perception is the standard, rather than the wearer's intentions and convictions.
- Symbols relating to local tradition 'strongly influenced by Christianity and humanism' are permitted.

Two things emerge from this: (a) the headscarf and Islam are incompatible with the liberal state; and (b) these Christianity-based arguments are being made at a time of dropping church membership in Germany as a whole (27 per cent non-members in 1997, lower now),[32] and that they were *not* made by governing parties in the states on the territory of the ex-German Democratic Republic, where Christian religious affiliation is particularly low (only 25–30 per cent of the population) and where Muslims are present in much lesser proportions. This would argue in favour of the view that the political instrumentalisation of the issue was enacted on purely pragmatic lines – to benefit the Christian parties in those states where (a) Christian religious affiliation is stronger; and (b) there are noticeable numbers of Muslims. In other words, circumstances controlled the arguments which were made very much for party-political advantage through the promotion of a certain vision of national identity.

France and Belgium

The legislative speeches in Belgium and France are simultaneously simple and complex: simple because of their one clear message; complex because of the disparate strands

---

[30] *Landtag von Baden-Württemberg, Drucksache 13/2793, Gesetzentwurf der Landesregierung, Gesetz zur Änderung des Schulgesetzes.*

[31] Details are to be found in Robert Gould, *Identity Discourses in the German Headscarf Debate*, Working Paper Series 15, Canadian Centre for German and European Studies/Centre canadien d'études allemandes et européennes: York University, Toronto, 2008, http://ccges.apps01.yorku.ca/wp/wp-content/uploads/2009/01/gould.pdf; and in Christian Joppke, *Veil, Mirror of Identity* (Cambridge: Polity, 2009).

[32] M. Minkenberg, 'Democracy and Religion: Theoretical and Empirical Observations on the Relationship between Christianity, Islam and Liberal Democracy', *Journal of Ethnic and Migration Studies*, 33:6 (2007), pp. 887–909. Further information is to be found in the data reports of 2002 and 2006 of the Federal Statistics Office of Germany.

which are brought together. The message is 'ban the *burqa*' – though the actual legislation does not say this: it prohibits only the covering of the face in public places. The disparate strands are:

- *Gendering* (the most frequently-used single argument).
- Human rights.
- National *identity* issues.
- *Social* issues (cohesion and social values).
- *Securitisation* – protection of the state and of persons other than the wearer.
- *Urgency* in the sense of the speed 'with which the bill has to be passed'.
- The need to *protect* the legislation *from legal challenges* – both internal and European.
- *Europeanisation and internationalisation* – (a) the extreme closeness of the French and Belgian positions and arguments, and parallels with arguments in Germany; (b) the desire to project a certain international image of the country; (c) explicit European comparisons; (d) troop losses in Afghanistan; and (e) Muslim countries as negative examples.

France

The literature on French *laïcité*, on the question of headscarves being worn by girls in schools, and on a visible Islam in France is legion and cannot be examined in detail here. However, Beaubérot's survey of the development of the concept in the period 1905–2005 outlines the ways in which it became inseparable from French identity and, for many, inseparable also from us-versus-them thinking.[33] Bowen explores the nature, and misunderstandings, of *laïcité*, at the same time as exposing themes in the public debates at the beginning of the decade on girls wearing headscarves in schools.[34] These themes became prominent again in 2010. A further perspective is provided by Roy who describes a point fundamental for the later debates on *le voile intégral*, namely that *laïcité*, as it is understood today, is founded on a myth of consensus, and in particular on that of the consensus of 'republican values'.[35] As will be seen below, 'republican values' played a key role in the debates. Amir-Moazami is valuable for examining the discourses around headscarves in both France and Germany at the time of the Ludin affair in Germany, the growing controversy in France leading to the Commission on the Application of the Principle of *Laïcité* in the Republic (*Commission sur l'application du principe de laïcité dans la République*) and the prohibition of headscarves for girls in schools.[36] At the same time, as Mas makes clear, the debates are taking place against the complex background of French post-colonialism which include in her view 'the discursive inflation of Islam to despotic proportions' and the deployment of *laïcité* in 'winning the war against the enemy'.[37]

As could be expected, the debates in the National Assembly (11 May 2010; 6, 7, and 13 July 2010) and Senate (14 September 2010)[38] made frequent reference to what is called the

---

[33] J. Beaubérot, *Laïcité 1905–2005: Entre passion et raison* (Paris: Seuil, 2004).

[34] J. Bowen, *Why the French Don't Like Headscarves: Islam, the State, and Public Space* (Princeton and Oxford: Princeton University Press, 2007).

[35] O. Roy, *La laïcité face à l'islam* (Paris: Stock, 2005), p. 43.

[36] S. Amir-Moazami, *Politisierte Religion: Der Kopftuchstreit in Deutschland und Frankreich* (Bielefeld: transcript verlag, 2007).

[37] R. Mas, 'Compelling the Muslim Subject: Memory as Post-colonial Violence and the Public Performativity of "Secular and Cultural Islam"', *The Muslim World*, 96:4 (2006), pp. 585–616.

[38] Vote in the National Assembly: 336 for, 1 against, 2 abstentions – but approximately 200 absences (the vote was held on July 13th); Senate vote: 246 for, 1 against, no abstentions.

Republican triptych of Liberty, Equality and Fraternity; the arguments contained in the references are revealing. Equally revealing is the way in which the debates also mention national, Constitutional and supranational European bodies.

The confrontation and irreconcilability of values is quite clear and was summarised on 11 May by two members of the National Assembly from opposing parts of the political spectrum:

'The alternatives are clear – the Republic or the *Burqa*' (Lionel Luca [*UMP*], quoting the statement of Sihem Habchi, President of *Ni putes ni soumises* [Neither Whores nor Housemaids], to *La Mission d'information sur la pratique du port du voile intégral sur le territoire national* [Fact-finding Mission on the Wearing of the *Voile Intégral* in France]),[39] and 'Marianne and *le voile intégral* express totally opposite views of the world' (Danièle Hoffman-Rispal; *Socialiste, radical, citoyen et divers gauche*).[40]

Not only is the state as currently constituted incompatible with the *voile intégral* and *burqa* and vice versa, but they are hostile to the state. Speaker after speaker returns to this fundamental conflict with references to *valeurs républicaines* (Republican values) and bases the argument on the 'native/alien' dichotomy, which is also on occasion the contrast between modern Enlightenment-based values and backward values, and between integration and *communautarisme* (withdrawal into separate communities).[41] In all this the *burqa* is a mark of hostility to what is 'modern'. It is also stated to be a profoundly political symbol deliberately being used against the Republic.[42]

The whole of the discussion in the National Assembly and Senate is based on the assertion, both implicit and explicit, that French national identity is threatened unless effective measures are taken to prohibit the wearing of the *burqa/niqab/voile intégral* in public. This argument of the threat to *valeurs républicaines* is in fact the starting point for the whole process of banning the *voile intégral*, beginning literally with the heading of the resolution passed on 11 May 2010[43] and in Michèle Alliot-Marie's opening statement of the debate which followed on 6 July 2010,[44] in which as Minister of Justice and Freedoms she piloted the bill and spoke in both the National Assembly and, later, the Senate.

Secondly, it emerges from the statements that not only are the foundations of the state involved, but so are fundamental societal values. These are unequivocally inseparable from the *triptyque républicain* (republican triptych of liberty, equality, fraternity), so much so that, speaking of the hearings leading up to the *Rapport d'information* (Report to the National Assembly) of 26 January 2010, it was asserted that what had emerged in the course of the hearings was that 'the best way of combating *le voile intégral* is the complete Republic [*la République intégrale*], as a violation of any of the three parts of the republican

---

[39]Éric Raoult, *Rapport d'information fait en application de l'article 145 du Règlement, au nom de la mission d'information sur la pratique du port du voile intégral sur le territoire national*, enregistré à la Présidence de l'Assemblée nationale le 26 janvier 2010 (Paris: Assemblée Nationale 2010), p. 322, http://www.assemblee-nationale.fr/13/rap-info/i2262.asp; *Journal Officiel de la République Française, Assemblée nationale*, 2ième séance du 11 mai 2010, p. 3192.

[40]Ibid., p. 3185.

[41]It should be noted that the characteristics of *communautarisme* outlined by Michèle Alliot-Marie to the Senate on 14 September 2010 correspond very closely to those of the equally hostile German term *Parallelgesellschaft*: withdrawal from and rejection of the majority culture, refusal of integration, non-acceptance of 'our' values and constitutional principles, non-egalitarian and non-participative practices: *Journal officiel de la République Française, Sénat, Compte rendu intégral*, Séance du mardi 14 septembre 2010, pp. 6731–6732.

[42]See particularly Jacques Myard (*UMP*), 7 July 2010.

[43]RÉSOLUTION *sur l'attachement au respect des valeurs républicaines face au développement de pratiques radicales qui y portent atteinte*. TEXTE ADOPTÉ n° 459 'Petite loi' Assemblée Nationale, Constitution du 4 octobre 1958, Treizième législature, session ordinaire de 2009–2010, 11 mai 2010.

[44]*Assemblée nationale – 3e séance du 6 juillet 2010*, p. 5367.

triptych is a violation of the Republican Pact'.[45] It is clear that the debate has not evolved since the act of 2004 banning headscarves on girls in schools.[46]

Invocation of republican values leads to the extremely frequently repeated references on all the days of the debates to the equality of men and women and the rejection of the notions of submission, subservience, dependence, inferiority, domination, isolation, marginalisation, humiliation, and even dehumanisation of women.[47] These highly emotive concepts and arguments are accompanied by a range of metaphors of imprisonment behind *le voile intégral*: *isoloir* (isolation cell), *prison* (prison) denying the fundamental value of liberty; they are accompanied by metaphors of death, *cercueil* (coffin), *spectre* (ghost), *fantôme* (phantom) – the final stage in the removal of identity, becoming an un-person, and destroying the ability to interact with society as a citizen.

Constant references (119 instances) to *le vivre ensemble* (living together/social cohesion) as the fundamental outcome to be constructed by all social and political values, and which is made quasi or completely impossible by face coverings, provide the fundamental argument to stigmatise the public wearing of the garments as 'un-French', completely unacceptable and inhibiting social and political life around a common core of values (*socle de valeurs*). Often referred to in the debates, the official figure of the number of women wearing the *voile intégral* in France in 2009 is 1900.[48] This means that the argument is being made that 1900 women threaten the whole of French social and political life.

To underscore the legitimacy of the bill when the matter came before the Senate on 14 September 2010,[49] Michèle Alliot-Marie re-emphasised the argument of the preservation of the constitutional value of *l'ordre public social* (public social order). This had been the starting point of her testimony before the Committee for Constitutional Laws, Legislation and the General Administration of the Republic of the National Assembly in June.[50] The following points from her opening statement to the Senate on 14 September summarise the argument and final public position of the government, a position which was not challenged by representatives of *any* party:

> Living in the Republic with an uncovered face is a question of dignity, a question of equality within the Republic, also, and a question of respect for our Republican principles... *Le voile intégral*... dissolves the identity of the individual in that of a community. It calls into question the French model of integration based on the

---

[45]Sandrine Mazetier, 11 May 2010, p. 3188. These categories are the same as those present in the 2004 debate banning the headscarf in schools.

[46]V. Amiraux, 'Headscarves in Europe: What is Really the Issue' in Samir Amghar, Amel Boubekeur and Michaël Emerson (eds) *European Islam: The Challenges for Society and Public Policy* (Brussels: CEPS, 2007), pp. 124–143; and V. Amiraux, '"L'affaire du foulard" en France: Retour sur une affaire qui n'en est pas encore une', *Sociologie et sociétés*, 41:2 (2009), pp. 273–298. See also F. Lorderie, 'À l'assaut de l'agenda public: La politisation du voile islamique en 2003–2004' [Attacking the Public Agenda: The Politicisation of the Islamic Headscarf in 2003–2004] in Françoise Lorderie (ed.) *La politisation du voile: L'affaire en France, en Europe et dans la monde arabe* (Paris, Budapest, Turin: L'Harmattan, 2005), pp. 11–36.

[47]In President Sarkozy's speech before both houses on 22 June 2009 asserting that the *burqa* was not welcome in France, he spoke of *des femmes prisonnières derrière un grillage, coupées de toute vie sociale, privées de toute identité* [women imprisoned behind a net cage, cut off from all social life, completely deprived of identity].

[48]*Commission des lois constitutionelles, de la législation et de l'administration générale de la République Rapport d'information*, p. 28. The figure is repeated on eight other occasions in the report.

[49]*Sénat, Journal officiel*, Séance du mardi 14 septembre 2010. Mercredi 15 septembre 2010, p. 6731 ff.

[50]Report dated 23 June 2010, p. 27. This reflects also the arguments made when prohibiting headscarves in schools: Cesari, op. cit. The statement to the Senate by François-Noël Buffet, *rapporteur de la Commission des lois constitutionnelles, de législation, du suffrage universel, du règlement et d'administration générale* went further into the details of the constitutionality of the bill (p. 6733ff).

values of our society and of the principles of our Constitution... It expresses the wish to put into practice a separate vision of society, that is, non-egalitarian and non-participatory... In this sense, *le voile intégral* is incompatible with our constitutional principles.

The general and unrestricted scope of the prohibition arises from its constitutional basis.

To summarise: the fundamental goals of the state are directly threatened by *le voile intégral*, as is 'the unity of our country, our most precious possession' (all the translations above are my own).

One must argue, then, that in the French case the *triptyque républicain* and *valeurs républicaines* are the functional equivalent of the German 'Christian-Occidental values': they are the basic exclusionary argument. One thing to note here is that the French position is not overtly based on religion. This is in stark contrast to the German case with its Christian vs. Muslim argument of 'Christian-Occidental' or even 'Christian-Jewish' culture, which continues to the present day in many German political statements (for instance 16 October 2011, when Chancellor Merkel and the Premier of Bavaria pronounced multiculturalism a failure or dead and emphasised *deutsche Leitkultur* [German foundation culture] with its Christian-Occidental component).[51]

In contrast to this German religion-based confrontational tone, both in 2004[52] and 2010 it was repeatedly argued in both the Senate and National Assembly that the bill avoids stigmatising any group by not referring to Muslim practices or to any garment by name. On the other hand, scepticism is justified in this connection as the members of the National Assembly and Senate do not hesitate to use *burqa* and *niqab* consistently as terms of obloquy,[53] though the bill itself does not employ these terms; it does not prohibit any large black or blue garment which envelops the body. It prohibits only covering the face (*la dissimulation du visage*).[54]

In the arguments supporting the French identity statements there are two elements completely absent from the German case – but present also in the Belgian ones. In France, it is consistently argued that the legislation must be in conformity with European norms and jurisprudence. Similarly, numerous references are made (not always accurately) to other EU countries which have, or are said to have, banned face and head coverings or which are considering such a ban. Following the example of the *Rapport d'information*,[55] a second, externally-oriented, argument is employed: the desire to set an example or to be an example for others as part of French identity. This practice is present in all the debates, from the resolution on 11 May, when Nicole Ameline (*Union*

---

[51]R. Gould, 'La "mort" du multiculturalisme allemand: Ce que cachent les propos chocs d'Angela Merkel', *L'Actualité fédérale*, décembre 2010, 1:2, http://ideefederale.ca/wp/wp-content/uploads/2010/12/Dec_2010.pdf. For information on the notion of *Leitkultur* [German foundation culture], see H. Pautz, 'The Politics of Identity in Germany: The Leitkultur Debate', *Race and Class*, 46:4 (2005), pp. 39–52; G. Hentges, 'Das Plädoyer für eine "deutsche Leitkultur" – Steilvorlage für die extreme Rechte?' in C. Butterwege et al. (eds) *Themen der Rechten – Themen der Mitte. Zuwanderung, demografischer Wandel und Nationalbewußtsein* (Opladen: Leske + Budrich, 2002), pp. 95–121.

[52]Annette Schavan, Minister of Education in Baden-Wurtemberg, introduced the headscarf bill in 2004 by saying '[By this means] the legal basis will be created for prohibiting the wearing of the headscarf by Muslim teachers while teaching'. *Landtag von Baden-Württemberg, Plenarprotokoll 13/62*, 4 February 2004, p. 4385.

[53]This includes André Gerin's statement (paraphrasing Brecht), 'the foul beast born of the fertile belly of the 1930s', *Assemblée Nationale*, 11 May 2010, p. 3186.

[54]*Loi n° 2010–1192 du 11 octobre 2010 interdisant la dissimulation du visage dans l'espace public:* Article 1: Nul ne peut, dans l'espace public, porter une tenue destinée à dissimuler son visage.

[55]Section II B: 'Reaffirming France's support for women persecuted anywhere in the world'.

pour un Mouvement Populaire) argued that France should 'provide a signal for women who, throughout the world, from Kabul to Sanaa and from Bamako to Buenos Aires, are fighting daily for their liberty, their dignity, and their equality',[56] to 14 September in the Senate when it was also argued that, 'by passing this bill, we will send a strong signal and give hope to the women of the whole world who are fighting and dying for the freedom to be able to live without wearing this humiliating covering'.[57] The external dimension is present also in explicit mentions of the European Court of Human Rights, in European jurisprudence and the EU Charter of Fundamental Rights. This has a double function: it anchors French identity within the process of European integration and provides further legitimisation of the principal arguments; and secondly it reinforces the distinction between French/European social and legal norms and those from outside Europe and the EU.

Finally, in all these arguments it has to be emphasised that their thrust and content closely follow the *Rapport d'information* of 26 January 2010. Its position is made very clear by some of the section headings, for example: 'Part II – A Practice Completely at Odds with the Values of the Republic', of which the following are subsections: 'Negation of Liberty', 'Rejection of the Principle of Equality', 'Refusal of Fraternity'; and 'Part III – Liberating Women from the Clutches of the *Voile Intégral*'. The debates contain quotations from the *Rapport* and include frequent references to it and to the testimony of its expert witnesses. Fed by the *Rapport*, the attitude of the debates was one of confrontation. Farhad Khosrokhavar put it clearly during his appearance as a witness before the commission, aware that his remarks would not be appreciated by the politicians he was addressing: 'the real problem lies in the confrontational way in which we approach these questions in France. This attitude is in the DNA of our political culture'.[58]

At the same time, the civic-values-based confrontational approach noted by Khosrokavar and, as outlined above, evident in statements in the National Assembly and Senate, has a further origin or justification outside the polarities of political language. Important testimony was given to the National Assembly's *Mission d'information sur la pratique du port du voile intégral sur le territoire national* (Commission of Enquiry on the Practice of Wearing the *Voile Intégral* in France) by Élisabeth Badinter,[59] one of France's leading public intellectuals. Her views, quoted frequently and favourably in the *Rapport d'information* and figuring in the debates, are founded on just such a polarity. Covering the face is completely destructive of each of the values enshrined in the *triptyque républicain*, and the state is literally engaged in a battle with an alien religiosity and view of society which seeks to impose its views on 'us';[60] compromise would be destructive;[61] complete rejection is the only reasonable course of action. Thus the arguments in the political arena received significant support from an intellectual source with very considerable ethos.

What Khosrokavar said of France is valid also for Belgium where the *Rapport d'information* also provided a range of arguments, references, and quotations to oppose the *voile intégral*. There, too, Badinter's views are cited in support of the arguments.

---

[56]*Assemblée Nationale – 2e séance du 11 mai 2010*, p. 3814.
[57]p. 6761.
[58]21 October 2009, *Rapport du 26 janvier*, p. 438.
[59]*Rapport d'information du 26 janvier 2010*, p. 333f.
[60]Ibid., pp. 335–337.
[61]Ibid., pp. 338 and 340.

Belgium

To look back on only the last decade (and in the wake of the headscarf affair in France which saw the wearing of Muslim headscarves banned in schools),[62] numerous bills were presented and questions raised in both chambers of the Belgian parliament on matters concerning the headscarf, *voile intégral/burqa/niqab*. Could lawyers wear a headscarf in court?[63] Could spectators in the Senate or senators themselves wear one or a kippa or a turban?[64] Could officials in polling stations wear a headscarf?[65] The tone was frequently hostile, even on headscarves, which had been banned in schools in a number of localities. This was occurring despite the fact that Belgium has no doctrine comparable to that of *laïcité* in France which, as Doyle points out in this issue, as a result of the previous dominance of the Catholic Church attempts to keep religion and the state entirely separate.[66] But as she indicates also, *laïcité* was the product of politics and has in fact become a tool of politics directed against Islam. Instead of *laïcité*, Belgium has a fundamental principle of neutrality towards religions, but one in which the state directly provides funds from general revenues to a total of six denominations, including Islam.[67]

The following discussion will be limited principally to three virtually contemporaneous documents: the proposal dated 25 March 2011 to the House of Representatives (*Chambre des Représentants*) by the Flemish neo-nationalist and extremist party *Vlaams Belang* to ban headscarves in the federal public service (absolutely identical with the bill it presented to the Senate on 1 May 2008),[68] the deliberations of the Committee for Home Affairs, General Affairs, and the Public Service of the House (*Commission de l'Intérieur des Affaires générales et de la Fonction publique*) on 30 March 2011 considering a face veil ban in all public places,[69] and the follow-up plenary debate on 28 April 2011 when the bill was passed.[70] The latter two have been chosen also because they repeat views expressed across the parties and the linguistic divide in attempts in 2010 to pass such legislation before parliament was dissolved four days later. The rationale for the *Vlaams Belang* bill to ban the headscarf on federal civil servants was completely confrontational; accommodation is impossible. The principal argument was that of 'the inferiority of women in Islam'. The bill was necessary to protect the equality of men and women and other fundamental western democratic values. These are totally irreconcilable with Sharia law; accepting the headscarf on federal civil servants would be equivalent to legitimising the whole of Sharia which denies the separation of religion and the state; it would be a step towards the 'Islamisation of our country'. The headscarf is a symbol of 'resistance to our society and way of life'. On the other hand, the cross is among the 'harmless symbols which… are part of our culture and traditions'. The proximity to the argumentation both in the German state parliaments and in France is evident.[71]

---

[62]See F. Brion, 'L'inscription du débat français en Belgique: Pudeurs laïques et monnaie de singe' in F. Lorderie, *La politisation du voile: L'affaire en France, en Europe et dans le monde arabe* (Paris: L'Harmattan, 2005), pp. 121–146.
[63]*Chambre des Représentants, Commission de la justice*, 21 October 2009, CRIV 52 COM 670, item 12.02.
[64]19 August 2010; 5-32/1 – BZ 2010.
[65]*Chambre des Représentants*, 1 October 2010, DOC 53 0256/001.
[66]Doyle in this issue, pp. 265–283.
[67]H. Bousetta and B. Maréchal, *L'islam et les musulmans en Belgique: Enjeux locaux & cadres de réflexion globaux* (Brussels: Fondation Roi Beaudoin, 2003). See also M. Tellier, *Islam et musulmans en Belgique. Défis et opportunités d'une société multiculturelle. Ceci n'est pas un voile* (Brussels: Fondation Roi Beaudoin, 2004).
[68]*Chambre des Représentants*, 25 March 2011, DOC 53 1324/001. It is identical to the rationale of the bill introduced by the *Vlaams Belang* on 1 May 2008.
[69]*Chambre des Représentants*, 18 April, 2010, DOC 53 0219/004.
[70]*Chambre des Représentants*, 28 April, 2011, CRIV 53 PLEN 030.
[71]For further details, see Gould, *Identity Discourses*; Joppke, op. cit.

The number of women in the federal civil service wearing a headscarf is not given, but one might assume it is very small; the proportion of these compelled to wear one by a husband, father or brother (lack of free choice was emphasised in the rationale) is probably even smaller. However, as the opening and frequent argument of protecting women's position in society is phrased so broadly and strongly, based on the argument that headscarf = Sharia, it is clear that the framers of the bill were giving the headscarf a symbolic value which applies beyond the federal public service, and beyond Belgium even. As in the dissenting opinion of the German Federal Constitutional Court and for many politicians at the level of the German states, the piece of cloth became the visible symbol of a set of utterly illiberal and hostile values, likely to undermine state and society.

The statements made in the committee meeting on the face veil bills on 30 March 2011[72] repeat, often verbatim, earlier ones made on 29 April 2010[73] in the plenary session of the Chamber when spokespersons for party groups presented their reasons for supporting a ban in connection with no less than four bills to this effect. The committee proceedings on 30 March 2011 also refer explicitly to the earlier committee examination one year earlier and to some of its arguments. Consequently, they are representative of an established discourse with a common position and common arguments against *le voile intégral*. As in all the other countries, the aim of the political statements made in both committee meetings is above all (but not exclusively) to protect local values from the influence of the new arrivals, rather than propagate local values to the new arrivals.

All speakers and bill proposers in Belgium share the same intention – across ideological and linguistic lines. This is the affirmation of common 'European' values against what the headscarf/*voile intégral*/*burqa* are deemed to represent. Similarly, to buttress their position, proponents (there are no opponents) make frequent references to arguments made in other EU member states. Consequently, as seen also in France and Germany, the argument operates in a system of polarities, us *vs.* them, 'native' *vs.* 'alien'. This united front against what are presented as alien values leads to a situation whereby, as in France, there is no attack on other parties; only in the reverse sense that the *Vlaams Belang* states its own worth in having persuaded other parties to act, and having introduced a similar bill as early as 2004, in addition to a comparable action in 1988.[74]

Across all parties, across the linguistic divide, and with a variety of arguments the point is made repeatedly and strongly that the *burqa* and face veil are contrary to the principals of gender equality and human dignity. It forces women into submission, deprives them of identity and forces them to live under constant threat; it is linked to humiliation and denigration. As in France, it is equated with a denial of liberty: it is a 'mobile prison', 'individual prison', 'cloth prison'. As a 'shroud of freedom' it is equated with death, it is 'liberticide', and represents the ultimate loss of participation in society. This public manifestation of religion is incompatible with modern notions of participatory citizenship.

There is, however, one significant difference: whereas, as was demonstrated for France, the arguments emphasised the danger to the fundamental principles of the state, in Belgium this is not the case. Here, predominantly, it is society and its values which are under threat. There is no Belgian formula equivalent to the *triptyque républicain* and *les valeurs républicaines* on which to base an overwhelming and appealing argument that the state itself is

---

[72] DOC 53 0219/004, dated 18 April 2011.

[73] CRABV 52 PLEN 151. A bill to ban *le voile intégral* was passed with no contrary votes and two abstentions, but failed to become law when parliament was dissolved after the government fell.

[74] On 29 April 2010 Filip De Man (*VB*), stated, 'In this connection, too, we were the trendsetters' (item 08.02). Annik Ponthier, repeated the view on 28 April 2011, saying that the *VB* had 'shown the way' (item 12.07). See also Bart Laeremans (*VB*) to the Senate committee mentioned below.

threatened. Nor is there a symbol such as *Marianne*. And the Kingdom (*le Royaume*) does not function as an equivalent to the French *la République*. However, mention of society and its values can be found 41 times in the plenary session and 21 in the committee.

The following two statements from the committee and plenary proceedings may be taken as representative of the repeated argument that covering the face is hostile to Belgian *societal* values.

> Catherine Fonck (*Centre démocrate humaniste*/Democratic Humanist Centre Party):
>
> For her group, wearing a *voile intégral* is a significant break with the fundamental principles of society, with 'social cohesion', civility and sociability. Being able to recognise each other is the foundation of 'social cohesion'.[75]
>
> Bart Somers (*Open Vlaamse Liberalen en Democraten*/Flemish Liberals and Democrats):
>
> It is connected to the question of the sort of society we want to live in, with our view of what a human being in fact is... Our group defends the values of a liberal and free society. Freedom goes together with diversity... A free society is one in which each person is important, unique, and has the chance to grow and develop.[76]

As in France, the goal is social cohesion (*le vivre ensemble*) on the basis of a common core of values (*un socle commun de valeurs*).

Although gender equality and the concomitant position on human dignity receive so much attention, it is the safety (*sécurité*) argument which is both explicitly stated to be the *ratio legis* and is a repeated argument (25 times in the Committee meeting, and some 16 times in the plenary session). This is an argument which, in addition to the danger to society, places the wearer of the *burqa/niqab/voile intégral* in the position of posing a threat both to individual (bodily) well-being and safety, closely related to the legal obligation always to be identifiable. Thus society and individuals are all at risk because of this expression of alien religiosity – although it is acknowledged that it is practised by only 200 women.[77] When the bill, passed by the Chamber, was briefly discussed in the Home and Administrative Affairs Committee of the Senate (it never went to the full Senate) on 10 May 2011, the Minister of the Interior repeated all the above arguments, including explicitly stating that 'there is no indication of a link between wearing a *burqa* and criminal activity or behaviour that would threaten the State'. She continued by emphasising 'as the debate in the House showed, wearing a *burqa* is above all a problem for human dignity and equality of the sexes'.[78]

As in France, also, it is argued that the legislation must be able to stand the test of European human rights principles, and that passing such a bill is important in sending a message on gender issues to other countries which accept or enforce the *burqa* or *niqab*.[79] Domestic legislation is given a global dimension.

It is argued in committee and in the plenary session that it is urgent to pass this bill. It is possibly this which also accounts for the insistence on safety/security, a concept explicitly linked to the question of public safety (*l'ordre/l'ordre public*). Both are contained in

---

[75] DOC 53 0219/004, page 6
[76] CRIV 53 PLEN 030, item 12.05.
[77] Eva Brems, 28 April 2011, CRIV 53 PLEN 030, item 12.13.
[78] *Sénat de Belgique*, 10 May 2011, Document 5-66COM.
[79] For example, the statement of Daniel Bacquelaine, item 12.04.

Paragraph 2 of Article 9 of the European Declaration of Human Rights as legitimate reasons for restricting a manifestation of religion. Together with the additional reason of 'protecting the rights of others', this is intended to make the bill contest-proof.[80] But the point here is, as in France, the claimed urgency of the need to act quickly to protect society (in France also the state) from what is consistently presented as a threat. This urgency even led to the decision not to request an opinion from the *Conseil d'État*, Belgium's highest administrative court, which also, as here, has a consultative function.[81]

Conclusions

Condemnation across parties of what is acknowledged as a minority expression of 'alien religiosity' (implicit in the German debates; 1900 wearers of the *voile intégral* in France; 200 in Belgium) is stated in such a way as to stigmatise the whole, variegated, group of Muslims.[82] The quantity and nature of the arguments against this public manifestation of religiosity are such that the much fewer generalised mitigating statements about the legitimacy and private practice of Islam are overwhelmed. The virtually total unanimity of politicians in Belgium and France, and to a lesser extent in Germany, in rejecting this public manifestation of a private matter illustrates the extent to which parties are convinced that political capital is to be gained by public condemnation. It is clear also that the ways in which politicians deal with Islam is inseparable from national identity,[83] itself now inseparable from a broader European identity and norms. Together, this is further evidence of the continued deliberate public reinforcement of Europe-vs.-Islam arguments noted by Shooman and Spielhaus for the period immediately preceding the debates in Paris and Brussels.[84] For the politicians and the public intellectual Élisabeth Badinter, these factors together place the situation outside the realm of any flexible approach such as was proposed by two scholars of Islam in France: Farhad Khosrokhavar who regretted the French confrontational approach (see above) and who, in contrast to the politicians, insisted that 'reality is made up of degrees and nuances',[85] and Jean Baubérot who spoke in terms of mediation and 'reasonable accommodations' along the lines of the Quebec model.[86]

The analysis thus reveals that the situation noted for the very first few years of the twenty-first century by Roy and Baubérot, namely the debate about French identity focused strongly on Islam, is continued also in 2010.[87] At the same time, the united opposition to the headscarf across party and ideological lines which both noted for the slightly earlier period[88] also continues and is even intensified for the *voile intégral*. The article

---

[80] However, proceedings to contest the act before the *Cour constitutionelle* on the grounds of undue restriction of fundamental rights guaranteed by the Constitution and the European Convention on Human Rights are continuing: *Cour constitutionelle, arrêt* [judgement] n° 148/2011 du 5 octobre 2011.
[81] Committee report, 12 April 2011, document DOC 53 0219/004.
[82] For evidence of this stigmatisation, as felt by women wearing headscarves, see Leyla Arslan, *Enfants d'islam et de Marianne: Des banlieues à l'Université* (Paris: PUF, 2010), p. 8 and pp. 169–173.
[83] Also J. Robine, 'La polémique sur le voile intégral et le débat sur l'identité nationale: Une question géopolitique', *Hérodote*, 136 (2010), pp. 42–55.
[84] Y. Shooman and R. Spielhaus, 'The Concept of the Muslim Enemy in the Public Discourse' in J. Cesari (ed.) *Muslims in the West after 9/11: Religion, Politics and the Law* (London and New York: Routledge, 2010), pp. 198–228.
[85] *Rapport d'information*, p. 438.
[86] *Rapport d'information* pp. 430–431.
[87] Olivier Roy, op. cit., p. 8; J. Baubérot, 'Existe-t-il une religion Républicaine?', *French Politics, Culture and Society*, 25:2 (2007), pp. 3–18.
[88] Roy, op. cit., p. 12; J. Baubérot, 'La Commission Stasi: Entre laïcité républicaine et multiculturelle', *Historical Reflections*, 34:3 (2008), pp. 7–20.

has revealed that this unanimity is not restricted to France alone. The all-party agreement in Belgium reaches across the linguistic divide. In other words, the opposition does not arise from specifically French phenomena such as *laïcité* or the Republican tryptich of values. These are slogans by means of which opposition to Muslim female face veils (and also headscarves) is rendered irresistible within the French context. As was seen, in Belgium the arguments were the same, but *laïcité* was not mentioned, nor, of course, were *valeurs républicaines*. However, complete agreement was achieved.

Furthermore, the similarity of argumentation against the headscarf in the civil service shared by the minority justices, the centre-left Social Democrats (*SPD*) in coalitions in the Sarre and Bremen, the centre-right Christian Democratic Union and Christian Social Union (*CDU/CSU*) in Germany, and the further right and populist *Vlaams Belang* in Belgium points in the same direction. In two countries with different languages, historical backgrounds, religious compositions, different social tensions, different political climates and structures, parties of different orientations which share only the desire of all parties – to achieve influence and power – have concluded that the way to these ends is promoted by a virtually identical set of exclusionary arguments directed against items of female clothing associated with Islam. The direction in which all this points is that the rejection of an 'alien' religion cannot be explained by 'national' factors alone. Indeed, the references in the debates and in the *Rapport d'information* to points of view, arguments, policies and practices in other European countries and elsewhere make quite clear that the politicians are aware that a visible Islam is a Europe-wide (and even world-wide) source of concern. On the other hand, parties function only on a national level and thus select arguments and slogans which fit their particular context.

The argument in Belgium and France that face veils/*burqas*/*voile intégral* suppress individuality, interchange, and hence civic citizenship (*citoyenneté*) can be related to another factor: as expressed by Bramadat (above) it is the view, also in the French and Belgian debates, that one function of the modern state is to enable its citizens to develop their individuality and autonomy fully. The argument was made that the face veil contradicts this interplay of the state and human potential. Writing of Germany, Müller assigns the *headscarf* the role of a double refusal: access to modernity to be achieved through personal autonomy and integration into the role of citizen, and as a difference marker between religiosity and secularity, between tradition and modernity, evoking fear of religion-based regulation, fundamentalism and loss of individual liberties.[89] In the French and Belgian debates the Muslim full-face or full-body veil has all these roles – but in a manner which is visually more radical, and hence the resistance is more radical. Like the minority justices in Germany with their reference to 'veil' (*Schleier*) and 'covering which hides the shape' (*Verhüllung*) the politicians in Belgium and France repeatedly present arguments utterly condemning something which they do not actually ban – the enveloping cloak. But the only thing which the new additions to the criminal code prohibit is covering the face. Politicians are talking about one thing and prohibiting another. This means that *burqa, niqab, Schleier, sluier, Verhüllung, voile intégral* carry such heavy negative connotations, linked to the visual and verbal association with terrorism and the safety/security argument, that it is politically advantageous to deploy them with such frequency. Put differently: it is impossible not to be overtly against them. And once more, the arguments are trans-border in nature. Roy advances the view that the French Republic developed and

---

[89] A. Müller, 'Das Kopftuch als Verdichtungssymbol', in Cristina Allemann-Ghionda and Wolf-Dietrich Bukow (eds) *Orte der Diversität: Formate, Arrangements und Inszenierungen* (Wiesbaden: VS Verlag für Sozialwissenschaften, 2011), pp. 145–159: p. 155. For France, Baubérot, 'La commission Stasi'; Joan Wallach Scott, 'Introduction', *The Politics of the Veil* (Princeton, NJ: Princeton University Press, 2007), pp. 1–20.

defined itself in the late nineteenth and early twentieth centuries by a strong and verbally harsh opposition to Catholicism. For the opening years of the twenty-first century he argues that this process is continuing with Islam. This is certainly the case for the debates of 2010. Although neither the Federal Republic of Germany nor Belgium has defined itself in any period in opposition to Catholicism or Christianity, it has been shown that politicians in these countries, too, define their visions of society and the state in opposition to Islam. In all three countries, also, the prohibition was treated as a matter of great urgency, in Belgium and France practically as a national emergency.

Tietze's statement on the semantics of religion cited in the introduction that religion, when defined as a political force, 'has to be excluded' applies to Islam. The exclusion of a Christian political force does not take place. In their election manifestos and statements of fundamental principles (*Grundsatzprogramme*) the *CDU/CSU* claim Christianity as their foundation;[90] the *Vlaams Belang* position is fundamentally that of the *CDU/CSU*, stating that the cross is among the 'harmless symbols which... are part of our culture and way of life'.[91] To refer to Tietze again, significantly also, no politician argued that Islam is 'an ethical contribution to social life' – even for those Muslims otherwise described as 'living peaceably among us'.

The arguments that the state is directly endangered (Germany and France) and that society's values are also endangered (Germany, France and Belgium) mean that any individual seeing these public manifestations of what is emphasised as an alien (in every sense of the word) religiosity can feel threatened, even though they have no contact with Muslims. The negative impacts of such statements are heightened by references to French and Belgian soldiers dying in Afghanistan, terrorist actions (Senate, 14 September 2011) and the forced wearing of *burqas* and face covering in Afghanistan, Kuwait, Saudi Arabia, Iran – and also France and Belgium. In this particular context globalisation means that the movement into Europe of values and practices is not to be tolerated, whereas the outward movement of values is to be encouraged, a position best summarised by the sub-section heading in the *Rapport d'information* to the National Assembly mentioned above, 'It is the mission of French values to extend beyond the borders of France'.[92]

The argument of personal safety is absent from the German statements, but concerns for the security of the state and its fundamental principles are present in the dissenting judgment and more strongly in the political debates, perhaps most notably in the words of the Hessian Minister of Education, 'but when in our state... religious minorities use the fundamental rights contained in our Federal Constitution against our state – we are certainly justified in protecting ourselves'.[93] In France and Belgium in 2010 and 2011 the references to extremist, fundamentalist, fundamentalist elements (*extrémiste, fondamentaliste, intégriste*) inevitably suggest threats to national security. In addition, the explicit references to safety (*sécurité*) as an endangered value within state and society, whether referring to personal safety or national (or European) security, form part of what is now a highly problematic and potent constellation of concepts and factors within national life. Through their emotional impact the arguments feed on each other to heighten the notion of danger – not as an abstraction, but rather as something which is already affecting both the collectivity and individuals. Such statements are being made by members of mainstream parties and consequently gain credibility.

---

[90]Emphasised at the 24th *CDU* Party Congress, 13-15 November 2011. *Beschluss: Starkes Europa, gute Zukunft für Deutschland*, p. 23; and *Sonstige Beschlüsse*, p. 8.
[91]DOC 53 1324/001, dated 25 March 2011.
[92]p. 150.
[93]Karin Wolf (CDU), *Plenarprotokoll des Hessischen Landtages*, 16. Landtag 30. Sitzung, 18 February 2004, p. 1908.

Writing of the national headscarf debates in the very early years of the twenty-first century, Ataç and colleagues note that 'the categorization of distinct groups follows mainly four major discursive "demarcation" lines – culture, gender, modernity and "Westernness", and fear and threats'.[94] This is valid for the German case and for the recent French and Belgian debates of 2010 and 2011 – plus, as outlined, the elements of urgency, protection of society and state, protection of the legislation from judicial contestation at home or in the European Court of Human Rights and European Court of Justice, and the 'export' of Western values across the globe. The fact that this cross-party rejection is present in Belgium and Germany, two countries with no doctrine of strict separation of state and religion comparable to French *laïcité*, points to broader roots of the rejection of globalising Islam in these liberal democratic states.

What emerges, then, is that these debates about a visible manifestation of 'alien religiosity' reach far beyond what Minkenberg and Willems called 'the relationship between religion and politics'. For the politicians they embrace not only the nature of the state, the nature of society, but also the very nature of the individual. Particularly as enunciated in the French and Belgian parliaments, but in Germany also, the arguments reflect what Triadafilopoulos has described as aggressive integrationism, in opposition to liberal multiculturalism.[95] Concentrating on phobias and fears, the politicians making these arguments consciously reject the approach based on accommodations and compromise, advocated by Khosrokhavar and Bauberot, in favour of conformity to certain principles defined as inseparable from the public good, defence of the state, and worldwide applicability. They do this with awareness of arguments employed in other European countries and supranational entities, thus reinforcing a strategic national and European identity within a given geopolitical context. By various arguments they seek to minimise the impingement on the freedom to practice religion, but nevertheless acknowledge that the measures restrict certain religious manifestations in spaces subject to government control and where, as they see it, the government *must* act. For these parliamentarians, the 'social compact' (*pacte social*) (Alliot-Marie), society and its values (Belgium) and society (Hassemer), not to mention *laïcité*, have reached their limits for 'bearing or enduring alien religiosity'. In their way of expressing this notion, the parliamentarians are using a 'method of political communication complicating the civic dialogue by its very non-dialogic nature'.[96] To speak with Triadafilopoulos, they are employing and legislating illiberal means to [would-be] liberal ends.

---

[94] I. Ataç, S. Rosenberger and B. Sauer, 'Discursive Europeanization? Negotiating Europe in Headscarf Debates' in Sieglinde Rosenberger and Birgit Sauer (eds) *Politics, Religion and Gender: Framing and Regulating the Veil* (London and New York: Routledge, 2012), pp. 74–93.
[95] T. Triadafilopoulos, 'Illiberal Means to Liberal Ends? Understanding Recent Immigrant Integration Policies in Europe', *Journal of Ethnic and Migration Studies*, 37:6 (2011), pp. 861–880.
[96] G. Mesežnikov and O. Gyárfášová, *National Populism in Slovakia*, Working Papers (Bratislava: Institute for Public Affairs, 2008), p. 33.

Swiss Shock: Minaret Rejection, European Values, and the Challenge of Tolerant Neutrality

DOUGLAS PRATT

University of Waikato

ABSTRACT *In 2009 Switzerland, for long an apparent beacon of European toleration and neutrality, voted to ban the erection of minarets. Internal religious matters are normally dealt with at the regional or local level – not at the level of the Swiss national parliament, although the state does seek to ensure good order and peaceful relations between different faith communities. Indeed, the freedom of these communities to believe and function publicly is enshrined in law. However, as a matter of national policy, now constitutionally embedded, one religious group, the Muslim group, is not permitted to build their distinctive religious edifice, the minaret. Switzerland may have joined the rest of Europe with respect to engaging the challenge of Islamic presence to European identity and values, but the rejection of a symbol of the presence of one faith – in this case, Islamic – by a society that is otherwise predominantly secular, pluralist, and of Christian heritage, poses significant concerns. How and why did this happen? What are the implications? This paper will discuss some of the issues involved, concluding the ban is by no means irreversible. Tolerant neutrality may yet again be a leitmotif of Swiss culture and not just of foreign policy.*

Since the end of November 2009 the erection of Muslim minarets in Switzerland has been forbidden by virtue of a vote of 1.53 million to 1.13 million, or 57.5 per cent to 42.5 per cent. A relatively high number of voters, 53.4 per cent of those eligible, turned out for this referendum, or 'Citizens' Initiative' (*Volksinitiative*). At the time there were some 200 mosques in Switzerland. Only four have minarets. The oldest, an Ahmadiyya mosque built in 1962, is in Zürich. The largest, built in 1975 with Saudi funding, but open to all Muslims, is in Geneva. The town of Winterthur has had an Albanian Muslim society mosque since 2005. The newest mosque with a minaret, in the village of Wangen bei Olten, was built in 2009 and belongs to the Turkish cultural society, which has only around 70 members. However, the building of this mosque was accompanied by much controversy, although purportedly reflecting more a matter of issues with Turkish symbolism and presence than necessarily specific religious issues as such. Two further mosques had sought planning permission to erect a minaret, and it was their applications which sparked a right-wing reaction aimed at, and eventually achieving the addition of a single sentence to article 72 of the federal Constitution: 'The construction of minarets is prohibited'. The 'new form of anti-Muslim discourse' that Doyle notes in the introduction to her paper is here given clear expression.[1]

---

[1] Doyle, this issue.

So long as this addition remains there will be no more minarets built in Switzerland. On the one hand it would seem a political overkill: building code restrictions and allied requirements at the local level had precluded, without rancour, the building of some minarets, just as they preclude new church towers or steeples. By the same token, right-wing moves to curtail liberal policies, or compromise a climate of relative tolerance are nothing new and had been regularly rejected.[2] The image of modern Switzerland as both neutral and tolerant had seemed secure. Nevertheless, reactionary forces in the face of ongoing wider changes within European society had been building even in Switzerland – and the image of tolerance may well be just that; an image that is perhaps not as deeply rooted in reality as assumed by an outsider. But Switzerland wasn't exactly at risk of being transformed overnight into a minaret-dominated landscape. So, what was the issue, really? And should it be taken seriously? Does the ban mark a 'retrenchment into a ghettoized mentality; of a fall-back to an exclusive fundamentalism?'[3] Or is it merely a localised quirk of Swiss democracy, a piece of misguided public opinion masquerading as an expression of quixotic self-assertion?

In order to explore the issues and implications pertaining to this event I will review the process and outcomes of the vote by, first, sketching the constitutional and Muslim context, then examining the genesis and outworking of the initiative. Some of the post-vote analysis will be discussed along with some salient issues, responses, and consequences that have emerged. Other European countries have their flashpoint issues with Islam – usually centred on female attire[4] – however, as Mayer notes, 'The symbolic nature of the minaret has acquired a central place in the political debate in Switzerland today: but larger anxieties and issues hide behind the minaret question'.[5] What are these, and how are they present in and through this Swiss affair?

Federal Constitution and Matters of Religion

The right of the population to vote upon a proposal that is the result of a Citizens' Initiative to amend the Swiss federal constitution is enshrined in article 139, notwithstanding some key limitations which would automatically rule out certain proposals. Otherwise, so long as a minimum of 100,000 registered voters signs a petition seeking leave to hold a referendum to vote on the proposal (the 'Initiative') then the Federal government is duty-bound to facilitate the vote. In this case the initiative seeking a determination on the issue of preventing the building of minarets was submitted to the Federal Parliament in July 2008 with some 115,000 signatures in support.[6] Although there is no specific article on religion in the Swiss Federal Constitution, in the section on 'education, research and culture' there is article No. 72, 'Church and State', which previously contained only two paragraphs. The first affirms that religious matters, particularly with respect to church–state relationships, are an issue for the cantonal (regional) level of government, not the federal (national) level. The second asserts that the state has a peace-keeping responsibility in respect to the

---

[2]Lathion notes that 'Initiatives rarely pass: fewer than 15 of the 160 initiatives submitted since 1891 have been successful'. S. Lathion, 'Citizen's Initiatives in Switzerland' in Patrick Haenni and Stéphane Lathion (eds) *The Swiss Minaret Ban: Islam in Question* (trans. Tom Genrich) (Fribourg: Religioscope, 2011), p. 17.
[3]Douglas Pratt, *The Church and Other Faiths: The World Council of Churches, the Vatican, and Interreligious Dialogue* (Bern: Peter Lang, 2010), p. 20.
[4]See Gould's 'Alien Religiosity', this issue.
[5]Jean-François Mayer, 'In the Shadow of the Minaret: Origins and Implications of a Citizens' Initiative', in Haenni and Lathion, op. cit., p. 10.
[6]Ibid., p. 14.

different confessions or faith communities – historically, of course, this refers to the need to maintain stability and peace between Catholic and Protestant interests arising out of the origins of Switzerland as a confederation of autonomous cantons (regions) initially either Catholic or Protestant. Thus the federal state has a duty to ensure the ongoing stability of the federation, although as with other European states such as Germany whose modern identity arose out of inner-Christian sectarian tensions, nowadays these tensions have been resolved by the twin processes of secularisation and ecumenism. Since the minaret vote there is now a third paragraph within the constitution, namely one which forbids their construction. Ironically, this new third paragraph takes the place of an earlier third paragraph that was rescinded over a decade ago, namely a prohibition on the formation of new Catholic dioceses – a provision which had been inserted in respect to the state's keeping of the peaceful balance between the two Christian communities.

Muslims in Switzerland

The Census of 2000 recorded just 4.26 per cent (310,807) of the population as Muslim. By comparison, Christians made up at least three-quarters, with almost 42 per cent recorded as Roman Catholic and a little less than a third as Protestant. A decade earlier, in 1990, there were 152,200 Muslims and in 1980 just 56,600. Today it is estimated that there are some 350-400,000 Muslims across Switzerland, mainly migrants from south-eastern European countries such as Turkey and the Balkans. The majority are Sunni (c. 75 per cent), some 7 per cent are Shi'a and 10–15 per cent comprises a combination of Turkish Alevites and Sufis.[7] Typically, they are very well integrated into Swiss society and for the most part are quite secular in outlook and practice. Factors in Muslim immigration include economic and political motivations: for instance, workers from Turkey and the former Yugoslavia; more recently refugees and asylum seekers. So, despite their still relatively small proportion of the total population of some seven million, Muslims comprise the third largest religious community after the Christian churches.[8]

Of the nearly 311,000 registered Muslims in 2000, the majority (88 per cent) were foreigners with different residence categories. Only 12 per cent were actually Swiss citizens. Those coming from other birth countries included Yugoslavian (especially from Kosovo) as the biggest group, at 39 per cent; Turks comprised 23 per cent; Macedonians made up 16 per cent; from Bosnia-Herzegovinia there was 9 per cent, and from upper east North Africa (Maghreb) 4 per cent. As at 2000, most Muslims in Switzerland lived in just five cantons: Zürich (65,000); Aargau (29,000); Bern (27,000); St Gallen (27,000) and Waadt (24,000). Some 90 per cent of Turkish Muslims and some 80 per cent of the Muslims from the former Yugoslavia were in German-speaking Switzerland. Although numbers have since changed, these patterns of relativity remain more or less.

Swiss Muslim social structure is today fairly well developed with some 150 Muslim cultural and social organisations. Muslims in Switzerland are reckoned, on the whole, to be relatively nominal vis-à-vis religious practices. There are many different forms of Islam in evidence, and differences of identity are linked to the countries of origin or to membership of a specific community. There is also evidence of a wide range of individual interpretation of the Quran and traditional Muslim texts. The majority of Muslims see no difficulty

---

[7]See Felix Muller and Mathias Tanner, 'Muslime, Minarette und die Minarett-Initiative in der Schweiz: Grundlagen' in Mathias Tanner, Felix Müller, Frank Mathwig and Wolfgang Lienemann (eds) *Streit um das Minarett: Zusammenleben in der religiöse pluralistischen Gesellschaft* (Zürich: Theologischer Verlag, 2009), pp. 21–43.
[8]Wolfgang Lienemann, 'Argumente für ein Minaret-Verbot? Eine kritische Analyze' in Tanner et al., op. cit., p. 123.

harmonising their Islamic identity with Swiss citizenship and values. In 2005 a qualitative study investigated four dimensions of Muslim life: religious practice; citizenship awareness; the understanding of integration into Swiss society; the understanding of cultural identity.[9] The main conclusion states that Muslims in Switzerland display a very heterogeneous profile and a highly individualised religious viewpoint. There is no single Islam or sole Muslim community within Switzerland. Islam in Switzerland is itself a diverse phenomenon, not a religious monolith.

Some 90 per cent of Muslims in Switzerland are categorised as alien, so they are ineligible to vote. Of course, as Muller and Tanner point out, Muslims in Switzerland would feel themselves to be better integrated if, indeed, they had the right to vote.[10] As it happened, they were disenfranchised from casting a vote on a matter that directly affected them. But to what extent were Muslims in Switzerland impacted by the vote to ban minaret construction? Rifa'at Lenzin notes that the minaret is a primary architectural symbol of Islam, alongside the tropes of dome and crescent moon.[11] She usefully explores the origins, etymology and structural styles of minarets and notes the reasons for minarets in any given situation are varied; so too is the self-understanding of Muslims with respect to the symbolic significance of their minarets. What is of primary importance to Muslims is communal prayer space – the mosque as such. Wherever Muslims live, they gravitate to the dream, then reality, of their own place to pray. Muslim reactions to the Initiative ranged from indignation to resignation. For many the anti-minaret initiative was viewed as a further expression within Switzerland of increasing Islamophobia and of hostility toward Muslims. Certainly most Muslims felt themselves silenced by the fact they are not Swiss but aliens in Switzerland, therefore their voices were largely absent. They were present, but talked about in the third person.

For many, as a purely practical matter of cost and building-code compliance, the erection of a minaret at their local mosque is a non-starter. It is not an issue; minarets are not seen by most Swiss Muslims as a 'must-have' feature of their place of prayer. Nevertheless, the negative and unsettling impact of the ban is of considerable significance. Many were deeply shocked; others took a more resigned stance. So what was this so-called 'initiative' to have the building of minarets banned all about?

The Citizens' Initiative: Background and Motivation

Two political parties, the far-right SVP/UDC (Democratic Union of the Centre) and the right-leaning EDU/EDF (Federal Democratic Union) formulated and promoted the initiative that would ban the building new minarets. The initiative process was launched in May 2007 and a petition of some 115,000 valid signatures was submitted in July 2008. Populist concerns were picked up and fanned into fires of fear by the right-wing politicians eager for grassroots support. Xenophobia and racism played a part in the negative discourse, alongside anxieties associated with immigration and asylum-seeker concerns, and diatribe about foreign-born criminals. However, for the most part, the attention of angst was Islam itself; the minaret the focal symbol so far as the discourse about Islam was concerned.[12] Construed as a symbolic motif of a presumably exclusivist and domineering religion, the

---

[9]Eidgenössische Ausländerkommission, *Muslime in der Schweiz. Identitätsprofile, Erwartungen und Einstellungen. Eine Studie der Forschungsgruppe 'Islam in der Schweiz'* (Geneva: GRIS, 2005).
[10]Muller and Tanner, op. cit., p. 31.
[11]Rifa'at Lenzin, 'Eine muslimische Perspektive auf die Minarett-Diskussion und das Zusammenleben in der Schweiz von morgen' in Mathias Tanner et al., op. cit., pp. 45–60.
[12]Cf. Mayer, 'In the Shadow of the Minaret', op. cit., p. 8.

response of the Swiss to an imagined Islamic take-over threat was to enact a domineering exclusivism of their own, by way of a blanket rejection of a rather little-found material feature. The architectural trope became the lightening rod of pent-up angst. As Lienemann notes, the motives and arguments of the initiative broadly reflect and echo concerns and prejudices widely held throughout Western Europe. The general question underlying much of the negative discourse, he suggests, is whether Islam, with its predominating legal perspective and approach, is in the end compatible with a free society?[13]

The Vote

So it was that in November 2009 the Swiss voted to ban the building of minarets. Representing 53.4 per cent of eligible voters, the total vote meant a clear majority of the electorate had their democratic right. The relatively low turnout has been largely attributed to the fact that earlier polling indicated the vote would be lost; thus a significant number of potential voters against the measure either assumed it would not pass in any case, or else did not regard it an issue worth voting upon. Nevertheless, democratic justice was seen to be done, even if many railed against the outcome as itself an unjust legislative action. Despite the fact that all major political parties, together with the Federal Council and the Churches, advised against a vote in favour of the ban, 57.5 per cent of those *who voted* did just that. Nevertheless, it was an absolute *minority* of all *eligible* voters who voted in favour. Thus, in reality, a minority vote brought about a constitutional ban on the building of minarets in Switzerland. The Swiss Federation of Protestant Churches (SEK–FEPS) acknowledges that, in the run-up to the vote, the initiative:

> ... was underestimated by most of the established political parties. Most rejected it very quickly, but in a pretty superficial way, and didn't attack it very strongly. This is also linked with the fact that political parties are not very comfortable with issues around religions.[14]

Indeed, all the polls leading up to the vote indicated the initiative would be lost. The fact they were so wrong indicates a substantial expression of private prejudice, or simple anti-Muslim conviction, where individual values and opinions took precedence over any party-line principle, other than with the supportive right-wing parties. Although the result was an unpleasant surprise for many, of deep significance is the underlying fact that the free democratic culture and practise of direct democracy, as it has evolved in Switzerland is not up for debate even though there might be some tensions or contradictions between direct democracy rights and human rights. Law by referendum is an important part of Swiss political culture.

Initiative Arguments – Analysis and Reactions

On the whole the rationale for the ban was very confused, indeed quite bizarre, and played deliberately upon an inchoate fear of an impositional Islam, drawing on popular prejudice. The minaret was portrayed as a symbol of aggression and power, an inherently negative symbolic edifice within Switzerland representing an inherent Muslim desire to live by,

---

[13] Lienemann, 'Argumente für ein Minaret-Verbot?' in Tanner et al., op. cit., p. 135.
[14] SEK–FEPS, *Background Paper on Switzerland's Vote on Minarets* (July, 2010). Schweizerischer Evangelischer Kirchenbund – Federation des Eglises protestantes de Suisse (SEK-FEPS), 'Background Paper on Switzerland's Vote on Minarets', November 2009, http://www.sek-feps.ch/sites/default/files/media/pdf/themen/minarett/110929_Backgroundpaper_Minaretfinal_update.pdf (accessed 2 May 2013).

and impose on others, Sharia law codes. As Lienemann notes, central to the anti-minaret argument is the claim that the building of minarets is an expression of Muslim pretensions of socio-political hegemony.[15] The reference to minarets as symbolising Muslim aggression was quite widespread and utilized by some right-wing politicians. Barbara Steinemann of the SVP/UDC party, even claimed they reminded her of rockets.[16] Also, the anti-minaret rhetoric drew heavily on 9/11 as a background context, and made references also to former European negative interactions with Islam, the general European history of perception and experience of Islam, as well as contemporary migration issues. Thus the motivation for the 'yes' vote was based on a perception of the global political Islamic world, with minarets regarded as the symbol of an aggrandizing power; and this power, and so its primary symbol, must be resisted. The one object was seen to represent symbolically both piety and power – with power emerging as the dominant motif, so provoking a fearful reaction. Muslims were portrayed invariably as religious fanatics; intolerant and unenlightened; indeed, resistant to Enlightenment and post-Enlightenment ideals and thought thus incapable of integration into the normal realms of western society.[17] As Muller and Tanner put it, 'the minaret is thus a symbol of a religio-political demand which wants to know nothing of fundamental religious freedom'.[18] Yet the genuinely religious aspect of the matter, and the question of religious freedom, was not particularly evident in the discourse leading up to the vote. Interreligious dialogue played no role, 'although there is a large consensus within the population that it is necessary'.[19]

Wolfgang Lienemann has analysed arguments in favour of the ban and found them to be mostly a mash of prejudicial assertions rather than coherent and reasoned arguments as such. However, some are of a more structured nature, drawing on apparent hard evidence and supportive opinions of scholars; but in fact slanting, twisting, and misinterpreting them to a large degree. The usual stratagem of taking things out of context and presenting them in an unfavourable light is liberally employed. He notes the EDU/UDF made use of a more specifically religious argument by spuriously distinguishing minarets from church-towers and referring to them as symbolic of Islam's presumably inherent drive to predominance and power, thus: 'Minarets, at the core of these arguments, are seen as symbolic of an intentional Islamic grasp for power and the ousting of the entire (liberal) Swiss legal system'.[20] On the basis that Swiss society is founded upon Christian values and principles, and that Islamic values and principles are something wholly alien, then Islam *per se* (and especially Islamic law) is entirely incompatible with Swiss society. But this ignores the reality of the secular contract: Swiss citizens can hold radically different, even incompatible, religious beliefs, and indeed take a critical perspective toward the state and at the same time concede, whether implicitly or explicitly, to live within the societal norms and abide by the legal expectations and framework of the state. Indeed, the state itself guarantees religious freedoms with respect to belief and practice.[21]

Paradoxically, the EDU/UDF endorses the active missionary engagement and presence of Christianity within Swiss society – even though it is a secular society – as beneficial for the health of the wider society; but any comparable activity by Muslims in respect to Islam

---

[15] See W. Lienemann, 'Einleitung' in Tanner et al., op. cit., p. 10.
[16] Samuel M. Behloul, Minarett-Initiative: 'Im Spannungsfeld zwischen Abwehr-Reflex und impliziter Anerkennung neuer gesellschaftlicher Fakten' in Tanner et al., op. cit., p. 109.
[17] Ibid., p. 107.
[18] Felix Muller and Mathias Tanner, 'Muslime, Minarette und die Minarett-Initiative in der Schweiz'. in Tanner et al., op. cit., p. 40.
[19] SEK–FEPS, op. cit., p. 3.
[20] Lienemann, 'Argumente für ein Minaret-Verbot? Eine kritische Analyze', in Tanner et al., op. cit., p. 129.
[21] Ibid., p. 130.

Table 1. Comparison of Swiss and Islamic values.

Swiss values	Islam
Tolerance	Intolerant world religion
Free, religious freedom	Compelling, forceful, impositional
Human/basic rights	Oppressive (towards women), anti-human rights, etc
Democracy, secularism	Impositional law and theocracy, political–religious
Individuality	Obligation for comparative obedience, submission
Neutrality	Committed to power and influence of religion
International, world-affirming	Fundamentalist, traditionalist, archaic
Egalitarian	No integrative potential; discriminatory; anti-women

is ruled out as unhealthy. Indeed, Islam is regarded as finding its strength to act directly in proportion to Christianity's propensity to inaction: 'The power of Islam is in the weakness of Christianity' is the mantra of the right-wing proponent of the ban.[22] The anti-minaret lobby appealed to an atavistic desire for an assertive, imperialist, even aggressive form of muscular Christianity that stands up to its enemies.

Another general argument of the anti-minaret lobby was that the presence of Islam in Europe threatens the secular status-quo; therefore Islam should be either 'tamed' or rejected.[23] But it is unlikely to be tamed, in the sense of becoming, like the churches, secularised vis-à-vis relations with the state. So it must be rejected. The very presence of Islam is regarded as threatening the religious freedom of others, thus the initiative sought 'to ban a religious-political symbol of that which represents the rejection of religious toleration thereby ensuring the freedom of belief for all'.[24] The presumed negative situation of women in Islamic countries also played a role for many in formulating their stance on the minaret ban issue. The fact that in some Muslim countries Christians are not allowed to build churches, or enjoy civic freedoms, was also made use of, but as a negative quid pro quo argument. The religious peace of this land (Switzerland) would be endangered were the unfettered erection of minarets to proceed; and besides, so long as Christians do not have the freedom to build churches and promote their religion in Muslim lands, then Muslims in 'our' land should be likewise denied.

Clearly, lying behind many negative arguments and opinions supporting the ban is the reality that many Swiss do hold fears concerning Islam and its perceived and presumed challenge to Swiss democracy. Some stated that the rising overt presence of Islam leads them to feel as foreigners in their own land; at least, that was the rhetoric employed. Thus Henry Both asks: 'Do we really have so many ignorant, frightened, uncritical or unenlightened voting citizens in our land?'[25] In the event, the Initiative's propaganda triumphed over sensible critical reflection, analysis and judgement. The negative press and dimensions of Islam were read as descriptive of normative Islam, and so of all Muslims, *per se*.

With respect to external perceptions of what was taking place in Switzerland, a headline such as 'Minaret Ban Challenges Tolerant Swiss Image' exemplified the reaction of the liberal US media: something is amiss in the state of Switzerland. However, the reaction of conservative media was conspicuously different: the Swiss are doing what others can

---

[22]Ibid., p. 131.
[23]Behloul, op. cit., p. 106.
[24]Ibid.
[25]Henry Both, 'Der Schock und seine Folgen' in Andreas Gross, Fredi Krebs, Martin Schaffner and Martin Stohler (eds) *Von der Provokation zum Irrtum: Menschenrechte und Demokratie nach dem Minarett-Bauverbot* (St-Ursanne: Editions le Doubs, 2010), p. 118.

only wish for – enacting a halt on things Islamic. But a clear critical point was made nonetheless, namely that, as there are only four minarets in Switzerland, with hardly a flood of applications to build more, the decision to ban further minaret building can only be interpreted as a symbolic action taken in sympathy with an anti-Muslim stance as such.[26] Further, the Swiss action was criticised as, paradoxically, mirroring an exclusivist Muslim stance, such as with Saudi Arabia, towards the religious 'other' which the west often fulminates against. Typically, in the west, the cry is that Muslim countries ought to display towards others (usually Christian and/or Jewish others) the same openness and freedom to practise one's faith that the (Judeo-Christian) west shows towards religious others, including in particular, Muslims. So, Switzerland was acting more like an exclusivist Muslim country than an inclusivist western one. Furthermore, as Yves Winter pointed out, the American media tended to the view the minaret ban as representing not so much a special Swiss case but rather interpreted it in the context of a growing European Islamophobia.[27] Switzerland has enacted something that a considerable portion of European society apparently feels – a generalised antipathy towards Islam as such.

Lienemann's summary of anti-minaret arguments is incisive.[28]

(1) The minaret is a symbol of power for Muslims in Switzerland inspiring them to carry out their demand for Sharia to be their own law independently of, and in this way to threaten and in the end to destroy the liberal Swiss legal system. This must be utterly resisted.
(2) Islamic norms are incompatible with the Swiss legal system.
(3) Religious freedom in Switzerland is threatened by the building of minarets which moreover are frequently financed or financially underwritten by fundamentalist Islamic groups or governments.
(4) In numerous Muslim lands there is no religious freedom for non-Muslims, or only a very limited freedom.

Although many individuals, organisations, and churches rallied behind the Muslims in reacting against the initiative to ban minaret construction, the vote for the ban was successful. Counter-arguments were based largely on legal and rights issues, issues of ethics and human rights, and freedom of religion. The question of what makes for a genuine multicultural society, as enshrined in laws and rights, was raised. All human persons, irrespective of the manifest diversity of human beings – ethnically, culturally, religiously and so on – are entitled to the dignity of being who they are.[29]

Post-vote Analysis

The vote has also been interpreted as the consequence of the failure of public opinion forming institutions.[30] In particular the media were criticised as having focussed solely on the negative global image of Islam – terrorism, Iraq, wars in Lebanon, Afghanistan, Gaza; unrest in Iran, strife in Yemen, conflict with Libya.[31] Thus Islam anywhere was identified with Hizbollah, Hamas, Taliban, al-Qaida, Iranian mullahs and so on. The image of fundamentalist and autocratic Islamic regimes overrode the reality of Muslims in

---

[26] Cf. Yves Winter, 'Kritik und Unverständnis: Medienreaktionen aus den USA', in Gross et al., op. cit., p. 176.
[27] Ibid.
[28] See ibid., p. 132.
[29] Cf. Muller and Tanner, op. cit., p. 41.
[30] Cf. Gross et al., op. cit., 2010, p. 11.
[31] See Roger Blum and Marlis Prinzig, 'Das Versagen der Medien', in Gross et al., op. cit., pp. 19–24.

Switzerland, the overwhelming majority of who are moderate and integrated. Blum and Prinzig argued that had the media played a proper critical role in the debate, instead of sensationalising the negative and pandering to reaction, the outcome may well have been different. Joris and Riederer[32] provided a trenchant feminist critique that explores the negative portrayals of the symbolism of the minaret, the narrow view of Muslim women's rights, and the linking of the minaret question with the Burka issue: does forbidding of one imply dealing with the other? Are religious architectural and clothing codes not part and parcel of human rights? And so does forbidding any of them trample on human rights?

The Swiss image of Islam, as analysed from 183 newspaper letters-to-the-editor on the subject of the vote, is marked by a diffused public anxiety that contributed to the outcome.[33] There was a predominance of negative image, rhetoric, and logic as, for example, in the putative argument that Muslims do not allow churches and church towers in their lands, so why should we allow minarets in ours? Minarets were treated not as a religious symbol, but as a symbol of power and the supposed Muslim desire to dominate. Islam and Muslim culture in general were regarded with anxiety as a foreign 'other', inherently resistant to true integration. So-called 'Swiss values' were posited in contrast to presumed 'Muslim values' with the clear implication that they cannot coexist in any contiguous fashion. Such values included: tolerance, freedom, religious freedom, human rights, democracy, individualism, neutrality, secularism, internationalism, egalitarianism, and so on. Based on an analysis of many letters, an insightful comparison of values leading to contrasting portrayals of the religions involved has emerged as follows.[34]

Swiss letters-to-the-editor revealed a view of Islam as inherently alarming and threatening. It was repeatedly asserted that Islam is a political–religious system that is simply not compatible with a democratic state. Nevertheless, some Swiss certainly did see the inherent paradox, if not danger, in the outcome: 'a minaret ban clearly contradicts the spirit of our liberal constitutional regulations'; and also that the ban 'offends also against the Swiss guarantee of religious freedom'.[35]

Some Issues and Responses

The minaret ban has certainly raised a number of social and political, as well as theological and philosophical, issues. The ban touches on a range of basic issues: human rights, the principle of non-discrimination, religious freedom, and the rule of law. As Muller and Tanner note, freedom of religion in conjunction with cultural identity is a central fundamental right with the minaret initiative pointing 'to the issue of dealing with cultural and religious minorities'.[36] Since more than 20 per cent of the Swiss population is foreign, there are always questions arising concerning integration policy, in this case particularly with regard to Muslims and Islamic culture centres. Ongoing questions include: What exactly is a mosque? What has to belong to it and what not? What are the appropriate academic and administrative requirements for working permits for imams? Can there be Muslim cemeteries – after more than hundred years of non-denominational cemeteries? What is the place of religious symbols in the public sphere? Can there be headscarves for students and teachers? The way Islamic countries honour – or not, as the case may be – religious freedom for churches was an important question for many, as already noted. In

---

[32]Elisabeth Joris and Katrin Riederer, 'Not in our Name', in Gross et al., op. cit., pp. 25–36.
[33]See Simon Landwehr, 'Das helvetische Bild des Islam', in Gross et al., op. cit., pp. 37–48.
[34]Ibid., p. 45.
[35]Ibid., p. 41.
[36]Muller and Tanner, op. cit., in Tanner et al., op. cit., p. 42.

response, the Swiss Council of Religions and the churches attempted to take into account the matter of non-Muslims in Islamic countries in a nuanced manner: 'We need to work toward a global "symmetry of justice"... [for a]... "symmetry of *in*justice" is not a solution'.[37]

A widespread sense of shock at the outcome continues to be felt and expressed. Swiss value their unique, highly participatory democratic system, but the outcome on this occasion was like nothing before. Any presumption that an open democracy tends naturally to produce 'liberal' outcomes was severely shaken: 'The minaret initiative was the first initiative in the history of Swiss democracy where it is the case that after the vote, as well as before, there has been ongoing intensive discussion'.[38] There is often expressed a sense of having now to learn from this event; that, indeed, the very functioning of Swiss democracy and political self-understanding as a nation is on the line. The democratic conundrum posed by the vote is quite stark: How could the Swiss vote against the very democratic freedoms enshrined in their own constitution and the convention on Human Rights? Interestingly, Josef Lang links the Muslim minaret issue to the 1893 anti-Semitic vote, which was also the result of a popular initiative.[39] In that case, on the basis of Switzerland being a Christian land, Jews living there were effectively compelled to fully integrate and so not stand out as 'different'. Given this history, Lang argues that the consequence of the minaret vote is that Switzerland needs a new debate about its democracy as such. This is echoed by Hans Widmer who remarks: 'Whoever wishes to consider the relationship between democracy and religion must first clarify the deeper meaning of democracy and religion'.[40] In other words, what are they and how are they related?

According to Lienemann, the chief issue of the minaret debate had to do with the perception of Islam and the meaning of minarets as such.[41] Are they representative symbols of belief and practice, or do they really represent pretensions to power and predominance? In other words, is the issue a matter of religious or political perception, or both? Certainly from out of the process and its aftermath there have been significant consequences for the churches in Switzerland and for interreligious engagement involving Muslims. Indeed, it can be asked: What does this vote mean for Christian–Muslim engagement in Switzerland at a time when the wider Christian church 'without any abandoning of its missionary mandate, has reached a position where interreligious relations and dialogue... has been affirmed and embraced?'[42] The fact that the ban occurred despite the clear critical opinion and advice of churches and allied councils, which otherwise enjoy good dialogical relations with local Muslims, throws into sharp relief the level of dissonance between formal and official stances and local attitudes. Lenzin, for example, is concerned that it will be difficult for the future of dialogical relations between Muslims and Christians and, furthermore, that it could contribute to the likelihood of increased radicalisation of young Swiss-born Muslims who may feel effectively rejected in their homeland.[43] As it happens, interreligious engagement with Islam has been at the forefront of official church engagements and statements ever since 9/11.[44]

---

[37]SEK–FEPS, op. cit., p. 2.
[38]Gross, op. cit., p. 12.
[39]Josef Lang, 'Gestern die Juden, heute die Muslime', in Gross et al., op. cit., pp. 78–82.
[40]Hans Widmer, 'Reflexions- und Qualitätsdefizite', in Gross et al., op. cit., p. 94.
[41]Wolfgang Lienemann, 'Einleitung', in Tanner et al., op. cit., pp. 9–19.
[42]Pratt, op. cit., p. 20.
[43]Lenzin, ibid.
[44]Frank Mathwig, 'Das Kreuz mit den Minaretten: Theologische Bemerkungen zur Rolle der Kirchen in der Minarett-Diskussion', in Tanner et al., op. cit., p. 145.

Dialogue with Muslims is regularly affirmed and the condemnation of the proposal to ban minarets was universal in terms of official church response and advice. Nevertheless, aside from asserting opposition to the ban, there was little in the way of active church engagement in the public arena in the lead-up to the vote. But the outcome led inevitably to a suggestion of a lack of credibility of the churches in their formal opposition to the ban. However, the Roman Catholic and the Old Catholic Churches, together with the Federation of Swiss Protestant Churches and the Swiss Council of Religions, did contribute to the pre-vote debate by focussing on the issue of the restriction of religious freedom which had the support of all member churches.[45] Indeed, both the Federation of Swiss Protestant Churches and the Swiss Council of Religions:

> ... resolved that the Minaret Initiative is untenable. There are problems and questions with regard to some fundamentalist groups, and there are for sure unsolved questions in the interreligious dialogue with Islam as such, not only in Switzerland. All this has to be discussed and seriously addressed. But the Minaret Initiative is definitely the wrong way to do it and the wrong answer to some existing difficulties.[46]

And elsewhere the Swiss Council of Religions made clear its rejection of the anti-minaret Initiative:

> The Council, which consists of leaders from the Christian, Jewish, and Muslim communities, is dedicated to protecting religious peace in Switzerland and to strengthening trust among the churches and religious communities... The Swiss Council of Religions views the freedom of religion as a basic universal right... [It] thus attempts, within the limits of its possibilities and contacts, to assert its influence in situations of religious discrimination, marginalization, and persecution in other countries.[47]

Opposition to the minaret ban has not only thrown up aforementioned social, political and religious issues, it also begs a range of philosophical questions. A key question has to do with the matter of religious freedom as a private right to self-expression, on the one hand, and the public right to determine political and corporate national identity in terms of what constitutes, both figuratively and literally, the (national) self-image, on the other. Wherein is true liberality to be found? And how is religious diversity to be construed? The Swiss Council of Religions notes that 'Switzerland, a country with a Christian background and a variety of cultures, confessions, and languages, is distinguished by its diversity (that) has, moreover... increased as the result of globalization and worldwide migration'.[48] The Council goes on to state:

> Switzerland has known cultural diversity for a long time. It is part of its history and characteristic of the Swiss identity. The people of this country have developed rules and systems of coexistence in the course of a long common history. The

---

[45] See SEK–FEPS, op. cit., p. 2.
[46] Ibid.
[47] Swiss Council of Religions, *For Religious Coexistence in Peace and Freedom: Statement of the Swiss Council of Religions on the Referendum Initiative to Ban the Construction of Minarets* (Berne: Swiss Council of Religions, 2009), p. 1.
[48] SCR, op. cit., p. 2.

resulting rules are such an integral part of the cultural tradition of the country that its people are hardly aware of them in explicit terms; and at the center of this democratic self-image lies the recognition of the freedom of each individual within the framework of a legal order that is equally binding for all... Cultural diversity thus serves to make Switzerland strong.[49]

Personal reflection of a self-confessed Swiss 'secular Muslim', Jasmin El-Sonbati gives a salutary perspective on the impact of the minaret ban upon Muslim life and sensibilities. Born of an Egyptian father and Austrian mother, raised in Egypt and Europe, for a long time now a resident in Switzerland whilst also regular visitor to Cairo, she asks by way of a response to the vote in favour of the Minaret ban, 'can I, a secular Muslim who is against religious fanaticism, live with a mosque that has no minaret?'[50] She is confronted with a personal conundrum: 'Egyptians were astonished as to why liberal Switzerland, a model of democracy and human rights, could in any case forbid minarets'.[51] She had never expected the Swiss to vote in favour, for to do so would give credence to the arguments and ideologies of the right-wing political forces: 'Nevertheless, on the evening of 29 November 2009 I was shocked and astonished, despite my unconditional faith in the Swiss democratic order'.[52]

The outcome of the vote prompted an inner quest and dialogue to decide where she stood and what kind of Islamic life she can now lead. Prompted by an uneasiness that she felt as a result of the vote, her book is a personal perspective, as one of the some 400,000 Muslims in Switzerland, to explore how Muslims have lived, and now can live, in Switzerland, or live as Swiss Muslims. What does the controversy mean for Muslim life and self-reflection? Her challenge to the Muslim and so also the Swiss community is a vision of inclusively tolerant and broadly accepting liberal religious and secular societies that can get on with one another. In her perspective, a mosque needs no minaret as such; it is the life of Islam which is the important thing: 'Our mosque has no minaret, for our God [Allah] does not need stone... yet if the building authorities approve, and our neighbours are agreed, we will build a small tower'.[53]

Consequences and Counter-policy Prospects

The promoting right-wing political parties had together received 30.2 per cent of the electoral vote in the 2007 general election. That their jointly sponsored initiative against minarets garnered a 57.5 per cent mandate was considered a considerable political victory. Interestingly, however, 57.5 per cent of a turnout of 53.4 per cent of eligible voters amounts to attracting support of just 30.7 per cent of the voting public. While the conclusion has been that a sizeable minority of voters who normally support other parties and their policies in fact voted against the party line in this case, it could equally be concluded that the appeal of the issue was such as to draw out an almost 100 per cent of right-wing party supporters who voted in favour, thus overwhelming the otherwise normal balances of the democratic process. Martin Mühlheim is certain that the anti-

---

[49]Ibid., p. 3.
[50]Jasmin El-Sonbati, *Moscheen ohne Minarett: eine Muslimin in der Schweiz* (Oberhofen am Thunersee: Zytgolgge Verlag, 2010), p. 8.
[51]Ibid.
[52]Ibid., p. 9.
[53]Ibid., p. 12.

minaret vote reveals the extent to which anxiety about Islam is rife.[54] The outcome resolves nothing other than to embed in law a measure of discrimination against a particular group that exists within Swiss society. Emil Brix raises the issue of the direct challenge of the Swiss democratically derived outcome for democracy in Europe.[55] There is a key issue to be addressed namely that of democratic process: representative decision making, versus direct (as in Switzerland) democratic vote, and how that plays out in terms of other democratic conventions and obligations.

Following initial surprise at the wide acceptance of the anti-minaret initiative, 'the view has been gaining ground that this decision on the part of the population entails an opportunity to begin a new discussion on questions of relevance' and in this regard 'the churches and religious communities had to recognize that their focus on religious freedom as main arguments against the initiative failed and didn't reach the heart of the majority of the voters'.[56] In fact the vote:

> ... showed indirectly too how much our population is secularized when it comes to decide on issues addressing religious issues, and how difficult it has become to talk on religious issues or religious symbols in the European public sphere. The danger of instrumentalization of religion was evident. It is to be seriously taken by the churches that their voice is more and more difficult to be heard.[57]

Subsequent to the vote, Swiss Christian leaders stated that:

> The result of the referendum was the expression of a search for identity in our country. The role religion plays for the identity of a secular society that reflects a Judeo-Christian past and in which 80 per cent of the population retains its membership in a Christian church is not that clear anymore. What does actually a 'post-secular' society mean? What does it mean, in concrete terms, that religion is a public matter? What should religion matter to the state? What holds our society together?[58]

For the churches, the signal consequence is the apparent and quite likely real intra-religious challenge of interreligious engagement, especially with respect to Islam. An earlier report from a meeting of the World Council of Churches (WCC) had made the point that a negative opinion of the religious other provokes negative responses. The challenge, in this case as elsewhere, is to connect grassroots Christianity with the theology and praxis of interreligious engagement. As Reinhold Bernhardt asserts, commitment to one's own tradition and the claim to universal validity are not mutually exclusive.[59]

In many ways, as noted above, the Swiss vote is an expression of a wider European tension.[60] Dietrich Fischer asks how a culture clash can be prevented and makes a plea for the pursuit of positive interrelations.[61] Hans Köchler sees the vote in the context of

---

[54] Martin Mühlheim, 'Vom Ernstnehmen der Ängste', in Gross et al., op. cit., p. 131.
[55] Emil Brix, 'Die Schweiz: Eine Enttäuschung für Europa?', in Gross et al., op. cit., pp. 189–196.
[56] SEK–FEPS, op. cit., p. 3.
[57] Ibid.
[58] Ibid., p. 4.
[59] Reinhold Bernhardt, 'Die Polarität von Freiheit und Liebe: Überlegungen zur interreligiösen Urteilsbildung aus dogmatischer Perspektive' in R. Bernhardt, *Kriterien interreligiöser Urteilsbildung* (Zürich: Beiträge zu einer Theologie der Religionen 1, 2005), p. 72.
[60] Cf the paper in this issue by Armando Salvatore, 'Islam and the Quest for a European Secular Identity'.
[61] Dietrich Fischer, 'Wie können wir die Konfrontation der Kulturen verhindern?', in Gross et al., op. cit., pp. 209–213.

the crisis of European identity in light of late twentieth century postcolonial immigration and so forth; what price diversity and homogeneity?[62] The Swiss initiative highlights key problems and questions of cultural identity, rights, and political processes. Köchler hopes the Swiss will eventually turn the decision around. Others draw comparisons with other earlier historical moments of stress between Europe and Islam, noting the need to distinguish today between Islam and Islamism. Muslims have a major problem with the negative portrayal of Islam, thus suggesting a need for better community education about this religion. Nevertheless, as the Swiss Council of Religions has asserted:

> The dialogue among the churches and religious communities of Switzerland shows that differences of religion, culture, tradition, and social–political views do not preclude a deep common belief that all people share the same inalienable dignity. The fundamental rights to the freedom of belief and conscience apply equally to all. The right to construct mosques and minarets can therefore not be made to depend on whether religious minorities enjoy the same religious freedoms in other countries. Answering injustice with further injustice would be a betrayal of Swiss values.[63]

Conclusion

Wolfgang Lienemann notes that the so-called Swiss culture of tolerance derives from the Edict of Nantes (1598) that ushered in a century of religious freedom: 'It was not tolerance in today's sense; rather that religious dissidence and plurality were no longer persecuted'.[64] Indeed, he avers that religious tolerance and the freedom of denominational identity lie ultimately at the very foundation of modern Switzerland. In point of fact:

> Permanent neutrality is a principle of Swiss foreign policy. It serves to preserve Switzerland's independence and the invulnerability of its national territory. In parallel, Switzerland undertakes not to take part in wars between other states. In principle, neutrality is an obstacle neither to participation in economic sanctions nor to membership of international organizations such as the United Nations (UN) or the European Union (EU). Even military involvement in peace-keeping operations authorized by the UN or the parties to a conflict is compatible with neutrality. But Switzerland cannot become a member of a military alliance such as the North Atlantic Treaty Organization (NATO).[65]

Tolerant neutrality is thus a long-standing hallmark of Swiss society vis-à-vis its relations with other states and, with it, a culture of acceptance of variety and difference within, including religious, which has been hard-won in regard to its own history. According to the Swiss Council of Religions, the Swiss tradition is very much that the:

> ... freedoms guaranteed by the Federal Constitution form a foundation for the peaceful and respectful coexistence of people of different religions and cultures in Switzerland. Everyone has the right in this country to live their faith visibly,

---

[62]Hans Köchler, 'Multikulturalität, Demokratie und Rechtsstaatlichkeit in Europa', in Gross et al., op. cit., pp. 214–220.
[63]SCR, op. cit., p. 5.
[64]Lienemann, 'Einleitung', in Tanner et al., op. cit., p. 9.
[65]Swiss Federal Department of Foreign Affairs, *Swiss Neutrality*, http://www.eda.admin.ch/eda/en/home/topics/intla/cintla/ref_neutr.html (accessed 2 May 2013).

freely, and in a community within the framework of the public order. This also includes the construction of places of worship that are typical for their respective religion.[66]

Nevertheless, the freedom of Muslim religious expression, unlike all others, is now constitutionally curtailed. And, as the Council has pointed out, the minaret ban does not solve any problem:

> On the contrary, it only contributes to suspicion, mistrust, and aggression against people of Muslim faith... Switzerland enjoys a long liberal tradition, one that seeks out dialogue and works towards a common learning process. The country recognizes that the true challenge lies in finding ways for all of the society's members to live together despite any differences among them.[67]

Without doubt, the minaret ban violates both the Swiss constitution and the European Convention on Human Rights in respect to the freedom of religion and belief and also freedom from discrimination. Yet Lienemann argues that the greater portion of society effectively rejected the Initiative which, in reality, flies in the face of Swiss liberal and tolerant cultural identity.[68] Perhaps the problem, politically, was that too many who did not agree with the Initiative did not bother to vote – most likely because lead-up polls, in suggesting the vote would be lost, had the effect of promoting a measure of apathy on one side whilst galvanising its proponents on the other. Yet, as noted already, this is not the first time that a clause on religion has been added to the Constitution only to be rescinded at a later time. At one time Catholic action to amend organizational structures – as in forming new dioceses – was likewise prohibited. This has since been rescinded. The Swiss may have compromised their heritage of tolerant neutrality and social liberality with respect to the current ban applying to the Muslim community, but this is not an irredeemable situation. It is possible yet that international pressure and persuasion, if not direct legal action, will effect change. It is more likely, given the particularities of the Swiss democratic process, that a new sensibility will eventually dawn, one that embraces Islam in Switzerland as part and parcel of the cultural landscape and so will not regard the continuing of a minaret ban as a propos, especially given regular building code restrictions, compliances and ordinances. There is never a prospect of Switzerland's landscape being swamped by a sea of minarets. Time, and wider issues of accommodating religious diversity and in particular the presence of Islam, will yet tell.

---

[66] Ibid., p. 1.
[67] Ibid., p. 6.
[68] Lienemann, ibid.

Something Varied in the State of Denmark: Neo-nationalism, Anti-Islamic Activism, and Street-level Thuggery

MARK SEDGWICK

Aarhus University

ABSTRACT *The article argues that categories such as 'Islamophobic' and 'Right Wing' are inadequate and even misleading descriptors of reactions to Islam in Europe, and should be replaced by a distinction between neo-nationalism, anti-Islamic activism, and street-level thuggery. Neo-nationalism is a well-established but underused descriptor; anti-Islamic activism and street-level thuggery are more novel and are explored in the article. The article applies this threefold distinction to the case of Denmark. It is argued that the neo-nationalist Danish People's Party can be understood as a response to neo-nationalist views that are widespread among the Danish population. It is then argued that street-level thuggery, of which a small movement called* Stop the Islamisation of Denmark *is taken as an example, may be eye-catching, but is ultimately unimportant. Anti-Islamism, in contrast, may be important. Two Danish examples are examined: the very Danish* Tidehverv *movement, which shows how Christianity can still matter even in an apparently secular society, and the* Free Press Society, *a more influential Danish organization that is shown to be part of an international movement.*

Introduction

Western European countries are widely perceived to have become hostile in various degrees to Muslim immigrants and residents in recent years, a phenomenon generally ascribed either to the rise of the Far Right or to some form of racism, xenophobia or Islamophobia. Explanation in terms of the Far Right focuses attention on politics, while explanation in terms of racism focuses attention on the people, or at least on some of them. This article takes the case of Denmark, and argues that a much better understanding is provided by three separate but overlapping phenomena: neo-nationalism, anti-Islamic activism, and street-level thuggery.

'Neo-nationalism' is not a new concept, but is not widely known. As André Gingrich and Marcus Banks argued in 2006, it is a good label for a widespread contemporary social phenomenon – a particular set of attitudes and concerns among voters – that may have political consequences[1] such as, in the case of Denmark, the rise of the Danish People's

---

[1] André Gingrich and Marcus Banks, *Neo-nationalism in Europe and Beyond: Perspectives from Social Anthropology* (New York: Berghahn Books, 2006), p. 3.

Party (DPP; *Dansk Folkeparti*).[2] Anti-Islamic activism is a term that has occasionally been used in the press but has not been much used in scholarly writing, though Arun Kundnani has written interestingly on 'anti-Islamism' in Britain, a related trend since, as he notes, Islam and Islamism 'can easily be conflated',[3] and a recent report by George Soros's Centre for American Progress sometimes uses 'anti-Islam' when discussing developments in America.[4] It is used in this article to describe groups or individuals that focus on raising public awareness of the threat that they see as posed by Islam and on encouraging measures to combat that threat. It does not include groups or individuals focusing on other issues (feminists, for example) who sometimes criticize Islam or Muslims. As this article will show, anti-Islamic activism is present within the DPP, but the DPP itself cannot be described as an instance of anti-Islamic activism, because the DPP is a multi-issue political party that aims ultimately at attracting votes, while anti-Islamic activism is single-issue and aims at changing opinion. Finally, street-level thuggery is also term that has been used occasionally, but not in scholarly writings. It is used in this article to distinguish anti-Islamic activism from activities based around street violence.

This article does not argue that neo-nationalism, anti-Islamic activism, and street-level thuggery provide a complete explanation of recent events in Denmark or in Western Europe. It ignores, for example, the role played by the media. It merely argues that two of these three phenomena are central, and also that all three are separate, and need to be examined separately.

Something that might be called Islamophobia is present in neo-nationalism, which includes fear of Islam, and in anti-Islamic activism and street-level thuggery, which promote fear of Islam. However, the term 'Islamophobia' will not be used in this article, for a number of reasons. It lacks any agreed definition,[5] it is more polemical than analytic, it confuses very different phenomena, and it implies that the issue is primarily one of fear.[6] As will be shown below, fear does in fact play some part in hostility to Muslims and Islam, but it would be wrong to understand this hostility only in terms of fear.

Similarly, this article will make only very limited use of the term 'Far Right'. This is also a term that lacks any agreed definition and is highly polemical.[7] If applied to phenomena as different as neo-nationalist politics, anti-Islamic activism, and street-level thuggery, it too confuses very different phenomena. As Gingrich and Banks point out, the Far Right has historically been opposed to the democratic political system, working outside it and against it. Today's neo-nationalist politicians accept and work within the system, at least in Western Europe.[8] As this article shows, both the forms of anti-Islamic activism that matter are distinct from the traditional Far Right and from street-level thuggery.

---

[2]This article follows standard English usage in translating the Danish prefix *folke-* as 'people's' in the name of the party. However, in actual usage rather than etymology, the prefix signifies 'national' more than 'people's'.

[3]Arun Kundnani, 'Islamism and the Roots of Liberal Rage', *Race and Class*, 50:2 (2008), p. 43.

[4]Wajahat Ali, Eli Clifton, Matthew Duss, Lee Fang, Scott Keyes and Faiz Shakir, 'Fear, Inc.: The Roots of the Islamophobia Network in America', Center for American Progress, 2011, http://www.americanprogress.org/wp-content/uploads/issues/2011/08/pdf/islamophobia.pdf.

[5]José Pedro Zúquete, 'The European Extreme-right and Islam: New Directions?', *Journal of Political Ideologies*, 13:3 (2008), p. 323.

[6]John Bowen, 'Commentary on Bunzl', *American Ethnologist*, 32:4 (2005), p. 524, quoted in Zúquete, 'The European Extreme-right', p. 324.

[7]This was well illustrated by the range of views expressed in *Fascism Past and Present, West and East: An International Debate on Concepts and Cases in the Comparative Study of the Extreme Right*, ed. Roger Griffin, Werner Loh, and Andreas Umland (Stuttgart: Ibidem-Verlag, 2006).

[8]Gingrich and Banks, *Neo-nationalism in Europe and Beyond*, p. 3. They also distinguish neo-nationalism from regional secessionism, which is not an issue in Denmark. This distinction may not work equally well in some of the newer EU countries.

While understanding the phenomena discussed in this article as 'Islamophobia' results primarily in lack of precision, understanding them in terms of the Far Right can be positively misleading. If what this article describes as anti-Islamic activism is identified as Far Right, as it often is, attention is then directed to the traditional Far Right, often understood as street-level thuggery. This is marginal in Western Europe, and has little or no impact on mainstream politics. Anti-Islamic activism, in contrast, is not to be found on the margins, and can have an impact on mainstream politics, as this article shows. The impact of anti-Islamic activism is not the topic of this article, but it seems likely that it is two-fold. On the one hand, it provides analyses that, when repeated in the media, can impact both DPP voters and street-level thugs. On the other hand, and perhaps more importantly, it also has an impact on those who would normally oppose DPP-supported measures, and certainly street-level thuggery, in the name of liberalism and decency. Put simply, the traditional Far Right and street-level thuggery are not of great importance, while anti-Islamic activism is of importance. Neo-nationalism, however, is even more important. All three are distinct phenomena, but they also overlap, and overlaps will be indicated below.

This article will focus on the two phenomena to which least attention has so far been paid, neo-nationalist sentiment and anti-Islamic activism. It will examine both street-level thuggery and political responses to neo-nationalist sentiment only briefly. It also argues that older phenomena are also important, for example in the way that one particular understanding of Christianity lies at the origin of one of the two forms of anti-Islamic activism that this article will consider.

The Danish neo-nationalism examined in the article is probably fairly typical of neo-nationalism elsewhere in Western Europe, though it will be argued that the nature of the Danish electoral system has amplified its political consequences by giving the DPP more influence than it would have under some other electoral systems. One form of anti-Islamic activism considered in this article is international rather than Danish, and so has wider relevance, in America as well as in Europe. The other form of anti-Islamic activism is specifically Danish, but may still be of wider significance, as it is likely that it is not only in Denmark that factors older and other than neo-nationalism or international anti-Islamic activism are of importance.

The central events in Denmark that this article seeks to explain are those between 2001 and 2011, on which there is already a considerable literature.[9] These dates are determined by the election in 2001 at which a Centre-Right coalition government under the Liberals (*Venstre*) took power, and the election in 2011 at which it then lost power. This was the period during which Denmark introduced some of Europe's toughest laws against any further immigration and also passed laws to promote the 'integration' of immigrants. These were announced immediately after the 2001 election[10] and then refined

---

[9] See especially Jørgen Nielsen (ed.), *Islam in Denmark: The Challenge of Diversity* (Lanham: Lexington Books, 2012); Peter Hervik, *The Annoying Difference: The Emergence of Danish Neonationalism, Neoracism, and Populism in the Post-1989 World* (New York: Berghahn Books, 2011); Peter Hervik, 'The Rise of Neo-nationalism in Denmark, 1992–2001' in Gingrich and Banks, *Neo-nationalism in Europe and Beyond*, pp. 92–106; Tom Bryder, 'The Xenophobic Theme in Danish Politics 2001–2005' in Pascal Delwit and Philippe Poirier, *Extrême-droite et pouvoir en Europe* (Brussels: Editions de l'Université de Bruxelles, 2007), pp. 291–308; Karen Wren, 'Cultural Racism: Something Rotten in the State of Denmark?', *Social and Cultural Geography*, 2:2 (2001), pp. 141–162.
[10] Danish Government, 'En ny udlændingepolitik', 17 January 2002. Available at: http://www.nyidanmark.dk/NR/rdonlyres/442728D5-C3FA-4CD8-8557-7350ECD53745/0/en_ny_udlaendingepolitik.pdf (accessed 6 February 2012). The policy made it much more difficult to claim asylum in Denmark, lengthened the period needed for refugees to gain permanent residence on the basis that they should normally return to their place of origin when possible, reduced welfare benefits for refugees and immigrants, placed severe limits on granting residence

18 times – on average, once every six months – between 2001 and 2011.[11] 2001–2011 was also the period during which the Cartoon Crisis occurred, and during which such symbolic steps as the closing the Commission for Ethnic Equality (*Nævnet for Etnisk Ligestilling*) took place.[12]

Neo-nationalism

Neo-nationalism, as Gingrich and Banks and their collaborators have argued, is a response to threats posed by globalization at the levels of sovereignty, identity, and economics. Neo-nationalism is the revival of nationalism in the face of globalization and, as is generally the case with most forms of nationalism, often has an important ethnic element. Globalization means the erosion of national sovereignty, a process to which the increasing scope of the EU has contributed in Western Europe. Globalization brings economic consequences that threaten the welfare state. And globalization also brings, most visibly of all, immigration. For some Europeans, these developments are unproblematic or even desirable, while for others they are deeply worrying. As Natalie Doyle argues in this journal, neo-nationalism is also a reaction to a 'crisis of political representation' of which the functioning of the EU is partly cause and partly consequence.[13] These are factors which Gingrich and Banks do not emphasize, but which are not incompatible with their explanation. The analyses of Gingrich and Banks and of Doyle, taken together, provide a convincing explanation of the origins and nature of neo-nationalism.

The political platform of the DPP, like that of similar parties in other countries, has four main planks that respond to the worries identified by Gingrich and Banks and their collaborators: protection of national identity, protection of welfare benefits, opposition to immigration, and opposition to the EU. In addition, a fifth plank is that they can be trusted, while mainstream politicians cannot be, a plank that may respond to the crisis of political representation identified by Doyle. In this, it will be argued, the DPP is responding to the concerns of part of the Danish electorate – though to some extent the response may also reinforce those concerns.

The history of Danish neo-nationalism

Although some authors have placed the rise of what Karen Wren called 'cultural racism' in Denmark in the 1980s,[14] and some of the individuals and organizations that would later become important in neo-nationalist politics were already active in that decade (as this article will show), Peter Hervik argues convincingly that it was really in the early 1990s that the neo-nationalist sentiment that would play such a large role in 2001–2011 first

---

permits to foreign spouses, and tightened requirements for permanent residence and naturalisation, requiring both better knowledge of Danish and of 'Danish society, principles and values'.

[11]Hilmar Vester, 'Udlændingelov ændret hvert halve år', *DR Indland*, 17 November 2010, http://www.dr.dk/Nyheder/Indland/2010/11/17/222723.htm. The forerunner of these laws was passed in 1998 by a Centre-Left coalition government under the Social Democrats (SDP; *Socialdemokraterne*) in an unsuccessful attempt to stem the rise of the DPP in opinion polls ahead of the 2001 election (Hervik, 'The Rise of Neo-nationalism in Denmark', p. 101). The law was first negotiated and put forward before the 1998 election and Brian Arly Jacobsen argues that the SDP partly won that election because of the law (personal communication).

[12]'Nævnet for Etnisk Ligestilling nedlægges', Ritzaus Bureau, 5 March 2002.

[13]Natalie J. Doyle, 'Islam, Depoliticization and the European Crisis of Democratic Legitimacy', *Politics, Religion and Ideology* 14:2 (2013), pp. 265–283.

[14]Wren, 'Cultural Racism', pp. 142, 152.

became visible,[15] initially focusing not on Islam or immigration but on the EU. In 2000, this neo-nationalist sentiment then shifted its focus from the EU to Islam and immigration.

The first clear sign of mass neo-nationalist sentiment was in 1992, when a Danish referendum rejected the Maastricht Treaty. This was the treaty that began the transformation of the European Economic Community into the EU and laid the framework for the creation of the euro and for cooperation in justice and police matters, as well as attempting (with less success) to establish a Common Foreign and Security Policy (CFSP). The Maastricht Treaty had been approved by 130 of 179 members of the Danish parliament, and a 'yes' vote was generally expected in the referendum required by the Danish constitution, but in the run-up to the referendum concerns emerged about the place of Denmark in 'a new Europe where borders disappeared and [European] integration increased'. 'Would the language and cultural identity disappear?' 'Who would "we the Danes" be in such a large entity?'[16] Objections to the treaty were especially strong among manual workers and public sector employees, and those telling pollsters that they had no interest in politics.[17] A subsequent re-referendum in 1993 accepted the Maastricht Treaty only with 'opt-outs' that exempted Denmark from the treaty's most important provisions – the euro, justice and police matters, and the CFSP – and also from the mostly symbolic common European Citizenship.[18]

The rejection of the Maastricht Treaty represented a victory for the two small parties that had, alone, campaigned against it: the leftist Socialist People's Party (SF; *Socialistisk Folkeparti*) and the maverick Progress Party (PP; *Fremskridtspartiet*). The PP is sometimes described as Far Right, but this is hardly an adequate description, since as well as campaigning against the Maastricht Treaty, it had campaigned after its foundation in 1973 not only for lower welfare benefits and lower taxation, but also for raising money by selling off Denmark's remaining overseas territories, Greenland and the Faroe Islands, and for saving money by replacing the armed forces with a recorded telephone message saying 'We surrender' in Russian.[19] These are not typical Far Right positions.

Mass neo-nationalist opposition to the EU was again visible in 2000, when in another referendum Danish voters rejected replacing the Danish krone with the euro. As in 1992, a 'yes' vote was generally expected, especially since the question was not substantial: the Danish krone had been pegged to the German mark since 1982, a peg that was transferred to the euro in 1999 and still exists.[20] However, the pre-referendum campaign did not focus on monetary issues as some had hoped, but rather broadened to include discussion of threats to welfare benefits, and the risk of loss of national identity and culture.[21] Again, objections to the euro were especially strong among manual workers, the less educated, and public sector employees.[22]

---

[15]Hervik, 'The Rise of Neo-nationalism in Denmark', p. 95.
[16]Ibid., pp. 95–96.
[17]Palle Svensson, 'The Danish Yes to Maastricht and Edinburgh. The EC Referendum of May 1993', *Scandinavian Political Studies*, 17:1 (1994), p. 78.
[18]Symbolic in that what really matters is still national citizenship. Despite this opt-out, Demark – like other EU countries – still allows citizens of other EU states to vote in local and EU elections. Denmark, however, applies special residence rules to citizens of other EU states, which other EU countries do not.
[19]Bryder, 'The Xenophobic Theme', p. 296.
[20]Eugenio Domingo Solans, speech, the 'Euro and Denmark' exhibition, Aalborg, Denmark, 10 September 1999, http://www.ecb.int/press/key/date/1999/html/sp990910_1.en.html.
[21]Roger Buch and Kasper M. Hansen, 'The Danes and Europe: From EC 1972 to Euro 2000: Elections, Referendums and Attitudes', *Scandinavian Political Studies*, 25:1 (2002), p. 12.
[22]Buch and Hansen, 'The Danes and Europe', pp. 17–18. One study emphasised worker/white-collar, while another found that 'if private/public-sector employment is included it cancels out the effect of worker/white-collar'.

A strong voice during the 2000 referendum campaign was that of the DPP, which had split off from the PP in 1995 after the leader of the PP had been jailed for tax evasion and fraud, and had dropped the PP's call for lower welfare benefits and lower taxation, as well as its maverick proposals regarding the armed forces, Greenland and the Faroe Islands (though it retained something of the PP's propensity for iconoclastic media stunts).[23] Support for the DPP is strongest among the same social groups where objections to Maastricht and the euro had been strongest, though public sector employees are no more likely to vote for the DPP than are other groups.[24] The strong showing of the DPP in the 2001 election, then, can be seen as a result of the continuation of the neo-nationalist sentiment that rejected replacing the krone with the euro in 2000, and was first visible in the rejection of the Maastricht Treaty in 1992. There are, of course, alternative understandings of these events, which this article does not provide space to consider.

The extent of neo-nationalist sentiment

The five main planks in the political platform of the DPP, as has been said, are protection of national identity, protection of welfare benefits, opposition to immigration, opposition to the EU, and opposition to a political establishment that cannot be trusted. Attitude surveys in 2001 and 2007 showed that these addressed concerns that were especially strong among DPP voters, but were also present among voters for other parties. Figure 1 shows views of DPP voters and of voters for Denmark's two largest parties, the Liberals and the Centre-Left Social Democrats (SDP; *Socialdemokraterne*), at the time of the 2001 election.[25]

As can be seen, the majority of DPP voters were neutral or even positive about the EU *as a whole*, but views on the EU as a whole are not the same as views on a possible expansion of powers by the EU, the issues considered during the Maastricht Treaty and Euro referendum campaigns. There was, however, some concern about the EU among voters for all three parties shown, and this concern was greatest among DPP voters. Views about welfare as a whole (not shown) did not differ greatly between DPP voters and other voters, reflecting the general Danish consensus in favour of generous welfare to which the PP had represented a brief and not always serious exception, but voters for all three parties were concerned about welfare spending on immigrants.[26] The pattern on this issue and on the two other issues relating to immigration and Islam was the same: 30 per cent–40 per cent of SDP voters were concerned, 50 per cent–60 per cent of Liberal voters were concerned, and 70 per cent–80 per cent of DPP voters were concerned. DPP voters thus share concerns with other voters, only more so. Taken together, these concerns measure neo-nationalist sentiment, and show that it was far from exclusive to DPP voters. DPP voters, however, were more neo-nationalist than Liberal voters, and Liberal voters were more neo-nationalist than SDP voters, save in their views of the EU and of the untrustworthiness of political leaders, where SDP voters were closer to neo-nationalist positions than Liberal voters.

This article will not attempt to analyse neo-nationalist sentiment with regard to the EU, which has little direct relevance for attitudes to Islam. Attitudes on remaining issues can be

---

[23]Bryder, 'The Xenophobic Theme', p. 293.
[24]Susi Meret, 'The Danish People's Party, the Italian Northern League and the Austrian Freedom Party in a Comparative Perspective: Party Ideology and Electoral Support' (PhD dissertation, Aalborg University, 2009), pp. 227, 234.
[25]Source: Aalborg University Danish Election Project, Valgundersøgelsen 2001 and Valgundersøgelsen 2007 – foreløbig, http://bank1.surveybank.aau.dk (accessed 14 March 2012). Data for similar figures below is taken from the same source. Meret uses similar data in 'The Danish People's Party', pp. 252, 254, 277.
[26]Meret, 'The Danish People's Party', p. 241.

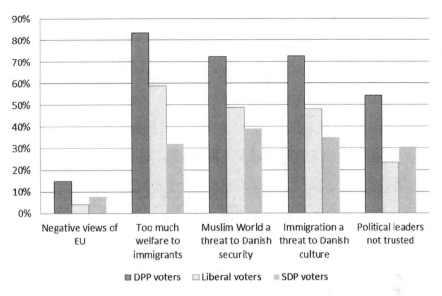

Figure 1. Voter sentiment.

divided between those for which there is some obvious empirical basis, and those for which an empirical basis is hard to find. Concern with immigrant use of welfare had some empirical basis. One study estimates that in 1998 non-western immigrants received almost 40 per cent of the main secondary unemployment benefit (*kontanthjælp*), despite making up only 5 per cent of the population,[27] and a 2005 report by a Commission on Welfare appointed by the Ministry of Finance found that the average total net cost to the Danish state of one non-western immigrant was $50,000 in the case of a male and $790,000 in the case of a female.[28] These calculations are open to dispute, but even, so there was clearly an issue with immigrant use of welfare.[29] As Figure 2 shows, concern with regard to this issue declined among all voters between 2001 and 2007 (though it declined less among DPP voters than among other voters), underlining the empirical basis of the concern, as welfare spending on immigrants did actually decline after 2001.[30]

Similarly, there is some empirical basis for the view of the Muslim world as a threat to Danish security, a concern which increased between 2001 and 2007 among DPP and Liberal voters, as Figure 3 shows. The 2001 election came in the immediate aftermath of 9/11. Between then and 2007, three more things happened to increase this fear: the engagement of Danish troops in support of US troops in Afghanistan and Iraq (with consequent

---

[27]S. Pedersen, 'Overførselsindkomster til indvandrerne' in G.V. Mogensen and P.C. Matthiessen (eds) *Integration i Danmark omkring årtusindskiftet. Indvandrernes møde med arbejdsmarkedet og Velfærdssamfundet* (Aarhus: Aarhus Universitetsforlag, 2000), quoted in Pedersen *Immigration and Welfare State Cash Benefits: The Danish Case*, Rockwool Foundation Study Paper 33, Odense: University Press of Southern Denmark (2011), p. 19.

[28]Denmark, Ministry of Finance, Velfærdskommissionen, *Analyserapport: Fremtidens velfærd og globaliseringen* (Copenhagen: Velfærdskommissionen, March 2005), p. 123. That is, a negative NPV of DKK280,000 and DKK4,400,000, taking into account all varieties of benefit received and taxes paid. Converted at 2005 rates and rounded.

[29]Also, *kontanthjælp* is a benefit that is received only by those who do not qualify for the more generous primary benefit, unemployment insurance. Many immigrants (but few non-immigrants) do not qualify for unemployment insurance.

[30]Peder J. Pedersen, *Immigration and Welfare State Cash Benefits*, p. 35.

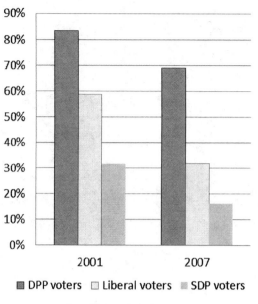

Figure 2. Voter sentiment: too much welfare to immigrants.

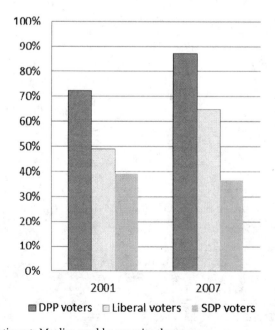

Figure 3. Voter sentiment: Muslim world a security threat.

Danish casualties), the Cartoon Crisis (which led to violent attacks on three Danish embassies in the Muslim world), and the emergence of 'home-grown terrorism' in Denmark after 2005. The author of this article does not himself consider that the Muslim world in reality constitutes a threat to Danish security, but accepts that there was an empirical basis for this view. Change in voter sentiment again reflects change in the empirical basis of this sentiment.

There is, however, no obvious empirical basis for the remaining fear, of Muslim immigrants as a threat to Danish culture. Changes in voter sentiment on this issue cannot be measured, as no question was asked about threats to Danish culture in the 2007 election survey, but responses to a question about immigration as a threat to Danish national character that was asked in both 2001 and 2007 were broadly similar, and did not decline significantly between 2001 and 2007. The concern that Muslim immigration constituted a threat to Danish culture, then, requires further explanation.

It is hard to tell to what extent there is an obvious empirical basis for the lack of trust in politicians that most DPP voters and some other voters for both other parties felt. Doyle's analysis of a crisis of political representation suggests one possible empirical basis: that politicians now represent voters less than they used to. A Danish journalist who covered immigration issues for many years has argued that lack of trust in the SDP government that was in power before 2001 was based on the negative personal experiences of certain voters, notably those who lived alongside poor immigrants in social housing and experienced crime and other hardships that they associated with immigration, and felt that the SDP government was more concerned with helping the immigrants than with helping them.[31] Immigrant crime is certainly a major concern among DPP voters, 98 per cent of whom told pollsters in 2003 that they thought that immigration increased criminality. This was a proposition that 78 per cent of DPP voters said they were fully in agreement with, as against 41 per cent of Liberal voters and 32 per cent of SDP voters.[32]

Again, no question was asked about trust in politicians in the 2007 election survey, but a question was asked in both 2001 and 2007 about whether people felt that politicians were paying attention to voters. The responses to this question in 2001 showed the same pattern as responses to the question about trust in politicians, with SDP voters being closer to the views of DPP voters than Liberal voters were. As Figure 4 shows, between 2001 and 2007, SDP voters did not become more convinced that politicians were paying attention to them, while Liberal and DPP voters did. One obvious empirical basis for this change in sentiment was that the SDP had been out of power, while the Liberals had been in power and the DPP had been an informal member of the coalition (as discussed below). This article will not investigate this concern any further, but will suggest that it is possible that it has an empirical basis in Doyle's crisis of representation, and in the negative experiences of certain voters, and that it is also possible that neo-nationalist political sentiment contains an element of anti-establishment sentiment.

The political impact of neo-nationalism

As has been said, Danish neo-nationalism is probably fairly typical of neo-nationalism elsewhere. One measure of neo-nationalist sentiment is voting in European elections, and in the 2009 European election, voting patterns in Denmark were not very different from those in Britain, another country that makes use of various EU opt-outs, as Figure 5 shows. 22.5 per cent of Danish votes in 2009 went either to the DPP or to the People's

---

[31] Pernille Ammitzbøll, personal communication, 17 March 2012.
[32] Aalborg University survey, National identitet – ISSP 2003, http://bank1.surveybank.aau.dk (accessed 14 March 2012).

(IL)LIBERAL EUROPE: ISLAMOPHOBIA, MODERNITY AND RADICALIZATION

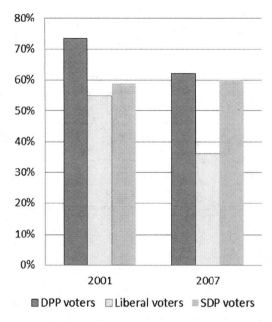

Figure 4. Voter sentiment: politicians not paying attention.

Movement against the EU (*Folkebevægelsen mod EU*), and 22.7 per cent of British votes went either to the UK Independence Party (UKIP) or the British National Party (BNP).[33] While neo-nationalist parties are almost invisible in British national politics, however, the DPP is far from invisible in Danish national politics. This is because of the different nature of the Danish electoral system.

In national elections, unlike European elections, Britain has a first-past-the-post electoral system similar to America's that discourages votes for small parties, so that in the 2010 national election the UKIP and BNP share of the vote was only 5 per cent. Neither party won any seats. Denmark, however, has a proportional system. No party has won an absolute majority in a Danish national election since 1890, and the Danish system at present divides parliamentary seats among about eight political parties. These parties can be classified as either first rank – the Liberals on the Centre-Right and the SDP on the Centre-Left – or second rank. The two first-rank parties have provided all but three of Denmark's prime ministers since 1920.[34] As the maximum share of the vote won by any one party since the 1960s has generally been in the region of 25 per cent–30 per cent, first rank parties depend on the support of second-rank parties, which can demand either formal inclusion in a coalition government or adoption of particular measures as the price of their support, as was the case with the DPP from 2001 to 2011.

The DPP's highest ever share of the vote in a national election was in 2007, when it won 13.9 per cent, a result that would doom it to insignificance in a country with a first-past-the-post electoral system. In Denmark, however, this share of the vote made

---

[33]Denmark's People's Movement against the EU and Britain's UKIP of course emphasize three of the standard four planks of neo-nationalist policies – national identity, opposition to the EU, and lack of trust in mainstream politicians – more than the other two planks – welfare and immigration.

[34]The exceptions were during the Second World War under German occupation, and on two occasions when the Liberals did extremely badly, 1968 and 1982.

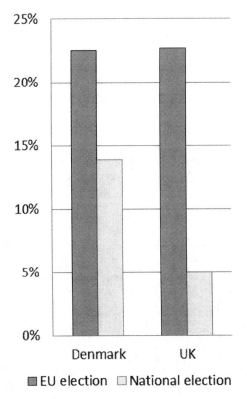

Figure 5. Neo-nationalist share of the vote.

the DPP a major political force. The nature of the Danish electoral system, then, meant that the political impact of neo-nationalist sentiment was greater than it would have been under another system. Neo-nationalist sentiment may well have been equally strong in other European countries where it had less political impact.

Neo-nationalism as understood by Gingrich and Banks, then, provides a good description of the sentiment among Danish voters that led to the rejection the Maastricht Treaty in 1992, the rejection of the euro in 2000, and the electoral success of the DPP in 2001 and 2007, and the nature of the Danish electoral system explains how the DPP's electoral success translated into political power. There is some obvious empirical basis for voters' concerns regarding welfare spending on immigrants and the Muslim world as a threat to Danish security. There is, however, no obvious empirical basis for the concern that was especially strong among DPP voters, that Muslim immigration posed a threat to Danish culture. To explain this, we must move on to other factors.

Street-level Thuggery

Before considering the anti-Islamic activism that is one central topic of this article, and which – it is argued – is separate from street-level thuggery, two examples of street-level thuggery will be considered for purposes of comparison.

One classic example of street-level thuggery is the National Socialist Movement of Denmark (*Danmarks Nationalsocialistiske Bevægelse*). This presents itself as the continuation of the original Danish National Socialist Workers' Party (*Danmarks National-Socialistiske Arbejder Parti*), a party founded in 1930 and inspired by the German Nazi Party,[35] but is in an entirely different league. The original Danish National Socialist Workers' Party might once have come to rule Denmark, since although it never won more than 2 per cent of the national vote and three seats in parliament (in 1943), there was at certain points a possibility that its rule might anyhow have been imposed by the German occupiers of Denmark. There is no prospect whatsoever of its self-appointed successor, the National Socialist Movement of Denmark, even winning a seat in parliament, let alone coming to power. In 2001 it stood in local elections in one municipality on the outskirts of Copenhagen, and attracted 73 votes.[36]

The National Socialist Movement of Denmark maintains a website decorated with a swastika, which includes its political programme, the first item on which is to 'protect and strengthen the Danish people's biological and spiritual health'.[37] This programme, however, also includes more topical causes: the protection of the environment and two neo-nationalist positions, opposition to immigration and to the European Union (EU).[38] At the street level, the National Socialist Movement of Denmark holds occasional small demonstrations that generally attract small numbers of anti-fascist counter-demonstrators. Violence may result. The long-term leader of the National Socialist Movement of Denmark was jailed after attacking some anti-fascist counter-demonstrators in 1999, and was again imprisoned after another demonstration in 2007, this time for assaulting a police officer.[39] The National Socialist Movement of Denmark, then, is an example of street-level thuggery, and is of significance primarily for its own members, and for some anti-fascist counter-demonstrators.

Only slightly less marginal than the National Socialist Movement of Denmark is Stop the Islamization of Denmark (SIAD, *Stop islamiseringen af Danmark*). This organization was founded in 2005 by Anders Gravers, a former member of The Danish Association (*Den Danske Forening*), an anti-immigration organization considered below. Gravers told the press that he decided that The Danish Association was no more than a talking shop, that action was needed, and that he therefore founded SIAD. He had not previously been politically active. The son of a slaughterhouse worker, he had worked as a butcher in a supermarket after dropping out of high school because, he told an interviewer, 'politics came into it'. He also served in the Danish army's UN contingent in Bosnia, during which period his young son was murdered by his former wife's drunken (and ethnically Danish) lover.[40]

Unlike the National Socialist Movement of Denmark, SIAD does not use the political rhetoric of biological racism. Its programme is neo-nationalist, calling for the expulsion of those who live in Denmark but 'do not follow and/or respect Danish manners and customs' and an end to further immigration,[41] but it claims not to be

---

[35]'Dansk NS-Historie', DNSB website, www.dnsb.info (accessed 13 March 2012).
[36]'Nazister stiller op til valg', Ritzaus Bureau, 28 September 2005.
[37]'Hvad vil Danmarks Nationalsocialistiske Bevægelse?', DNSB website, www.dnsb.info (accessed 13 March 2012).
[38]Ibid.
[39]'Jonni Hansen trækker sig som nazileder', Ritzaus Bureau, 19 October 2010.
[40]Jakob Sheikh, 'Han passer på danskheden – og sig selv', *Politiken*, 19 September 2010, p. PS-7. Press reports of the time confirm the murder of the son and the conviction of the murderer, whose name indicates Danish ethnicity. Curiously, the former wife was identified by Sheikh as a Christian Lebanese, and in press reports of the time as a Greenlander.
[41]'SIAD's politik', SIAD website, http://siaddk.wordpress.com/siads-politik/; (accessed 13 March 2012).

racist.[42] However, its size and methods are not so different from the National Socialist Movement of Denmark. It also holds occasional small demonstrations. In 2006, a SIAD demonstration in an immigrant-dominated quarter of the provincial city of Aarhus was expected to pass quietly, as the usual anti-fascist counter-demonstrators were occupied by a neo-Nazi demonstration elsewhere, but some local anti-SIAD counter-demonstrators of immigrant origin attacked the police who were present, resulting in a number of arrests.[43] Even when SIAD demonstrations do not result in violence, they still attract press coverage that refers to the risk of violence. In advance of a 2008 demonstration in the northern town of Aalborg, television news reported some 50 Muslims who 'invaded' the local police station, and interviewed a Danish convert to Islam who, dressed in Salafi style in sandals and short robe, seemed to threaten a violent reaction.[44] In the event, some 30 SIAD supporters were separated from about 50 counter-demonstrators on the opposite side of the road by about 20 police. The SIAD supporters, one of whom was seen refreshing himself from a beer bottle, shouted some simple slogans (such as 'out, out, out!'), the counter-demonstrators also shouted some slogans, and everyone went home.[45]

Both SIAD and the National Socialist Movement of Denmark, then, are examples of street-level thuggery. They are small, and come to public attention primarily because of demonstrations which are associated with violence. Gravers has never been imprisoned for violence, unlike the leader of the National Socialist Movement of Denmark, but the demonstrations he has organized have produced violence, and one of his former associates in SIAD was imprisoned in 2010 for making death-threats against a leftist Member of Parliament.[46] Both organizations advance positions that are neo-nationalist, but they are very different in nature from the other organizations that will be considered below. They are completely marginal to Danish politics.

Anti-Islamic Activism

The one phenomenon remaining to be examined, then, is single-issue anti-Islamic activism, which may be especially relevant as the source of concerns with Muslim immigration as a threat to Danish culture. During 2001–2011, the leading representatives of this in Denmark were two cousins, Søren Krarup and Jesper Langballe, both priests (*præster*), and Lars Hedegaard, a prominent journalist.[47] The anti-Islamic activism of Krarup and Langballe, however, differs significantly from that of Hedegaard. The anti-Islamic activism of Krarup and Langballe is a function of a certain variety of pro-Christian activism, has primarily Danish roots, and can be dated to the 1980s. It shows that while the role played by Christianity may often be 'as a marker of cultural identity, rather than as a source of dogmatic truth', as Doyle has argued,[48] this is not always the case. The anti-Islamic activism of Hedegaard, in contrast, is not a reflection of a pro-Christian stance, can be dated to 9/11,

---

[42]SIAD supporters interviewed during Aalborg demonstration in 2008. I did not attend the demonstration. The interviews are heard on an amateur video posted on YouTube, available at http://www.youtube.com/watch?v=jWiQwanh7Yo (accessed 13 March 2012).
[43]Pernille Ammittzbøll, 'Demonstration: Nazi-demo betyder ro i Århus', *JP Århus*, 10 June 2006, p. 2; 'Krav om strenge straffe efter optøjer mod politiet', Ritzaus Bureau, 26 October 2006.
[44]TV2/Nord News, 14 March 2008, http://www.youtube.com/watch?v=zCHQhgx1_5k (accessed 13 March 2012).
[45]This description is based on the amateur video posted on YouTube.
[46]'Højreekstremister i Danmark: Hærværk, bomber, vold og trusler', *Ekstra Bladet*, 25 July 2011, p. 10.
[47]The word *præst* is sometimes translated as 'minister', 'vicar' or 'clergyman'. Given the use of 'minister' in a political context, the etymologically closer translation 'priest' has been preferred.
[48]Doyle, 'Islam, Depoliticization'.

and has primarily non-Danish roots. What the two forms of anti-Islamic activism share, however, is that they are propounded by intellectuals, not by street-level thugs.

Krarup, Langballe, and Tidehverv

Søren Krarup was the son of Vilhelm Krarup, a priest who from 1926 contributed to a journal, *Tidehverv* [Epoch] that gave its name to a theological movement within the Danish National Church. Vilhelm Krarup edited *Tidehverv* from 1974 to 1984, when Søren Krarup took over.[49] The *Tidehverv* movement was initially a revolt by young theology students against the Church establishment (including Grundtvigianism), and especially the Church's Evangelical 'Inner Mission' wing, and against bourgeois Christianity with its conceptions of the correct moral Christian lifestyle. It was in some ways a Danish parallel to the dialectical theology of Rudolf Bultmann. *Tidehverv* emphasized the essentially sinful nature of man and the fact that salvation came through God's freely given grace, not through man's acts.[50] It took aim at sentimentality and an understanding of Christianity as 'childcare for adults', so as to free the gospel from 'idealism, progressive optimism (*udviklingsoptimisme*), and churchiness' and from the self-righteousness that came with this.[51] This position was accompanied by an emphasis on the value of speaking truth in plain speech.

The positions taken by *Tidehverv* were initially theological, but during the German occupation of Denmark during the Second World War the journal began to take more political positions, and in the post-war period took aim against 'social pietism', the humanist consensus of the period that it thought had almost become a replacement religion, offering the false promise of heaven on earth, for example through the creation of the modern welfare state.[52] Another reason for this shift in focus was that what had started as a protest movement in the 1920s had by the 1950s almost become the establishment, a position which it began to lose after the 1980s.[53]

Søren Krarup (hereafter, Krarup) followed in this tradition, writing in *Tidehverv* and in other publications from the 1960s against the consequences of 1968: 'contempt for the family, Danish self-contempt in relation to the European Community, the benefits society (*behandlersamfund*) and tone-setting neo-Marxism'.[54]

The political position for which Krarup became famous, however, was his opposition to the very liberal Law on Foreigners of 1983, which he saw as opening the door to a *Völkerwanderung* (*folkevandring*, migration of peoples) into Denmark from the Middle East, Asia and Africa that would inevitably change Denmark's nature. In 1986, he and Langballe founded a Committee against the Refugee Law (Komite mod Flygtningeloven), and some associates began the foundation of what, the following year, was established as The Danish Association, which published a newspaper, *Danskeren* (*The Dane*).[55] The Danish Association and its newspaper, with Krarup's support, agitated against the consequences of the Law on Foreigners.[56] It was the organization to which Gravers, whose SIAD was

---

[49] Søren Krarup, '*Tidehverv*', *Tidehverv*, 2006, p. 114.
[50] Christian Houlberg Skov, '*Tidehverv*', *Danmarkshistorien*, http://danmarkshistorien.dk/leksikon-og-kilder/vis/materiale/tidehverv/; (accessed 7 February 2012).
[51] Søren Krarup, '*Tidehverv*', pp. 113–114.
[52] Ibid.
[53] Skov, '*Tidehverv*'.
[54] Søren Krarup, 'National værnepligt', *Tidehverv*, 2009, pp. 69–70.
[55] Krarup, 'National værnepligt'.
[56] Mette Klingsey, 'Den danske forening: Dansk Folkeparti i strid om Den Danske Forening', *Information*, 20 March 2007, pp. 6–7.

given above as an example of street-level thuggery, once belonged, but was not itself a street-level organization or involved in thuggery, as will be shown later in this article.

In a later essay, Krarup shows his anti-Islamic activism to be based partly in nationalism – the idea of Danes as one large family, united in their membership of the Church – and partly in theology: the opposition to self-righteousness and the doctrine of redemption by faith alone, which *Tidehverv* had been emphasizing since the 1920s. In one essay, Krarup argued that Danes were 'one large family, which collectively belongs to the [National] Church', a family which meets in churches at Christmas as a family meets for someone's sixtieth birthday.[57] This situation was under threat from immigration, Islam, Danish leftists, and the European Union, so that 'the National Church has many odds against it, just as many as the Danish people. Just as many as the national community'.[58] This view is nationalist more than theological, as it sees the Church as ancillary to the national community.

A second view, however, was theological. Danes are free to attend church rarely or never, wrote Krarup, because this is the freedom that (Lutheran) Christians have, since salvation comes through God's freely given grace, not through following some set of rules.[59] God gives freedom because he is not 'a tyrant, a pope'.[60] This freedom, however, presupposes 'a Christian land', since the freedom is to have faith in God, not freedom in the sense of 'total spiritual emptiness' or that all gods are alike.[61] And this was a situation that was threatened by the growing number of 'Mohammedans' (*mohammedaner*, a deliberate use of an obsolete term), who believe they can achieve salvation through their own acts, and attempt to 'reduce Jesus to a third- or fourth-rate prophet'.[62] Muslims do not, in fact, believe that they can achieve salvation through their own acts, but rather that no-one is saved except by God's mercy, and Krarup's understanding of Islamic theology seems grounded mostly in the condemnation of 'religions of the law', from Judaism[63] to Roman Catholicism to various forms of pietism and the Danish National Church's Evangelical 'Inner Mission' wing. Islam is, in Christian terms, undoubtedly a religion of the law, but it is not *only* a religion of the law. However weak Krarup's grasp of Islamic theology, however, the Christian theology of *Tidehverv* justifies his anti-Islamic position.

A further theological basis of Krarup's anti-Islamic position was his conviction that the contrary of the false promise of heaven on earth was to be 'true to the earth' – and not just to the earth in general, but specifically true to one's own circumstances, and so to that particular bit of the earth where one was born.[64] This – 'true to the earth' – has been *Tidehverv*'s slogan. Though the idea ultimately derives from Nietzsche,[65] not the New

---

[57] Søren Krarup, 'Kirke og folk i Danmark' in Krarup, *Kristendom og danskhed: Prædikener og foredrag* (Højbjerg: Hovedland, 2001), pp. 84–85.
[58] Krarup, 'Kirke og folk i Danmark', p. 86.
[59] Ibid., p. 83.
[60] Ibid., p. 89.
[61] Ibid., p. 89.
[62] Ibid., p. 90.
[63] Krarup's objections to Islam should logically apply also to Judaism, and indeed in 1960 he did write of Judaism as un-Danish. Rasmus Lindboe and Sandy French, 'Krarups dans om antisemitismen', *Information*, 12 January 2004, p. 5. His subsequent statements on Judaism have, however, generally been uncontroversial.
[64] Søren Krarup, 'Hvem er konservativ?', *Berlingske.dk*, 6 October 2010, http://www.b.dk/kronikker/hvem-er-konservativ.
[65] 'Ich beschwöre euch, meine Brüder, bleibt der Erde treu und glaubt Denen nicht, welche euch von überirdischen Hoffnungen reden!' Friedrich Nietzsche, *Also sprach Zarathustra* (Berlin: Walter de Gruyter, 1968), p. 9. Pointed out by Hans Hauge, 'Den sorte fætter', *Information*, 5 June 2002, p. 8.

Testament, it effectively makes something almost sacred of one's place of birth and the people to which ones belongs, and in Krarup's case effectively made the defence of Denmark's identity as Denmark, as a country 'inhabited by a people, not population',[66] a sacred cause. 'At its heart', wrote Krarup, 'Christianity is about being true to your neighbour, and thus to your country'.[67]

Krarup's Christian-based anti-Islamic activism, which started with his objections to the Law on Foreigners of 1983 and his support for The Danish Association in 1986-87, moved on in 1995 to his joining the DPP along with his cousin and colleague in *Tidehverv*, Langballe,[68] and in 1997 to active participation in a campaign in the popular tabloid newspaper *Ekstra Bladet* for Danes to express their (negative) views on immigration, a campaign which Hervik credits with increasing significantly the neo-nationalist sentiment to which the DPP responded.[69] In 2001, Krarup and Langballe both stood for election as DPP candidates, and spent the years 2001–2011 as members of parliament, providing much of the intellectual content of the DPP's programme, and being active in parliament, in the DPP's relations with the press, and in their own writing.[70] The anti-Islamic activism of Krarup and Langballe, then, made a definite contribution to neo-nationalist sentiment.

Hedegaard and Eurabia

Hedegaard, in contrast, was not originally well disposed towards the Danish National Church. Once on the Far Left, he became editor-in-chief of the mainstream leftist daily newspaper *Information*, and then a columnist in the Centre-Right newspaper *Berlingske Tidende*. He was originally neutral in the Danish media's 'values debate' that was one consequence of the growth of neo-nationalist sentiment and of the rise of the DPP, and was promoted by Krarup, in which Islam and Danish culture were rhetorically pitted against each other.[71] As late as 1999, three years after the *Ekstra Bladet* campaign and two years before 73 per cent of DPP voters were to vote in accordance with the neo-nationalist concern that Islam posed a threat to Danish culture, Hedegaard was pointing out in *Berlingske Tidende* that neither Danish culture nor Islam was a unique, unitary entity, and asking sarcastically quite how Islam was thought to threaten the Danish language, Danish music, and Danish literature.[72] Before 9/11, he occasionally made fun of those he saw as excessively politically correct, but no more.

After 9/11, however, Hedegaard shifted his position, asking in his column on September 13, 2001 how we actually *knew* that terrorism had nothing to do with Islam,[73] and in his column the next week doubting the loyalty of immigrant Muslims in a time of war.[74] The following year he contributed an essay on '9/11 as history' ('Den 11. september som historie') to a collection of somewhat anti-Islamic articles, *Islam in the West: On the*

---

[66]'Beboet af et folk, ikke af en befolkning'. Søren Krarup, 'Vestlig/ikke-vestlig', *Tidehverv*, 84:8–9 (October 2010), p. 145.
[67]Søren Krarup, quoted in Else Marie Nygaard, 'Søren Krarup: Disse ord betyder noget for mig', *Kristeligt Dagblad*, 8 November 2011, http://www.kristeligt-dagblad.dk/artikel/439551:Seniorliv–Soeren-Krarup–Disse-ord-betyder-noget-for-mig.
[68]Krarup, 'National værnepligt'.
[69]Hervik, 'The Rise of Neo-nationalism in Denmark', pp. 98–99.
[70]Krarup, 'National værnepligt'.
[71]Mona Kanwal Sheikh and Manni Crone, 'Muslims as a Danish Security Issue' in Nielsen (ed.) *Islam in Denmark*, pp. 174–176.
[72]Lars Hedegaard, 'Frikadellens flugt', *Berlingske Tidende*, 1 October 1999, p. 18.
[73]Lars Hedegaard, 'Tid til besindelse', *Berlingske Tidende*, 13 September 2001, p. 8.
[74]Lars Hedegaard, 'Midt i en krigstid', *Berlingske Tidende*, 20 September 2001, p. 12.

Path of the Quran? (*Islam i Vesten – på Koranens vej?*), that was edited by two less established, freelance writers with a longer history of writing that was critical of Islam,[75] Helle Merete Brix and Torben Hansen.[76] This collection was welcomed by Krarup in *Tidehverv* for being honest about Islam's 'demonic and hateful nature'.[77] In 2003, Hedegaard then co-authored with Brix and Hansen a book, *In the House of War: Islam's Colonization of the West* (*I krigens hus: Islams kolonisiering af Vesten*), which is the central Danish expression of what may be called 'the Eurabia narrative' (though the book does not actually use the term 'Eurabia').

The Eurabia narrative is, in essence, the apocalyptic threat of the Islamization of Europe. It emerged in America, Britain and Israel in 2002–2003 in the context of the reluctance of 'Old Europe' – principally France and Germany – to join the US in the part of the War on Terror that involved invading Iraq, and also in the context of strong European criticism of Israeli actions during Operation Defensive Shield (March–May 2002), which included what was at the time feared to be a massacre in Jenin (but proved not to have been) and the entry of Israeli forces into Yasser Arafat's compound in Ramallah. Some American and Israeli commentators explained what they saw as Europe's anti-Semitism and betrayal of the West in terms of Europe's Arabization and Islamization. This was ascribed in a seminal article by one of the leading proponents of the Eurabia narrative, Gisèle Littman (writing under the pseudonym Bat Ye'or), to political arrangements between the France and the European Union on the one hand and Arab states on the other hand that aimed at 'influencing European foreign policy against Israel and detaching Europe from America' and at 'establishing permanently in Europe a massive Arab–Muslim presence by the immigration and settlement of millions of Muslims with equal rights for all… to integrate Europe and the Arab–Muslim world into one political and economic bloc, by mixing populations (multiculturalism)', a project assisted by various measures to make European public opinion more favourable towards Muslims.[78] The Eurabia narrative was also popularized by journalists such as Mark Steyn, writing in the British *Spectator* and in various North American publications. Steyn was responsible for the majority of uses of the term 'Eurabia' in print during 2003.[79] Since then the Eurabia narrative has expanded much further in the Anglophone world, as Kundnani has shown, but this lies beyond the scope of this article.[80] Neither Littman nor Steyn have any significant connection with the Far Right. Littman can be placed politically on the Israeli Right, and Steyn (though a Canadian) can be placed politically on the American Right, as can the editor of the online magazine in which Littman published her seminal article, David Horowitz. Both these political positions are distinct from the European Far Right, and have nothing to do with street-level thuggery.

The Eurabia narrative contains one element for which there is some obvious empirical basis – the growth of the Muslim population of Europe – and other elements for which there is little or no empirical basis. This article does not provide space for examining these elements in any detail, but it will note that while it is not necessarily the case that

---

[75]The earliest, tone-setting article by Brix that I have found is Helle Merete Brix, 'Svaret fra Gud', *Information*, 20 January 1999, p. 8.

[76]Helle Merete Brix and Torben Hansen, *Islam i Vesten – på Koranens vej?: en antologi* (Copenhagen: Tiderne Skifter, 2002).

[77]Søren Krarup, 'Mediestorm', *Tidehverv*, 2002, pp. 157–158.

[78]Bat Ye'or, 'European Fears of the Gathering Jihad', FrontPageMagazine.com, 21 February 2003, http://archive.frontpagemag.com/readArticle.aspx?ARTID=19633.

[79]As reported by Lexis-Nexis.

[80]Kundnani, 'Islamism and the Roots of Liberal Rage'.

the demographic projections of the Eurabia narrative are entirely wrong,[81] almost no serious scholars of Islam accept the other elements. For the proponents of the Eurabia narrative, of course, this just shows how right they are about the measures taken to make European public opinion more favourable towards Muslims. As was seen above, distrust of politicians was more widespread among DPP voters than among other voters, and it is possible that neo-nationalist political sentiment is also anti-establishment sentiment.

This Eurabia narrative is, in essence, the narrative followed by Hedegaard et al.'s *In the House of War*, which draws both on mainstream scholarly proponents of the Clash of Civilizations narrative (Bernard Lewis and Samuel Huntington), and on Littman (four works in the bibliography) and her husband (one work in the bibliography). Steyn himself does not appear in the bibliography, but another *Spectator* columnist, Theodore Dalrymple, does (two works), so evidently one of the co-authors, probably Hedegaard, was a reader of *The Spectator*, and so presumably also of Steyn's articles there. The book also draws on Ibn Warraq, author of the popular anti-Islamic *Why I Am Not A Muslim* (two works in the bibliography). The use of these sources may owe something to a private reading group, the Giordano Bruno Society, of which Hedegaard and Brix were members, along with a political commentator from the Centre-Right daily *Jyllands-Posten* and the Liberal minister of social affairs, which according to Hedegaard was motivated by the feeling that the Danish discourse on Islam was incomplete, and needed to be supplemented by 'what is being written around the world'.[82]

At a different level, the book also draws at one point on an alleged fatwa by 'Holy Jihad Denmark', calling on Danish Muslims to establish and expand a Muslim-only zone in Copenhagen as a means of achieving 'Islam's goal Caliph [sic]'. The fatwa also seems to encourage the rape of Danish girls, as 'unclean girls are not protected by the Holy Koran'.[83] This fatwa is almost certainly an anti-Islamic fabrication, as it can hardly be of Muslim origin.[84] The fatwa is closer to the anti-Islamic Eurabia narrative than to anything else. Its precise origins are not known.[85]

In the House of War was welcomed by a reviewer in *Tidehverv* as a book which said concisely what *Tidehverv* had been saying for years.[86] This was not exactly true, since *Tidehverv* had never referred to Littman or the Eurabia narrative, but *Tidehverv* had become as outspoken as *In the House of War* in the aftermath of 9/11. In a sermon given on the Sunday after 9/11 and reprinted in *Tidehverv*, Krarup's cousin Langballe almost welcomed 9/11 for waking people, if only briefly, from 'the false dream... of the fundamental good of man which will bloom and spread if only we learn to meet all men and peoples with trust, whether they believe in Christ, Mohammed, or the devil', before returning to the theme of salvation as God's freely given gift, contrasting this with

---

[81] See Mark Sedgwick, review of *God's Continent: Christianity, Islam, and Europe's Religious Crisis* by Philip Jenkins (Oxford University Press, 2007), *Nova Religio*, 13:3 (February 2010), pp. 134–137. A forthcoming argument in the opposite direction is Brian Arly Jacobsen, 'Projections of Muslim Populations in Europe: A Danish Case Study'.
[82] Hervik, *The Annoying Difference*, p. 172.
[83] Brix, Hansen and Hedegaard, *I krigens hus*, pp. 164–165.
[84] It is possible that an extremely ignorant Muslim might think that Islam's goal was a universal Caliphate, and be unable to distinguish between a Caliphate and a Caliph, and it is just about conceivable that an extremely ignorant Muslim might think that 'unclean' girls were not protected from rape, but even the most ignorant Muslim could hardly make the mistake of understanding the Quran as the work of the Prophet Muhammad rather than of God, as this alleged fatwa does. Hellig Jihad Danmark, 'Meddelelse til alle muslimske indvandrere, muslimske kulturcentre, moskeer og muslimske støtter i Danmark', http://www.7xs.dk/diverse/muslimsknoerrebro.htm and quoted in part in Brix et al., *I krigens hus*, pp. 164–165.
[85] The authors of *In the House of War* admit that the fatwa's authenticity had been questioned, but dismiss these questions. Brix et al., *I krigens hus*, p. 165.
[86] Alex Ahrendtsen, review of *I krigens hus*, *Tidehverv*, 2004, p. 19.

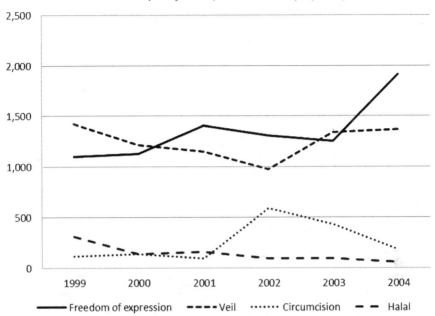

Figure 6. Cultural topics relating to Islam.

'Muslims' crazed self-righteousness', which turned God's gift into law.[87] Krarup subsequently referred to *In the House of War* with approval, accepting for example its argument that to tolerate the veil was to tolerate the first stage in a process of Islamization,[88] and both Littman and the Eurabia narrative appeared in *Tidehverv*.[89] The newer anti-Islamic discourse of Hedegaard, then, partly merged with the older anti-Islamic discourse of Krarup and Langballe.

The Free Press Society

The international discourse reflected in the contents of *In the House of War* was further promoted in Denmark by the Free Press Society (FPS, *Trykkefrihedsselskabet*), established by Hedegaard in 2004. The FPS was an indirect consequence of the publication of *In the House of War*, as after the publication of that book Hedegaard was refused admission to the Danish section of PEN, the international writers' club that has often worked for freedom of expression.[90] In response, he founded his own alternative organization, together with Krarup and Langballe.[91] The FPS was later joined by MPs from two other parties, the Liberal Søren Pind and the Conservative Naser Khader.

The issue of press freedom was a good choice, since – as Figure 6[92] shows – interest was declining in what had previously been the most popular cultural topic for

---

[87] Jesper Langballe, 'Når Gud vækker os', *Tidehverv*, 2001, pp. 194–196.
[88] Søren Krarup, 'Neutralitetens umulighed', *Tidehverv*, 2004, pp. 113–114.
[89] Claus Thomas Nielsen, 'Postkort fra Eurabien', *Tidehverv*, 2005, pp. 153–156; Monica Papazu, 'Islam', *Tidehverv*, no. 7 (September 2006), pp. 87–108.
[90] Marianne Juhl, 'Det frie ord: Værn for ytringsfriheden', *Jyllands-Posten*, 2 November 2004, p. 12.
[91] Marianne Juhl, 'Ytringsfrihed: Til kamp mod tabuer', *Jyllands-Posten*, 17 March 2005, p. 16.
[92] Source: Infomedia analysis.

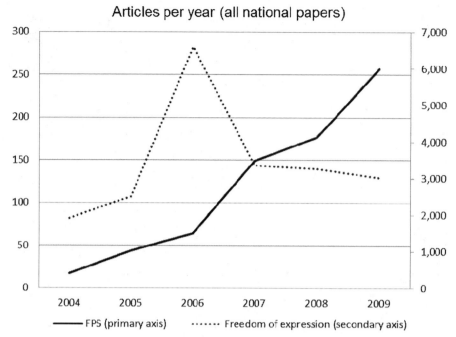

Figure 7. FPS and freedom of expression.

newspaper articles on Islam, the veil, while other topics such as FGM/female circumcision and halal meat were attracting relatively little attention. Freedom of expression, in contrast, was a topic of increasing interest in Denmark, or at least among Danish journalists.

Freedom of expression became a topic of great importance in the year following the establishment of the FPS, 2005, when Flemming Rose, the cultural editor of *Jyllands-Posten*, published the now famous cartoons of the Prophet Muhammad as an exercise in establishing to what extent fear of Muslim reaction was limiting the freedom of expression of Danish cartoonists.[93] To what extent Rose's action was influenced by the discourse promoted by the FPS is unknown: there were connections between him and Hedegaard, but Rose was not part of the FPS milieu. After this, Danish newspaper articles mentioning the issue of freedom of expression increased from 1914 in 2004 to 6589 in 2006. Press mentions of the FPS increased accordingly, as Figure 7 shows, and continued to increase even after interest in freedom of expression began to decline.[94]

The FPS and its magazine *Sappho* awarded annual prizes to a number of Danish and international figures who shared its perspectives: Daniel Pipes of the US Middle East Forum (which publishes *Islamist Watch*), Melanie Phillips of the British *Daily Mail*, Steyn, Rose, and Kurt Westergaard, the cartoonist whose *Jyllands-Posten* cartoon of the Prophet with a bomb in his turban became emblematic. Prizes were also given to prominent Muslims or ex-Muslims who criticized Islam: Ibn Warraq of *Why I Am Not A Muslim*,

---

[93]There may, of course, have been other motivations as well, but the origin of the Cartoons Crisis was an invitation to 42 cartoonists to contribute cartoons of the Prophet for publication in *Jyllands-Posten*. 12 accepted, 3 declined, and 27 did not respond. Jytte Klausen, *The Cartoons That Shook the World* (New Haven: Yale University Press, 2009), pp. 14–15.
[94]Source: Infomedia analysis.

Ehsan Jami of the Netherlands, and Shabana Rehman of Norway.[95] All these events received press coverage, as did other events that the FPS staged, such as a sale of prints of Westergaard's famous cartoon, and lectures by Littman and Dutch politician Geert Wilders.[96] No significant FPS events included persons unconnected to Islam. On this basis, the FPS can be classified as an instance of anti-Islamic activism, not of another variety of activism that sometimes focused on Islam, despite its name.

The FPS, then, was a successful Danish expression of anti-Islamic activism. Its roots were in the international discourse rather than in that of *Tidehverv*, as is indicated by the composition of the six-person board[97] and 32-strong 'board of advisors'[98] of the International Free Press Society (IFPS), established by Hedegaard in 2009. The Danish members of these boards were persons already associated with the FPS, such as Brix. Non-Danish members included former winners of the FPS's and *Sappho's* prizes, notably Steyn, and other international figures such as Littman and Wilders. They also include the authors of two popular anti-Islamic blogs, Ned May ('Baron Bodissey') of *Gates of Vienna* and Robert Spencer of *Jihad Watch*, both of which are placed by one analysis in the top 100 world politics blogs in terms of their readership and influence,[99] and the author of a less popular blog, Paul Belien of *Islamist Watch*. These blogs all promote versions of the Eurabia narrative, and *Jihad Watch* is financed by the David Horowitz Freedom Centre, which runs the website that published Littman's seminal article on Eurabia in 2003.[100]

Non-Danish members of these boards include members of two overlapping US organizations, the Committee on the Present Danger and the Centre for Security Policy. The Committee on the Present Danger was a 2004 recreation of a famous hawkish Cold War body, and aimed to stiffen American public resolve in the face of the Islamist danger.[101] It included prominent Washington figures such as George Shultz, Secretary of State under President Reagan (and presumably not very active on the Committee given his advanced age),[102] and R. James Woolsey, a neo-conservative who had briefly been director of the CIA for two years under President Clinton.[103] It also included less prominent but still

---

[95]'Trykkefrihedsprisen', *Trykkefrihedsselskabet*, http://www.trykkefrihed.dk/trykkefrihedsprisen.htm (accessed 7 February 2012) for the Free Press prizes; 'Om Sappho', http://www.sappho.dk/om-sappho.htm (accessed 7 February 2012) for the Sappho prizes.

[96]Carina Fogsgaard Jacobsen, 'Omstridt tegning sælger godt', *Kristeligt Dagblad*, 18 April 2009, p. 3. Bent Blüdnikow, 'Europa – et kontinent uden identitet', interview with Bat Ye'or, *Berlingske Tidende*, 19 September 2005, section 2, p. 14. Michael Enggaard, 'Wilders: For mange svage ledere', *Jyllands-Posten*, 15 June 2009, p. 5.

[97]'The International Free Press Society: Policy Statement', *Sappho*, 1 January 2009, http://www.sappho.dk/the-international-free-press-society-policy-statement.htm. Internet caches confirm that the same list was formerly given on the main IFPS website, but has now been removed.

[98]'Board of Advisors', *IFPS-Canada*, http://www.ifpscanada.com/about-ifps-international/board-of-advisors/ (accessed 7 February 2012). Internet caches confirm that the same list was formerly given on the main IFPS website, but has now been removed.

[99]In 2011, *Gates of Vienna* came 59th in Technorati's list of the 100 most influential blogs on world politics, and *Jihad Watch* came 79th; http://technorati.com/blogs/directory/politics/world/ (accessed 16 February 2012). For the identity of 'Baron Bodissey', 'Ned May', *FrontPage*, http://frontpagemag.com/author/ned-may/ (accessed 7 February 2012).

[100]'Staff', David Horowitz Freedom Center website, http://www.horowitzfreedomcenter.org/about/staff/; (accessed 7 February 2012).

[101]'History', CPD, http://www.committeeonthepresentdanger.org/index.php?option=com_content&view=article&id=51&Itemid=58 (accessed 7 February 2012). 'Mission', CPD, http://www.committeeonthepresentdanger.org/index.php?option=com_content&view=article&id=50&Itemid=53 (accessed 7 February 2012).

[102]Born in 1920, he was 84 in 2004.

[103]'Our members', CPD, http://www.committeeonthepresentdanger.org/index.php?option=com_content&view=article&id=1744&Itemid=89 (accessed 7 February 2012).

influential figures such as Daniel Pipes and Frank J. Gaffney, Jr, a former Deputy Assistant Secretary of Defense for Nuclear Forces and Arms Control Policy and founder of the Centre for Security Policy.[104] Neither Schultz nor Woolsey were on an IFPS board, but Pipes and Gaffney were, as was Christine Brim, Chief Operating Officer at Gaffney's Centre for Security Policy.[105]

The David Horowitz Freedom Centre and the Centre for Security Policy are identified in the recent report of the Centre for American Progress as two of eight key US anti-Islamic think tanks.[106] These think tanks are major players in America, and between them received $42.6 m in funding from seven major donors between 2001 and 2009. In the case of the David Horowitz Freedom Centre and the Centre for Security Policy, the two key donors were the Richard Mellon Scaife foundations and the Lynde and Harry Bradley Foundation, both of which are major supporters of conservative causes. For the Harry Bradley Foundation especially, financial support for anti-Islamic think tanks is one among many activities, including significant contributions to such respectable and well-established organizations as the Cato Institute and the Hoover Institution, and also to the Project for the New American Century.[107]

Among IFPS board members were also several authors in a collective book published by the Center for Security Policy entitled *Shariah: The Threat to America*, the introduction to which was signed by, among others, Woolsey.[108] This book adjusts the Eurabia narrative to the US, and argues that 'non-violent' jihadists, defined as Muslims who do not disavow the sharia, are even more dangerous than violent ones, as they are preparing 'the ultimate, violent seizure of the U.S. government and replacement of the US Constitution with Shariah'.[109] In order to address this threat, a US organization inspired in part by Gravers's SIAD, Stop Islamization of America (SIOA), was founded in 2010. SIOA was the key organizer of the resistance against the so-called 'Ground Zero mosque' in New York, and was funded partly through Spencer's *Jihad Watch* and partly through the Fairbrook Foundation, a significant contributor to the David Horowitz Freedom Centre.[110] Another response was the passing of laws at state level prohibiting the application of the sharia in American courts, a measure against what a *New York Times* correspondent described as a 'a problem more imagined than real'.[111] The passing of such anti-sharia laws was supported with some success by the American Public Policy Alliance, an organization set up for this purpose[112] that included among its named supporters most of the contributors to *Shariah: The Threat to America*, including four American members of the boards of the IFPS.[113] SIAO and the American Public Policy Alliance are classified

---

[104]'Frank Gaffney', Center for Security Policy website, http://www.centerforsecuritypolicy.org/1231.xml (accessed 7 February 2012).

[105]'Center Staff', Center for Security Policy website, http://www.centerforsecuritypolicy.org/staff.xml (accessed 7 February 2012).

[106]Ali et al., 'Fear, Inc.', pp. 15–16.

[107]Ali et al., 'Fear, Inc.', pp. 15–16, 17–19.

[108]Center for Security Policy, *Shariah: The Threat to America: An Exercise in Competitive Analysis – Report of Team B II* (Washington: Center for Security Policy Press, 2010), pp. vi–vii, xxiv. Book downloaded from http://shariahthethreat.org/wp-content/uploads/2011/04/Shariah-The-Threat-to-America-Team-B-Report-Web-09292010.pdf (accessed 7 February 2012).

[109]*Shariah: The Threat to America*, pp. 15–16.

[110]Ali et al., 'Fear, Inc.', pp. 15–16, 45, 70.

[111]Andrea Elliott, 'Behind an Anti-Shariah Push', *New York Times*, 31 July 2011, section A, p. 1.

[112]In July 2011, three states had passed laws on the model proposed by the American Public Policy Alliance. Elliott, 'Behind an Anti-Shariah Push', p. 1.

[113]'List of Supporters', American Public Policy Alliance website, http://publicpolicyalliance.org/?page_id=464 (accessed 7 February 2012).

by the report of Soros's Centre for American Progress as 'grass-roots organizations', a category that has no precise equivalent in Denmark, but is probably closer to anti-Islamic activism than to street-level thuggery.[114]

These international anti-Islamic networks supported Hedegaard in various ways, most obviously ideologically. To what extent they also provided financial support is unknown; they may have provided no financial support at all, but equally they might have provided some support easily enough, given the very considerable resources at their disposal.

Hedegaard in return provided support for his international colleagues, featuring for example alongside Littman and the bloggers discussed above as a speaker at a European Counter Jihad conference held in Brussels in 2007, and appearing in New York in 2011 for the 9/11 Tenth Anniversary Rally, of which Spencer of *Jihad Watch* was one of the main organizers.[115]

The impact of the FPS in Denmark, however, was lessened by some comments made by Hedegaard at a pre-Christmas dinner (*julefrokost*) in December 2009. Large quantities of alcohol are normally consumed during Danish pre-Christmas dinners, and Hedegaard was not speaking for publication, but his comments were filmed by an admirer and posted on a website. They included the assertion that Muslims 'rape their own children. You hear about it all the time. Girls in Muslim families are raped by their uncles, their cousins or their father'.[116] When these comments came to public attention, Hedegaard was charged with hate-speech[117] and fined $890[118] (a verdict finally reversed on appeal, in 2012).[119] More importantly, press interest in the FPS peaked, and was not favourable. The two MPs in the FPS who were not from the DPP, Pind and Khader, resigned from it,[120] as did Brix,[121] who had been a member of the original Giordano Bruno Society with Hedegaard, had co-authored *In the House of War* with him, and who had been the editor of *Sappho*. As one blog post regretted, Hedegaard and the FPS has lost the opportunity they had been so close to seizing, of moving from the periphery into the mainstream.[122] Langballe, however, did not resign from the FPS, and deliberately repeated a version of Hedegaard's statement in an article in *Berlingske Tidende*.[123] He too was fined

---

[114] Ali et al., 'Fear, Inc.', p. 63.

[115] 'Speaker Biographies', *CounterJihad Europa*, http://counterjihadeuropa.wordpress.com/conferences/counterjihad-brussels-2007/counterjihad-brussels-2007-biographies/ (accessed 7 February 2012). 'September 11th Ten-Year Anniversary Memorial & SIOA Freedom Rally', *Urban Infidel*, 11 September 2011, http://urbaninfidel.blogspot.com/2011/09/september-11th-ten-year-anniversary.html (accessed 7 February 2012).

[116] Andreas Lindqvist, 'Lars Hedegaard: Muslimer er voldtægtsmænd og løgnere', *Politiken*, 21 December 2009, http://politiken.dk/indland/ECE865702/lars-hedegaard-muslimer-er-voldtaegtsmaend-og-loegnere/. Re-translated into English from the Danish translation of the interview, which was conducted in English, and is no longer available on the internet. He is still appealing against his conviction at the time of writing.

[117] Under §266b of the criminal code (*straffelov*). This is often called the 'Racism paragraph', but in fact criminalises denigration on grounds of race, colour, ethnicity, faith, or sexual orientation.

[118] Michael Engaard, 'Lars Hedegaard dømt for racisme', *Jyllands-Posten*, 4 May 2010, p. 17. Also DKK5000, at 2010 rates.

[119] The verdict was reversed on appeal on the basis that Hedegaard had never intended his comments to be made public. Pia Buhl Andersen, 'Lars Hedegaard bliver frifundet for udtalelser om muslimer', *Politiken.dk*, 20 April 2012, http://politiken.dk/indland/ECE1602017/lars-hedegaard-bliver-frifundet-for-udtalelser-om-muslimer/; (accessed 22 April 2012).

[120] Andreas Lindqvist, 'Naser Khader forlader Trykkefrihedsselskabet', *Politiken*, 22 December 2009. 'Pind forlader også Trykkefrihedsselskabet', Ritzaus Bureau, 22 December 2009.

[121] Helle Merete Brix, 'Biografi', http://www.hellemeretebrix.com/biografi/; (accessed 13 February 2012).

[122] 'Trykkefrihedsselskabet har tabt det hele på gulvet', *180Grader*, 23 January 2010, http://www.180grader.dk/Leder/trykkefrihedsselskabet-har-tabt-det-hele-paa-gulvet (accessed 7 February 2012).

[123] Jesper Langballe, 'Islams formørkede kvindesyn', *Berlingske Tidende*, 22 January 2010, http://www.b.dk/kommentarer/islams-formoerkede-kvindesyn.

$890.[124] Both he and Krarup had previously announced that they would not be standing in the 2011 elections,[125] and presumably felt they had little to lose.

The FPS, then, was a vehicle for international anti-Islamic activism that for some time succeeded in inserting elements of the Eurabia narrative into Danish newspapers, and presumably also in increasing neo-nationalist concern with Islam as a threat to Danish culture and security. The IFPS, in contrast, had no direct impact in Denmark, but was one of the ways in which the international network of anti-Islamic activism was held together.

Organizations compared

This article has now considered one neo-national political party – the DPP – and three Danish anti-Islamic organizations – SIAD, the FPS/IFPS, and The Danish Association. There are overlaps between these. Krarup was involved with three of them: as well as being a DPP member of parliament, he was at one point a supporter of The Danish Association, and remained a member of the FPS. Gravers also involved with three of them: as well as founding SIAD, he was at one point a member of The Danish Association, and clearly derived the message of SIAD – that Denmark is in danger of Islamization – from the Eurabia narrative, developing links with one member of the advisory board of the IFPS. This was Spencer of *Jihad Watch*, the co-founder of SIAO.[126]

Despite these overlaps, however, the four Danish organizations are very different. The DPP, as has been said, is a multi-issue political party, whereas the other three are single-issue groups. Among these, SIAD, led by a former butcher, lies at one end of a scale, with its amateurish websites and small and potentially violent street demonstrations. The FPS, led by the former editor-in-chief of a national daily, lies at the other end of the same scale, with its members of parliament and widely covered press conferences. The Danish Association lies somewhere in between the two. It was led neither by a former butcher nor a former editor-in-chief, but (from 1990 until 2000) by a professor of employment law, Ole Hasselbalch. It never got involved in street-level demonstrations, but did receive negative press attention for numerous 'stupidities' (*dumheder*), the word used by Krarup in 2002 when announcing his resignation from the Association.[127] On that occasion, The Danish Association's deputy leader had referred to Muslims as a 'plague'.[128] On other occasions, Hasselbalch had failed to come up with a convincing explanation for the presence of marginal notes in his handwriting on a bomb-making manual that had fallen into the hands of a tabloid newspaper,[129] and had also failed adequately to disown an article in The Danish Association's newspaper which appeared to call for violence against centres where asylum seekers were being held.[130]

These incidents may be classified as stupidities, following Krarup, or as indications of potential street-level thuggery. More important than the position of The Danish Association on the continuum between respectable single-issue organizations like the FPS and street-level organizations like SIAD, however, is the clear difference that exists between the FPS and SIAD. This distinction is also made by the people involved. Hedegaard is

---

[124]Marianne Fajstrup, 'Jurist: Langballe-dom er tegn på skærpet praksis', *Berlingske Tidende*, 4 December 2010, p. 7. DKK5000 at 2010 rates.
[125]Krarup, 'National værnepligt'.
[126]Anne Barnard and Alan Feuer, 'Outraged, and Outrageous', *The New York Times*, 10 October 2010, p. MB-1.
[127]Hans Bjerregaard, 'Klar udmelding', *Ekstra Bladet*, 25 March 2002, p. 15.
[128]'DF-medlemmer melder sig ud af Den Danske Forening', Ritzaus Bureau, 19 March 2002.
[129]'Professoren med bombeopskrifterne', *Ekstra Bladet*, 16 August 1991, p. 4.
[130]Søren Krarup, 'Sin egen fjende', *Ekstra Bladet*, 7 January 1993, p. 20.

not to be found sharing a platform with SIAD, and Westergaard, who allowed the FPS to raise money through the sale of his famous cartoon, sued SIAD to prevent them even displaying it during a demonstration.[131] To understand the FPS and SIAD as being the same thing – which is what would be implied by simply classing both of them as Far Right – would be a real mistake.

Conclusion

Neo-nationalist sentiment, then, is the main driving force behind the hostility towards Muslim immigrants to, and residents of, Denmark during the period 2001–2011. This sentiment is distinct from Islamophobia or racism, though it does include fear of Islam, and is not felt only by DPP voters. It was first visible in the Maastricht Treaty referendum of 1992, and then in the euro referendum of 2000 and the election results in 2001. It is ultimately a function of globalization, which raises concerns relating to identity and welfare among some voters, especially manual workers and the less educated, who are in fact those with most to lose from globalization. Similar sentiment is probably found, for similar reasons, in countries such as the UK, but the proportional nature of the Danish electoral system means that it has more political impact in Denmark than in the UK. In the end, though, neo-nationalist sentiment gave rise to the Danish People's Party, not the other way round. The discourse of the DPP may well have increased neo-nationalist sentiment, but that sentiment had empirical grounds when it came to concern about high levels of welfare spending on immigrants, and seemed to have empirical grounds when it came to concern about Islamic threats to Danish national security, and perhaps even when it came to politicians ignoring the views and needs of 'ordinary' voters. These concerns were stronger among DPP voters than among Liberal or SDP voters, but were far from exclusive to DPP voters.

Anti-Islamic activism, which is distinct from political responses to neo-nationalist sentiment such as the DPP, probably raised fear of Islam as a threat to Danish culture. Initially, this activism was represented by Krarup and Langballe, in whose case anti-Islamic sentiment had roots that were in part nationalistic, but also in part theological, and were consistent with theological positions taken by *Tidehverv* since the 1920s, and a general stance against leftists that had started in the 1950s and increased after 1968. This pro-Christian Danish anti-Islamic activism preceded 9/11, but after 9/11 was joined by, and to some extent combined with, the international anti-Islamic narrative of Eurabia which Hedegaard accepted, itself promoted by an international network of anti-Islamic activists joined by bodies such as the International Free Press Society, the Committee on the Present Danger, the Centre for Security Policy, and the European Counter Jihad network.

Anti-Islamic activism, then, is a distinct phenomenon from the traditional Far Right, and is also distinct from street-level organizations such as SIAD, despite overlaps between them. Anti-Islamic activism has had an impact in the Danish media and Danish politics, made receptive by neo-nationalist sentiment and politics. It is far from being the prime cause of neo-nationalist sentiment, and probably has little impact on the stereotypical DPP voter in a social housing project. Its most important impact may in fact be on those who are not DPP voters, and who might be expected to stand against neo-nationalism in the name of liberalism. Just as neo-nationalist sentiment and politics is distinct from Islamophobia and racism, so is anti-Islamic activism, even though it promotes fear of Islam.

---

[131]'Tegning: Muhammed i fogedretten', *Information*, 14 March 2008, p. 10.

Krarup's activism has Christian roots, and Hedegaard's has international roots which this article has only been able to sketch, but which include elements not related to Islam.

As has also been said, to understand all the varied things that have been going on in the state of Denmark since 2001 in terms of the Far Right is positively misleading. Only SIAD really fits within any understanding of the traditional Far Right, and SIAD matters little more than the National Socialist Movement of Denmark, which does not really matter at all.

Acknowledgements

My thanks to Pernille Ammitzbøll, Brian Arly Jacobsen, Shenaz Bunglawala, Anders Klostergaard Petersen, and Jørgen S. Nielsen for their helpful comments on the draft of this article, and also to Anders Klostergaard Petersen for drawing my attention to the importance of *Tidehverv* in the first place.

In Defense of Ho(s)tels: Islamophobia, Domophilia, Liberalism

IRFAN AHMAD

Monash University

ABSTRACT   *I foreground the reconstituted notion of 'nation-state-as-home' as central to our understanding of the hostility to and fear of Muslims, Islamophobia, in the contemporary west and beyond. The reconfiguration of the quest from a 'heavenly home' into an 'earthly home' – a prime signature of secular modernity – led to the consolidation of the nation-state as sort of a 'natural' home generating a new kind of love:* domophilia – domo + philia, *love for home. This love for home, domo, stemming from the Indo-European linguistic root, dem – a zone of possession and imagined security – derives its sustenance from its constitutive obverse,* foris/foras, *outsider and stranger. What simultaneously connects and separates the two is hostility often manifest,* inter alia, *in war. Discussing the condition of Muslims in the west and in India, this article aims to demonstrate the complex intimacy between domophilia and Islamophobia. Public expression of Islamophobia, I argue, is not a deviation from but constitutive of liberalism. It is my contention that much of the talk about Muslims' 'integration', verily a moderate word for assimilation, is less than adequate to meet the ever-growing challenge of Islamophobia. We need a significantly new way of imagining politics anchored in a ho(s)tel, not in the hegemonic established sense of a 'home-as-nation-state' which carries seeds of violence.*

> When... many companies support mass immigration... including Muslim immigration, this means that they contribute to Islamisation, at home and abroad.
>
> We should rather be protecting our own democracies at home against Islam.
>
> It is unrealistic to believe that we can save Europe through democratic struggle from a future reality where Muslims will be in the majority.
>
> Just like in Lebanon, the Muslims will become overconfident in Germany, the UK and France... Europeans...will begin to wage a guerrilla war... We [European nationalists] will win [for]... we have nowhere to go, while our colonisers [Muslims] still have their homelands intact.
>
> When the Muslim populations have been expelled from Europe, we will have rather large unpopulated areas in Albania, Western Anatolia and Lebanon with

the capacity to offer a permanent home (territory) to several Christian minorities. (Andrew Berwick [Anders Behring Breivik])[1]

Introduction

Amsterdam: April 2008. I boarded the Berlin-bound train. After it passed the Dutch border, the train stopped. Two security personnel entered the train. In my compartment I was the only non-white. And I alone was asked to show my passport and residence permit. After a few halts when the train again stopped, a lady arrived to take her seat beside mine. Let me call her Gudrun. We exchanged a smile. I continued reading until Gudrun gently interrupted me to ask where I was from. 'Holland', I said. Dissatisfied with my response, she asked, 'Where are you originally from'. 'India', I replied.

My response evoked a deep interest in Gudrun. She told me how great Indian culture was and that she loved it. In particular, she liked the image of lord Ganesha and practiced yoga. She had never been to India, however. She had briefly lived in Sri Lanka. She asked me which god I worshipped. Without awaiting my reply she continued her admiration of India. Gudrun knew about Sikhs too. She saw a Sikh for the first time when the Indian Prime Minister P.V. Narasimha Rao's entourage passed (in the early 1990s) through the neighborhood of Berlin where she lived. Seeing the 'strange-looking' Sikh security official accompanying Rao's cavalcade, she felt 'awkward'. She had lived in that neighborhood since her birth. It was only during World War II that she temporarily lived out of Berlin when Gudrun's father had sent her to her relations in Bavaria. As a Protestant she was dismissive of the 'superstitious' Bavarian Catholics with whom she spent her late childhood. She described herself as 'rational' and 'secular'.

As our conversation went on, Gudrun said how unsafe she felt 'now' living in Berlin. 'There are many women with strange dress in the streets. Wearing scarves is not in our culture. Islamic faith represses women... Until late in the evening Turkish boys hang out in the streets. They cast suspicious glances at us'. 'Why do you feel unsafe; have they attacked you', I asked. 'No, but they beat their own women', she said disgustingly. Even though she herself had never been attacked she felt unsafe because they wanted, as she put it, 'to impose Islam on Germany'. 'Turks want to make our home like theirs', she held.

During our conversation I was mostly a listener. When I asked her if any Turk had said that he desired taking over Germany, she answered it in the negative, elaborating that Turks had two 'tongues' – one they use when talking to 'us', the other when they talk among themselves. For Gudrun, unlike me, it was too obvious to be stated. If I had been to Berlin before, she said, I must have observed the tremendous rise in number of mosques in the city. 'Their minarets are getting taller than our churches', she observed. At this point, I noticed a dash of unease on her face. She abruptly turned silent. After a while, she asked me if I was a Muslim. 'Is it relevant?', I said. What followed was an eerie silence until the train reached Berlin and we went our own way.

Lucknow, India: April 2007. For the UP state elections, with much fanfare the Bharatiya Janata Party (BJP) – the key proponent of anti-Muslim Hindu nationalism in the democratic-electoral arena – released a CD to woo voters. The idea for 'a high voltage short film [CD] targeting Hindu sentiments in a big way' was well under way at its Lucknow

---

[1] All quotes from Andrew Berwick [Anders Behring Breivik], *2083: A European Declaration of Independence* (place and name of publication not given, 2011), pp. 411, 572, 1294, 1312, 1324, http://www.kevinislaughter.com/wp-content/uploads/2083+-+A+European+Declaration+of+Independence.pdf (accessed 18 November 2012).

convention (in December 2006) where the BJP resolved to regenerate its ideology of Hindutva, or Hindu nationalism.[2] The film opens with the BJP's flag unfurling, and announcing: 'The BJP... presents *Bhārat kī pukār* [The Call of India]'.[3] Its symbol – the lotus – is shown blooming and it remains on the top left of the screen throughout. The female voice-over is juxtaposed with an assemblage of images – beginning with the image of a Hindu goddess inscribed in the heart of the territorial map of India (with the Hindutva saffron flag implanted in the map), and trains, jeeps, settlements set on fire by 'Muslim terrorists'. Thus begins the voiceover:

> Mother India is crying aloud today. Oh my sons, protect me from being torn asunder. I no longer have the strength to be enslaved again. Through terrorists and by spreading fear and dividing us, Pakistan wants to tear India apart... Now... people of India have to decide if they again desire slavery or Ram Rajya [the Hindu rule] in their independent India.[4]

The voiceover ends with the image of the god Ram, armed with an arrow and bow. A new chorus voiceover begins to sing the anti-Muslim nationalist song '*vanda matram*'.[5] This is followed by another male chorus voiceover singing 'o' mother India, we bow your head at your feet' and that 'today we swear that we will never let the tricolor [the Indian flag] be lowered'. The chorus is accompanied with images of the top BJP leaders, a few of them pictured with Indian landscape in the backdrop and making passionate speeches.

With this preface, the story unfolds. A newspaper vendor shouts: bomb explosions in Kashmir, attacks on Akshardham temple, a train exploding. In response, an elderly man says: 'the terrorists will but destroy this nation (*desh*)'. A pair of bloodthirsty eyes (with face veiled) is shown throwing a bomb, causing explosions and cries for help. Instantly there appears a text on the screen: 'The Indian nation in the grip of terrorism'.

The film refers to India as a nation, depicting it as a neat cartographical entity, and equating it with Hinduism. Those determined to tear the nation asunder are Muslims. This is shown through a series of tropes. In a news clip inserted into the story, a Hindu female leader in saffron robe roars: 'Hindus produce two kids but Muslims marry five times, produce 35 puppies and thus want to make this country into an Islamic state'. Notice the words. Hindus produce kids, Muslims produce puppies, which will convert India into an Islamic state. This demographic bomb is lethal not only to Hindus but also to Muslim women waiting to be liberated from the tyranny of their religion. The female leader's speech is prefaced with an encounter between a Muslim woman (in black chador) and a Hindu schoolmaster, the key protagonist campaigning for the BJP. He asks her to vote for the BJP as 'the government of the Congress and the Samajwadi [parties] is the government of the mullahs'. The camera then shows a conversation amongst Muslim women (in black chador) one of whom says that their leaders have 'ordered them to produce more than 10 children' and 'increase the [Muslim] population'. The conversation ends with the camera back to the encounter between the schoolmaster and the Muslim woman who says: 'This religion [Islam] regards us as sheer objects of

---

[2] 'BJP: CD meñ kyā hai?', *BBC Urdu*, 2007, http://www.bbc.co.uk/urdu/india/story/2007/04/printable/070405_bjp_cd_sen.shtml (accessed 4 November 2007); 'BJP Campaign Film Targets SP, Congress', *Financial Express*, 2006, http://www.financialexpress.com/printer/news/187384/ (accessed 15 June 2009).
[3] In transliterating Urdu and Hindi words, I have largely followed the *Annual of Urdu Studies* journal guidelines, also available online, http://www.urdustudies.com/pdf/22/01TitleTranslit.pdf (accessed 18 November 2012).
[4] The CD is in Hindi; all translations into English are by the author.
[5] Irfan Ahmad, 'Contextualizing Vande Matram', *Manushi. A Journal about Women and Society*, 111 (1999), pp. 29–30.

use'. The schoolmaster joyfully responds: 'Bravo (*shābbāsh*) my child! If all women become educated and wise like you this country's fate will radically alter'.[6]

This article is divided into three sections. In the first section, I lay out key elements of my argument. I suggest that the reconstituted notion of 'nation-state as home' ought to be pivotal to our understanding of the hostility to and fear of Muslims, Islamophobia, in contemporary west and beyond. Both in India and west prejudices against Islam have long existed; however, with the onset of nation-thinking they became at once national and civilizational. Here I engage with recent anthropological writings on Islamophobia to critique the dualism between nation and civilization. I contend that the nation-state continues to be relevant in the face of globalization. In the second section, I use a historical anthropological approach to situate the rise of the nation-state and how it became synonymous with 'society' and 'home'. Based on the histories of Australia and India, I show how the equation of home with the nation-state came about. This equation, however, was neither simple nor peaceful. It was fraught with violence for while in Australia it rendered the Aboriginal population 'homeless', in India it generated the demand for a separate 'home' for Muslims, Pakistan. Here I stress how nation became the axis of our thinking to the extent that knowledge itself became nation-statized. The rest of the section is devoted to the Indo-European linguistic exposition of the constitutive 'other' of home, the outsider/the foreigner/the stranger and its link with territory, property and possession. To this end, I critically discuss writings on Islam in Europe. Drawing on Hannah Arendt, I conclude this section with an alternative genealogy of home which, in the wake of atom bomb and the consequent possibility for the entire humanity to commit suicide, conceives of the entire earth as home (*domo*). In the third and concluding section, I argue that Islamophobia is not a deviation from but constitutive of liberalism. I caution against the doxa that Muslims' 'integration' will lessen Islamophobia and that they will get integrated into 'home (the west)'. As an alternative and inspired by Franz Kafka's thought, I suggest replacing the dominant notion of nation/home with *hostel*, if not *hotel*.

The Argument: Why Domophilia?

How does one unpack the portrayal of Muslims in the BJP's film and in the discourse of Gudrun? Importantly, is there a connection between the depictions of Muslims by the BJP in India and those by Gudrun in Germany – two vastly different countries separated by thousands of miles? Most writings on Islamophobia in the west rarely make a connection to the Indian situation and vice versa. Forging the connection between the two might offer a new window to unpack the phenomenon of Islamophobia. Both in the west and India, it is the movements and discourses of nation-making and nation-preserving – the quest for and crafting of a pure, cohesive and cozy home, nation – which predominantly accounts for Islamophobia. Prejudices against Islam and Muslims obviously predate nationalism. However, with the onset of nationalism the prejudices assumed a specific form; they became at once national and civilizational (see below). The key difference between Islamophobia in India and in the west is this: while in India Muslims for over two centuries have been made to serve as both historical symbolic and empirical other of the nation, in the west Muslims also became an empirical, non-distant other only in the post-World War II era with their migration as cheap, docile labor from the erstwhile colonies. That which had been so far away became so close. Brought as temporary guests, circumstances made them permanent residents of a home/nation historically fashioned with Islam and Muslims as one of the significant others.

---

[6]The BJP election CD, given by Yoginder Sikand, is in my personal library.

(IL)LIBERAL EUROPE: ISLAMOPHOBIA, MODERNITY AND RADICALIZATION

By Islamophobia if we mean hostility to and fear of Muslims, there is barely new substance to this phenomenon. From Martin Luther through Karl Barth to Geert Wilders, there is an established tradition of 'othering' of Islam in the west.[7] And this by no means is simply born out of sheer ignorance. In my view, what is new and distinct about current Islamophobia is that, unlike in the past, from 1960s onwards, Muslims as the significant other are no longer there far-away – in the Middle East, Asia, Africa – they have come to 'our home' called Europe and its different nation-states. It is this century-old notion of home or nation and its perceived de-stabilization by Muslims' residence and presence that may enable us to better understand the current Islamophobia. In the west, non-state terror and suicide bombings are fervently discussed not because they are primarily novel political phenomena; after all terror has been part of the non-west for decades in places like India, Sri Lanka and Uganda. Rather they are also discussed publicly (privately as well) because terror has reached 'home', the west, in the same way commentators discuss Islamophobia today because Muslims no longer live just in the Middle East, Africa or Asia; rather, they have come home, the west. Australian Prime Minister Kevin Rudd's statement succinctly captures how the threat of terrorism is primary to the west, home, and only secondary to the non-west, overseas. 'As the Australian government has said consistently there is an enduring threat from terrorism, at home, here in Australia, as well as overseas'.[8] The distinction of my argument will become more evident with an engagement with Matti Bunzl's writing on Islam in Europe. In 2005, Bunzl wrote an article 'Between Anti-Semitism and Islamophobia: Some Thoughts on the New Europe', to which many anthropologists responded. According to Bunzl, 'at the heart of the Islamophobic discourse... is the notion that Islam engenders a worldview that is incompatible with and inferior to western culture'.[9] In Bunzl's view, 'Islamophobia has emerged quite recently. It is a phenomenon of the late twentieth and early twenty-first centuries'.[10] But if 'othering' of Islam/Muslims and the fear thereof is central to Islamophobia, then surely it is not as novel as Bunzl makes it out to be. Edward Said's *Orientalism* (absent from Bunzl's discussion) demonstrates the working of this attitude in the western discourses for centuries. Gingrich is thus right in critiquing the novelty Bunzl assigns to Islamophobia. He asks us to go back to the colonial era to trace the discourse of orientalism in different forms in Central, Eastern and Southern Europe and the history of different European nationalisms to understand the ways in which their 'wider ideological inventory' was shaped by the figure of the 'bad Muslim alien'.[11] Likewise, John Bowen contends that 'the whole complex of anti-Islamic sentiments is far older than one might think by reading Bunzl's piece'.[12]

Central to Bunzl's argument is the shift from nation to civilization. Differentiating Islamophobia from anti-Semitism, he contends that while the latter emerged in conjunction with the nineteenth-century European nation-state formations and the (im)possibility of Jews to be included therein, the former is an upshot of a more recent discourse the pivot of which is the 'civilization' of Europe, not the nation-state. He writes:

---

[7]Irfan Ahmad, 'Haunting the West: Plural Narratives of a Singular Figure', *Australian Book Review*, March (2011), pp. 56–57.
[8]Rudd: 'There is a Threat from Terrorism', *BBC*, 4 August 2009, http://news.bbc.co.uk/2/hi/asia-pacific/8182704.stm (accessed 4 August 2009).
[9]Matti Bunzl, 'Between Anti-Semitism and Islamophobia: Some Thoughts on the New Europe', *American Ethnologist*, 32:4 (2005), pp. 499–508: p. 502.
[10]Bunzl, op. cit., p. 502.
[11]Andre Gingrich, 'Anthropological Analyses of Islamophobia and Anti-Semitism in Europe', *American Ethnologist*, 32:4 (2005), pp. 513–515: p. 515.
[12]John Bowen, 'Commentary on Bunzl', *American Ethnologist*, 32:4 (2005), pp. 524–525: p. 524.

> Islamophobes are not particularly worried whether Muslims can be good Germans, Italians or Danes. Rather, they question whether Muslims can be good Europeans. Islamophobia, in other words, functions less in the interests of national purification than as a means of fortifying Europe.[13]

Bunzl's point that the nation-state stands irrelevant, if not dead, seems to echo Gerard Ruggie's contention that the current European project of integration reflects 'unbundling of territoriality' thus marking a postmodern turn, propelled by globalization.[14] In my view, the EU is a 'rebundling' of territorialities rather than its 'unbundling'. Clearly, the EU project does have some novelty. And the novelty lies not in the 'unbundling' of territory but unbundling of authority. Nationalism continues to be relevant, rather more important than in the past, both in Europe and elsewhere. In fact, nationalist sentiments have heightened with the processes of globalization. The demands, institutions, and languages of globalization thus don't subvert but rather dovetail into the ideologies of respective nation-states. Bunzl's stress on Europe also ignores the fact that pan-European projects are institutionally and legally anchored in the national spaces and authorized by the organs of the nation-state. Though influenced and shaped by the processes and forces outside of it, the nation-state is the site of legal, educational, and economic distributions.[15] It is useful to remind ourselves that as a citizen of global south, one applies for visa to a specific nation-state, not to Europe writ large.

More importantly, Bunzl's dualism between nationalism and civilization is false. Under modernity, it is the nation-state that became the motor and career of civilization. As nations, both the French and British saw themselves as flag-bearers of *the* (not *a*) civilization and thus justified colonization of the non-west in terms of civilizing it. Is it not the case that nationalist discourses in the late nineteenth century and subsequently already contained vital elements of civilization and pan-European identity? For instance, August Wilhelm, brother of Fredrick Schlegel, was a German nationalist simultaneously wedded to the 'European patriotism'.[16] Thus d'Appolonia is on the mark when she asserts that 'one must recognize that there is no necessary contradiction between European ideals and national identities, between European unification and national nationalism'.[17] To capture these simultaneous strands of thought, she uses 'European nationalism', a term also deployed by Anders Behring Breivik, the Norwegian terrorist who killed over seventy innocent people. To d'Appolonia, 'European nationalism' does not have a single meaning as it at once encapsulates the national and the supranational as long as the pivot remains Europe.

Breivik described himself and his like-minded fellows as 'European nationalists' (see epigraphs). My point is that discourses of the nation and civilization/Europe don't have to be diametrically opposed; rather they co-habit together. Bunzl's own ethnographic evidence

---

[13] Bunzl, op. cit., p. 502.

[14] John Gerard Ruggie, 'Territoriality and Beyond: Problematizing Modernity in International Relations', *International Organization*, 47:1 (1993), pp. 139–174.

[15] Saskia Sassen, 'Spatialities and Temporalities of the Global: Elements of a Theorization', *Public Culture*, 12:1 (2000), pp. 215–232.

[16] Dietrich Von Engelhardt. 'Romanticism in Germany' in Roy Poter and Mikulas Teich (eds) *Romanticism in National Context* (Cambridge: Cambridge University Press, 1988), p. 117; Mary Anne Perkins, 'Cosmopolitanism and Nationalism in the Writings of August Wilhelm and Friedrich Schlegel' in Mary Anne Perkins and Martin Liebscher (eds) *Nationalism Versus Cosmopolitanism in German Thought and Culture, 1789–1914* (Lewiston: Mellon Press, 2006).

[17] Arian Chebel d'Appolonia, 'European Nationalism and European Union' in Anthony Pagden (ed.) *The Idea of Europe: From Antiquity to the European Union* (Cambridge: Cambridge University Press, 2002), p. 172.

goes against his dualism between nationalism and civilization. According to the Freedom Party of Austria, where Bunzl conducted his fieldwork, Islam is a threat 'penetrating Europe' and, therefore, it needs to be checked 'both at the national and European level'.[18] As pointed out by many, national identities and loyalties continue to be salient in Europe; and these identities are not in violation of but mostly in consonance with a European identity.[19] Bunzl's contention that in the contemporary discourses on Europe the nation-state has gotten replaced by 'European civilization'[20] is therefore simply untenable in much the same way as his premise of Europe being driven by 'secular forces'. We should remind ourselves that the Cold War was not all that secular. 'The threat of communism was not just to capitalist economic systems, but to Christian society as expressed in western bloc democratic nations'.[21]

Nation-state as Home: Its Valence and Violence

Contra Bunzl, if the nation-state continues to be relevant and salient, two things follow. First, nation-state is ultimately a territorial concept: without territory there is no nation-state. Liberalism and democracy, when institutionalized, are also territorial projects. In the words of Walzer: 'liberalism is above all a domestic theory, designed to address the relationships of individuals to one another and to the state'.[22] The same is largely true for the working of democracy; it is territorially anchored. Second, at least since the nineteenth century nation-state has been the prime signature of 'home'. As a matter of fact we use 'society' and 'nation-state' interchangeably;[23] likewise verily we substitute 'nation' and 'home'. Manning seems to have aptly captured this dynamic between home and nation: 'The home provides not only a tangible example of how we perpetuate the vocabulary of the nation in our daily utterances, it offers also a visceral instance of our desire for attachment and belonging'.[24] In fact, one can go a step further to say that knowledge itself is nationalized. Ideally, disciplines like sociology and history were supposed to historicize and sociologize nation-states. However, under the monumental weight of nationalism these disciplines themselves got unrecognizably nation-statized.[25] Consider a few names of the established journals: *British Journal of Sociology*, *Australian Journal of Political Science*, *American Journal of Sociology*, *Contributions to Indian Sociology* and so on. These are not

---

[18]Bunzl, op. cit., p. 506.

[19]Christopher Ansell, 'Restructuring Authority and Territoriality' in Christopher Ansell and Giuseppe Di Palma (eds) *Restructuring Territoriality: Europe and the United States Compared* (Cambridge: Cambridge University Press, 2004), pp. 2–18; Pierre Beckouche, 'Division of Man, Division of Men: Why is the Territory a Strong Component of Contemporary Collective Identity?', *GeoJournal*, 60 (2004), 381–387.

[20]Bunzl, op. cit., p. 506.

[21]Gary D. Bouma, 'Religious Resurgence, Conflict and the Transformation of Boundaries' in Peter Beyer and Lori Beaman (eds) *Religion, Globalization and Culture* (Leiden: Brill, 2007), pp. 187–202; also see Irfan Ahmad, *Islamism and Democracy in India: The Transformation of Jamaat-e-Islami* (Princeton, NJ: Princeton University Press, 2009), ch. 1.

[22]Michael Walzer, *Politics and Passion: Toward a More Egalitarian Liberalism* (New Haven and London: Yale University Press, 2004), p. 138.

[23]Anthony Smith, *Nationalism in the Twentieth Century* (Oxford: Martin Robertson, 1979), p. 191; Anthony Giddens, *The Consequences of Modernity* (Stanford: Stanford University Press, 1990). p. 13.

[24]Erin Manning, *Ephemeral Territories: Representing Nation, Home and Identity in Canada* (Minneapolis and London: University of Minnesota Press, 2004), p. xvii.

[25]Irfan Ahmad, 'Anthropology of Nationalism, Nationalism of Anthropology: Notes on the Idea and Practice of Indian Anthropology', paper presented at the Anthropology Colloquium, Macquarie University, Sydney, Australia (20 October 2011); also see Daniel Chernilo, 'Social Theory's Methodological Nationalism: Myth and Reality', *European Journal of Social Theory*, 9:1 (2006), pp. 5–22.

simply learned journals; they are *national* journals. Thus knowledge is national.[26] Likewise, our use of the term 'home' is equally national. What is currently called BBC Radio 4 was previously called 'Home program' run under the larger title of Home Service as opposed to the BBC's Foreign Service.[27] As I argue that nation has been mainly conceived as home and vice versa, let me further explain what I mean by it.

> Dr Annie Besant is one of those foreigners who inspired the love of the country among Indians. She declared in 1918: 'I love the Indian people as I love none other... My heart and my mind... have long been laid on the alter [sic] of the Motherland'. Annie Besant, born of Irish parents in London on 1 October 1847, made India her home from November 1893. Dr Besant started the Home Rule League in India for obtaining the freedom of the country and reviving the country's glorious cultural heritage.[28]

This pithy description of Besant, taken from a non-academic nationalist website, illustrates well my point about how nationalism and home are intimate bedfellows. Mohandas Gandhi was part of this drama of Home Rule Movement.[29] A theosophist wedded to spiritual politics containing elements of race theories and opposed to adult franchise, sources and resources for Besant's dream home lay primarily in the history of pre-Muslim India, in the ancient Hindu scriptures and traditions.[30] It is this kind of politics of nation and home-making which subsequently resulted into competing demands for Pakistan, the so-called 'homeland' of Indian Muslims. 'One man's imagined community' became 'another man's political prison'.[31] In significant ways, the Partition of India was a historically monumental drama with a series of preceding non-linear acts over the longue durée of colonial-nationalist modernity:

> ... which sought to secure riddance of that which it christened as 'outcast'; it was the gory manifestation of the dominant theory and practice of Indian nationalism to design a hygienic, orderly home believed to have been contaminated with a threatening outcast – the Muslim 'Other'.[32]

The idea of a homeland of Jews is not radically different.

The fantasy of nation is driven by the idea of an orderly, nice, cozy home where heart resides and which heart longs for when it finds itself distant from home. In fact the distance from home may generate more intense longing for it. One of the most powerful expressions of such a longing for home is the nationalist song of Peter Allen, an Australian entertainer of some repute. The song 'I Still Call Australia Home' Allen composed became a major hit

---

[26]For a fuller elaboration of this argument in relation to sociology and Indian nationalism, see Ahmad, op. cit., 'Anthropology of Nationalism'.

[27]*Oxford English Dictionary: The Definitive Record of the English Language*, 'home, n.1 and adj.', OED Online, www.oed.com.ezproxy.lib.monash.edu.au/view/Entry/87869?rskey=mezQcm&result=1&isAdvanced=false (accessed 11 June 2011). The change from 'Home program' to 'Radio 4' took place in 1967.

[28]'The Home Rule', Indianhistory.com, http://www.indhistory.com/home-rule.html (accessed on 13 June 2011).

[29]Judith Brown, *Gandhi's Rise to Power: Indian Politics 1915–1922* (Cambridge: Cambridge University Press, 1972), p. 149.

[30]Hashim Qidwai, *Jadīd hindustān ke seyāsī aur samājī khayālāt* (New Delhi: Taraqqi Urdu Bureau, 1985), pp. 105–119.

[31]Arjun Appadurai, *Modernity at Large* (Minneapolis: University of Minnesota Press, 1996), p. 32.

[32]Irfan Ahmad, 'Modernity and Its Outcast: The Why and How of India's Partition', *South Asia: Journal of South Asian Studies*, 35:2 (2012), p. 478.

(versions of this song on YouTube have hundreds of thousands of viewers).[33] Notably, Allen imagined Australia as 'home' primarily in relations to imperial centers such as old London and New York as well as the 'nature', the sun and the vast sea. Allen's song, an 'Australian classic', which the Australian airline, Qantas, subsequently used in its 'hugely popular campaign' from 1997 to 2009,[34] is not merely about Australia as home; it is a *white home*. As such, it is criminally silent about how this white home has historically been built by demolishing the home of the Aboriginal population. In contrast to Allen's white racist imagination of an Australian home, Moreton-Robinson, herself an aboriginal Australian, beautifully and poignantly writes about the simultaneous dispossession and homelessness settler colonialism unleashed. 'The non-Indigenous sense of belonging is inextricably tied to this original theft: through the fiction of Terra Nullius the migrant has been able to claim the right to live in our land' thereby rendering the indigenous people 'homeless and out of place'.[35] Larissa Behrendt's *Home* is another powerful attempt to write a different narrative of home as experienced by the Aboriginal actors[36] (but for long silenced in the public domain, including in the curricula of Australian schools).[37] It should be evident how the politics of home is deeply enmeshed in and reflective of the simultaneous possession and dispossession, both often awfully secured through the greasy arms of law (lawfully).

Home as nation is nearly inconceivable without its constitutive 'other' – internal as well as external – from which it needs to be constantly guarded off. At times internal other, to the German philosopher Johann Gottlieb Fichte (d. 1814) 'interior frontiers'[38] was the essence of the nation, might be regarded as dangerous as the external one. In the wake of India–Pakistan War of 1965, an Indian Urdu poet, Jañ nisār akhtar exhorted Indians, particularly Muslims, with the following words: 'This [India] is our home; safeguarding (*hifāzat*) this home is our compulsory duty'.[39] This poetic act of claiming India as 'our home' has barely met with much success, however. In the winter of early 2002, I was engaged conducting ethnographic fieldwork in India when over 2000 thousands Muslims were killed, in absolute complicity with the government officials, in the western state of Gujarat.[40] In the wake of this massacre, a national conference was organized in the north Indian town of Aligarh, the main site of my fieldwork. In the conference a prominent Indian politician said: 'Muslims should not be considered as tenant

---

[33]Aileen Moreton-Robinson, 'Still Call Australia Home: Indigenous Belonging and Place in a Postcolonising Society' in Sara Ahmed, Claudia Castanda, Anne-Marie Fortier and Mimi Sheller (eds) *Uprootings/Regroundings: Questions of Home and Migration* (Oxford: Berg, 2003), p. 23. The song is also available at http://www.youtube.com/watch?v=hV78XFdBTsk (accessed 16 June 2011).
[34]Qantas.com.au, 'I Still Call Australia Home', http://www.qantas.com.au/travel/airlines/i-still-call-australia-home/global/en (accessed on 13 January 2013). Obeying the unethical capitalist ethic of copyright, I don't cite the song which the reader can listen to by clicking the URL in this note.
[35]Moreton-Robinson, op. cit., pp. 25, 24.
[36]Larissa Behrendt, 'Home: The Importance of the Place to the Dispossessed', *South Atlantic Quarterly*, 108:1 (2009), pp. 71–85.
[37]The historian Mark McKenna of the University of Sydney made this point in the Annual History Lecture aired on ABC Radio National, 28 January 2013, http://www.abc.net.au/radionational/programs/specialbroadcasts/annual-history-lecture3a-professor-mark-mckenna/4484202 (accessed 30 January 2013).
[38]Ann Stoler, 'Sexual Affronts and Racial Frontiers: European Identities and the Cultural Politics of Exclusion in Colonial South East Asia', *Comparative Studies in Society and History*, 34:3 (1992), p. 516.
[39]Cited in Jagannath Azad, 'Hindustān ke tahzībī 'anāsir ki tashkīl meñ Urdu ka hissa', *āhang* (Gaya; January 1983), p. 22. The full couplet read as follows: 'is fizay-e-husn parwar kī hifāzat farz hai/ye hamara ghar hai is ghar kī hifāzat farzh hai'.
[40]Prasun Sonwalkar, 'Shooting the Messenger: Political Violence, Gujarat 2002 and the Indian News Media' in B. Cole (ed.) *Conflict, Terrorism and the Media in Asia* (New York: Routledge, 2006), p. 86.

(*kirāyadār*) in this country, *mulk*' (this statement made headlines in the local Hindi newspapers).[41] That is to say, India is their 'home' – does not one also become a tenant in her own home?

The argument I have been developing is further illustrated when we dwell on violence – war and the idea of home by way of exploring the biography of the Indo-European linguistic equivalent of home. To this end, I use the work of the French historical socio-linguist Emile Benveniste. For house the root word in Iranian, Latin, Greek and Sanskrit is *dam*, *domus*, *dòmos* and *dama* respectively.[42] While noting the commonality across the four languages, Benveniste underlines the difference between its Greek and Latin lexical employment. In Greek it refers to a house as a physical structure and it also has a verbal form meaning 'to construct' (the root being *dem*). In Latin, in contrast, *domus* denotes 'house' in the sense of 'family' and it has no verbal form.[43] Again, in contradistinction to its Greek usage, in Latin *domo*, *domi*, *domum* signify the family and home as a moral, social idea, not as a material one in the sense of a 'house'.[44] The derivative *domi* means peace and is contrasted with *militiae* meaning war the purpose of which is to monopolize or expand possession: the possessive pronoun *domus* signifies 'possession'. Derived from the common Indo-European root *dem*[45], *domāre* in Latin, *damàò* in Greek and *damayati* in Sanskrit means 'to do violence; to tame'.[46] And the logical opposite of *domo/domi* – home – is the outside or stranger called *foras* or *foris*.[47] What dialectically (dis)connects home and outside is war. After the end of the seventeenth century civil war fought along religious lines in Europe 'was diverted to the outside, so to speak, and many Absolutist theoreticians saw it as a permanent institution for the prevention of civil war [at home]'.[48] Peace at home and war abroad were not seen as contradictory; rather they mutually complimented each other. To better illustrate this constitutive interrelationship between *domi* and *foris* let me give a longer quote from Benveniste I have been citing at length:

> We can understand why in Latin *foris* is the opposite of *domi*; the outside begins at the door and is called *foris* for the one who is at home, *domi*. This door, according to whether it is open or shut, becomes the symbol for separation from and communication between, one world and the other. It is through the door that the secure and enclosed space... opens on an extraneous and often hostile world... The rites of passage through the door, the mythology of the door, give a religious symbolism to this idea [of home].[49]

As this quote shows, in addition to moral and social aspects, the simple yet gigantic entity called home has an inbuilt notion of a hostile 'outside' world with a clear territorial anchoring (though Benveniste does not elaborate on the territorial aspects). Territory has Latin origin – '*terratorium*, meaning earth (*terra*), and *terrere* meaning to frighten (suggesting

---

[41]*Amar uajāla* (Agra edition), 22 April 2002.
[42]Emile Benveniste, *Indo-European Language and Society*, translated by Elizabeth Palmer (London: Faber, 1973), p. 241. I am thankful to Ghassan Hage for directing me to this work.
[43]Ibid., p. 243.
[44]Ibid., pp. 244–245.
[45]Ibid., p. 239.
[46]Ibid., p. 251.
[47]Ibid., p. 244.
[48]Reinhart Koselleck, *Critique and Crisis: Enlightenment and Pathogenesis of Modern Society* (Cambridge, MA: The MIT Press, 1988 [1959]), p. 44.
[49]Benveniste, op. cit., p. 255.

terratorium as a place from which people are warned off)'.[50] By the eighteenth century it acquired a juridical bent connoting property; in fact, territory and property (hence the control over them) became more or less the same thing. The 1789 Constitution of the US authorized the Congress to pass laws 'respecting the Territory or other Property belonging to the United States'.[51] With the Treaty of Westphalia, the term territory became crucial to European politics. With the intensification of the movement of nationalism from the eighteenth century on, territory, nation and home became almost one and the same. Nationalism generated the idea of citizen inside and alien outside thus inaugurating the field of international studies. It is worth mentioning that it was not 'until Bentham coined the phrase *international* in late eighteenth century that *foreign* came to be firmly associated with the different character of other nations'.[52] When used first in the English language, the 'thirteenth-century term *chamber foreign* referred to private room in a house'.[53] In subsequent centuries the meaning of term foreign as something outside of a definite territory became certain to the extent that any fidelity with it was considered legally punishable and morally reprehensible. Perhaps the best illustration of this complex transformation of European political philosophy is the term 'naturalization'. To join a new nation, one needs to be naturalized. The premise is clear: she who moves from one territory to another becomes 'unnatural'. Hence the oath of allegiance to become a US citizen reads: 'I hereby declare, on oath, that I absolutely... renounce and abjure all allegiance and fidelity to any foreign prince, potentate, state, or sovereignty, of whom or which I have heretofore been a subject or citizen'.[54]

What I mean by all this is that our thought is notably ontopological. In Derrida's reading, ontopology signifies an 'axiomatics linking indissociably the ontological value of present being... to its *situation*, to the stable and presentable determination of a locality, the *topos* of territory, native soil, city, body in general'.[55] It is this solid, holy alliance between ontology and territory-nation, which finds expression in terms such as 'homeland security', 'home ministry' and 'home ground'. In sports, 'home' means a place of security 'free from attack by the opposition';[56] in cricket when a batsman rushes for a run after hitting the ball and he has planted his bat within the crease before the throw from the fielder hits the stumps commentators routinely say 'the batsman is safely home'.[57] There is no nation without a threatening 'other' or what Derrida calls 'some ghost'.[58] Since I regard 'home' and 'nation' as largely synonymous, we can likewise think of national culture, national music, national bird, national anthem, national curriculum, national dress, national cuisine, national sports and so on. Even air stands nationalized: think of the airlines – Air France, Air India, Air Italy and British Airways.

It is this notion of home/nation, which informs not only the statements and practices of Islamophobes such as Geert Wilders and Jorg Haider but also many scholarly analyses. In

---

[50]Linda Bishai, *Forgetting Ourselves: Secession and the (Im)possibility of Territorial Identity* (Lanham, MD: Lexington Books, 2007), p. 61.

[51]Ibid., p. 61

[52]David Campbell, *Writing Security: United States Foreign Policy and the Politics of Identity*, cited in Bishai, op. cit., p. 78, italics in original.

[53]Ibid., italics in original.

[54]Bishai, op. cit., p. 79.

[55]Jacques Derrida, *Specters of Marx: The State of the Debt, the Work of Mourning and the New International* (New York, London: Routledge, 1994), p. 82, italics in original; also see Jacques Derrida, 'Onto-Theology of National Humanism (Prolegomena to a Hypothesis)' in Barry Stocker (ed.) *Basic Writings* (London: Routledge, 2007), pp. 305–323.

[56]*Oxford English Dictionary*, 'home, n.1 and adj.'.

[57]This is based on my observation as a fanatic fan who has watched cricket for over a decade.

[58]Derrida, *Basic Writings*, p. 316.

discussion on Islam in Europe, the most often used term is 'Muslim presence'. The logical opposite is 'Muslim absence'. But have not Muslims been present for the last fourteen hundred years? If so, this term means that Muslims have become present *now* in the territory called France, Italy, the UK or Netherlands. My point is that there is a territorial ideology behind this term 'Muslim presence'. And this territorial ideology is the idea of home; until recently Muslims have been out there, far-off – in the Middle East, Asia, Africa; now they have come to invade 'the home' called Europe, the civilization, or the Netherlands, the nation-state. Some examples are in order here. Effie Fokas writes that the:

> ... hackneyed dichotomous representation 'liberal' versus 'traditional', 'moderate' versus 'radical'... Islam are clearly insufficient. A more nuanced approach is necessary, taking into account a number of key factors... including whether Muslim groupings are *autochthonous or immigrants*.[59]

In my view, this is far from a nuanced approach because the alternative of autochthonous and immigrant Fokas proposes is implicated in the language of nation–home–territory thinking. Do words like autochthonous and immigrant make any sense without a prior assumption of what is home and the necessary elements which (un)make it? Fokas urges readers to examine the givenness of a Muslim identity; the same urge is somehow missing in examining what after all is Europe; she takes Europe as a 'given'. Another example is Jocelyn Cesari who in fact uses the term 'home'. Applauding that 'there now exists a French Islam, an English Islam, a Belgian Islam', she writes that Muslims' 'daily concrete practices reveal an acculturation generating a "*homemade*"... *version of Islam*'.[60] If analyzed in relation to the distinction between *domo/domi* and *foris* and *foras* I discussed above, Cesari's argument renders Islam foreign while arguing for a *homemade version of Islam*. In Melbourne (in 2011), some Muslim women pleaded for a revision of the dress code in swimming pools. It generated heated reaction from the 'autochthonous' white women one of whom said, on TV Channel 7, that if Muslim women did not want to confirm to 'our ways', they should go 'home'. Bassam Tibi's claim that he fathered the term 'Euro-Islam'[61] squarely belongs to this language of home I am unpacking here in the same way as the lament of Xavier Bougarel that there is still not a 'European' Islam.[62] In the legal domain, America's 2002 Homeland Security Act is a robust example. Financed by America's Department of Homeland Security, in 2010, one think tank published a report titled 'Protecting the Homeland from International and Domestic Terrorism Threats'.[63]

In a variety of catalogues and media, this growing theme of 'Muslims Go Home' has appeared in the west, including in such important media as YouTube. A YouTube video exposition titled 'Muslims Go Home' – with no sound and picture – simply shows a short paragraph of text which simultaneously advises and chastises Muslims in the

---

[59] Effie Fokas, 'Introduction' in Aziz Al-Azmeh and Effie Fokas (eds) *Islam in Europe: Diversity, Identity and Influence* (Cambridge: Cambridge University Press, 2007), p. 2, italics added.
[60] Jocelyn Cesari, 'Muslim Identities in Europe: The Snare of Exceptionalism' in Al-Azmeh and Fokas, op. cit., p. 56, italics added.
[61] Jorgen Nielsen, 'The Question of Euro-Islam: Restriction or Opportunity' in Al-Azmeh and Fokas, op. cit., p. 35.
[62] Xavier Bougarel, 'Bosnian Islam as "European Islam": Limits and Shifts of a Concept' in Al-Azmeh and Fokas, op. cit., pp. 96–124.
[63] Laurie Fenstermacher et al. (eds), 'Protecting the Homeland from International and Domestic Terrorism Threats: Current Multi-disciplinary Perspectives on Root Causes, the Role of Ideology, and Programs for Counter-radicalization and Disengagement', http://www.start.umd.edu/start/publications/U_Counter_Terrorism_White_Paper_Final_January_2010.pdf (accessed 11 April 2011).

Figure 1. Anti-Muslim slogan 'Go Home' on the wall of Islamic Centre of America, Dearborn, Michigan. Bill Pugliano/Getty Images News/Getty Images. © Getty Images 2007.

following words: 'Muslims, shut up and grow up, or go home'. This exposition at YouTube is posted by an Australian, Michael Hunt.[64]

In recent times, the love for home and homeland (*domophilia*) has indeed become the signature of politics, both in 'east' and 'west'. Take France, for instance. In a 2007 election meeting, Nicolas Sarkozy said: 'France is our country and we have no other. France is us. It is our heritage. Our common good. Hating her would mean hating ourselves'.[65] 'If foreigners want to remain in France', he went on, 'they have to love France; otherwise, they should leave'.[66] Having presided over the brutal suppression of Tamil militancy (entailing massive violation of human rights), the triumphant President of Sri Lanka, Mahinda Rajapaksa, announced joyfully in 2009:

> We have removed the word minorities from our vocabulary... No longer are the[re] Tamils, Muslims, Burghers, Malays and any other minorities. There are only two peoples in this country. One is the people who love this country. The other comprises the small groups that have no love for the land of their birth.[67]

The need for this declaration of love for home has only increased as we have come to late modernity. If in the last two centuries nation as a territorial entity has been the dominant mode of organizing our lives and thinking, what Marc Auge calls 'non-places' of late modernity or supermodernity[68] have only accentuated the urge for a definite, familiar

---

[64]http://www.youtube.com/watch?v=c1EV_IVpYew (accessed 13 January 2013).
[65]Eric Fassin, 'National Identities and Transnational Intimacies: Sexual Democracy and the Politics of Immigration in Europe', *Public Culture*, 22:3 (2010), p. 526.
[66]Alain Badiou, 'The Communist Hypothesis', *New Left Review*, 49 (2008), p. 39.
[67]Nira Wickramasinghe, 'After the War: A New Patriotism in Sri Lanka?', *The Journal of Asian Studies*, 68:4 (2009), p. 1045.
[68]Marc Auge, *Non-places: Introduction to an Anthropology of Supermodernity* (London: Verso, 1995).

place, home included. The mythology of a secular Europe – that the quest for a heavenly home has got transformed into an earthly home – does not lessen the love for home. Rather it enhances the love for home in such a way that it assumes divine valence. Steve Bruce, the continuing advocate of Europe's secularization thesis (which has come under serious doubts in recent scholarship), makes an intriguing argument. In his view, even in a so-called secular society religion can take on non-religious roles of defending a national identity in the face of a national threat. He writes: 'modernity undermines religion except when it finds some major social role to play other than mediating the natural and super-natural world'.[69] Is it the case that religion in the west has come to be invested in the idea of home to serve as the reference point for politics? Geert Wilder's comment on Turkey's membership to EU probably exemplifies it cogently. He said: 'I am against the joining of Turkey [to EU]. I have nothing against Turkey. It is a very respected ally within NATO. ... But I believe it is not a member of the family. A good neighbor is not the same as being a member of the family'.[70] It scarcely requires mention that Wilder's usage of family presupposes and reinforces a distinct conceptualization of Europe as home/family which dates back to the eighteenth century when, to quote Koselleck, 'The Society of European states seems to have been transformed into one large family'.[71]

So far, I have argued how nation as home has conditioned our thinking of modern politics in general and of Muslims in Europe and India in particular. To this end, I have given short genealogies of the concepts of territory, nation, and home. There is another genealogy of home with which I wish to conclude this section of the article. This genealogy is admittedly preliminary and brief. Thoughts and practices about nation-as-home often assume this vast earth as a stable entity and then proceed to carve out of it a specific piece/tract called home. That is, a segment of human population seeks to build a home – *domo* – against another segment of population, *foris*, the strangers. But what if humanity at large becomes strange to itself? Who would, then, be the other against whom the idea of home will become meaningful? Has not the entire earth itself become home? Indeed it has become. It is the atom bomb and the moon landing, the latter enabling the viewing of the globe as an object from elsewhere, which fashioned the concept of a global home linking people – regardless of their multiple diversities – together. Hannah Arendt wrote:

> It is true, for the first time in history all peoples on earth have a common present: no event of any importance in the history of one country can remain a marginal accident in the history of another... Every man feels the shock of events which take place at the other side of the globe.[72]

With the lethal threat of the atom bomb, for the first time in history it dawned on humans that what was at stake was not the killing of one segment of human population by another but the possibility that humanity itself could commit suicide. This was a new realization in that it questioned the split between *domo* and *foris*: either the whole earth is *domo* or *foris*: in no way could it be both.[73] Surprising though it may seem, Osama bin Laden and Aiman

---

[69] Steve Bruce, *Religion in the Modern World* (Oxford: Oxford University Press, 1996), p. 96; and Steve Bruce, 'Social Process of Secularization' in R.K. Fenn (ed.) *The Blackwell Companion to Sociology of Religion* (Oxford: Blackwell).
[70] http://www.youtube.com/watch?v=KBnLa6Llz2g (accessed 12 July 2009).
[71] Koselleck, op. cit., p. 49.
[72] Hannah Arendt, *Men in Dark Times* (London: Harcourt, 1995), p. 83.
[73] Here I am indebted to Faisal Devji's *The Terrorist in Search of Humanity* (Delhi: Foundation Books, 2008); my reading of Arendt is somewhat different from Devji's, however.

Al-Zawahiri exemplify this new realization of home whereas the western plutocracies continue to operate in the old language of home as nation-state or a conglomeration of select western nation-states. In a VDO release of 2011, Al-Qaeda leader Aiman Al-Zawahiri reportedly said: 'you shall not dream of security until we enjoy it'.[74] Zawahiri's statement was a reiteration of what Osama bin Laden had said after the Madrid bombing of 2005: 'It is well-known that security is a vital necessity for every human being. We will not let you [the west] monopolize it for yourselves'.[75]

(In)Conclusion

The dominant liberal explanation for the public visibility of Islamophobia in the west runs as follows: Islamophobia is in some ways a betrayal of west's liberalism, at least in its 'pure', 'classical' formulations. Contemporary western legislations embodying Islamophobia is thus explained in terms of employing 'illiberal means to liberal ends'.[76] Islamophobia, I argue, is neither a deviation from nor a distortion of 'true' liberalism; Islamophobia is indeed constitutive of western liberalism from its unfolding to the present. In a thoughtful publication, which historically surveys the Cold War and Post-Cold War world in relation to Islam, John Trumpbour concludes: 'Alas, liberalism as a child of Enlightenment is shot through with Islamophobia'.[77] As an example, he cites the views of Voltaire (1694–1778) 'representing the apogee of Enlightenment reason and tolerance'. To Frederick the Great, Voltaire said: 'You may still have the pleasure of seeing Muslims chased out of Europe'. And to Catherine the Great, Voltaire unambiguously expressed his ardent desire as follows: 'I wish I had at least been able to help you kill a few Turks'. 'It does not suffice to humiliate them', Voltaire went on, 'they [Muslims] should be destroyed'.[78]

Notwithstanding its specificity, the history of Indian liberalism is not vastly different from that of the west. Described as the 'father of the Indian Renaissance' and of 'modern India', 'the... Christ of the Indian Renaissance' and in the words of historian Chris Bayly 'the first Indian liberal',[79] Rammohun Roy (1772–1833) unambiguously displayed, as did Voltaire more than a century earlier, ample hostility to Islam while showering praise on imperial Britain which had then freshly colonized India. Roy was deeply sad to have seen Hindustan 'for several centuries subject to Mohammadan Rule, and the civil and religious rights of its original inhabitants being constantly trampled upon'. Mark that, to Roy, Hindus were the 'original inhabitants'. And Muslims (*yaāvana* in Bengali)? 'Provisional inhabitants' at best! And this is how he liberally welcomed colonialism: 'Divine Providence at last, in its abundant mercy, stirred up the English nation to break the yoke of those tyrants, and to receive the oppressed Natives of Bengal under its

---

[74]'Zawahiri Praises Osama Bin Laden, Vows to Continue Jihad', *Times of India*, 8 June 2011, http://timesofindia.indiatimes.com/world/middle-east/Zawahiri-praises-Osama-bin-Laden-vows-to-continue-jihad/articleshow/8778372.cms (accessed 9 June 2011).

[75]Cited in Irfan Ahmad, 'Is There an Ethics of Terrorism? Islam, Globalisation, Militancy – Review Essay', *South Asia*, 33:3 (2010), p. 496.

[76]Robert Gould, this issue.

[77]John Trumpbour, 'The Clash of Civilizations: Samuel Huntington, Bernard Lewis, and the Remaking of the Post-Cold War World Order' in E. Qureshi and M. Sells (eds) *The New Crusades: Constructing the Muslim Enemy* (Columbia: Columbia University Press, 2003), p. 118.

[78]Ibid. Terry Eagleton notes the link between Islamophobia and current advocates of liberalism such as Salman Rushdie and Christopher Hitchens; see Irfan Ahmad, *Islam as Critique: Reason, Revelation, Tradition* (in progress).

[79]Ahmad, 'Modernity and Its Outcast', p. 483

protection'. As if this was insufficient, Roy went on: 'Your dutiful subjects have not viewed the English as a body of conquerors, but rather as deliverers, and look up to your Majesty not only as a Ruler, but also as a father and protector'.[80]

With liberalism yoked to and enshrined into the institutional matrix of the nation-state, Islamophobia began to be embodied in the figure of the 'Other' threatening and contaminating the purity, order and coziness of nation, home. India serves as its good illustration. Unlike Muslims in the west (called 'immigrants'), ancestors of most contemporary Indian Muslims were local Hindus who converted to Islam centuries ago. They are not immigrants/foreigners. In appearance seldom are they distinguishable from the Hindu population. They speak myriad Indian languages. Yet even in current post-colonial India Muslims are regarded as 'outsiders' and 'foreigners';[81] hence the recurring calls for the 'Indianziation' of Muslims and Islam. This call for Indianization, spearheaded by Hindu nationalist parties, is not limited to them; it goes far beyond to include even elements of the Left. Three years ago, in 2010, Mr L.K. Advani, key leader of the BJP who narrowly missed being India's Prime Minister, held that Muslims were not integrated into the nation and that only after the Allahabad High Court's politicized judgment vindicating the Hindu Right position on the Babri Masjid issue, he said that the judgment opened 'a new chapter for national integration and a new era for inter-community relations'.[82] The assumption of Muslims not being part of the 'national mainstream' abounds in public domain.[83] In order to integrate Muslims into the nation, in 1970, Balraj Madhok, President of the Bharatiya Jana Sangh (BJS), which subsequently became the current BJP, wrote *Indianization*.[84] Though it also concerned minorities such as Christians, Madhok's key target was Muslims. He regarded Muslims steeped in backwardness which prevented them from being Indianized. In his scheme, the modernization of Islam was a prerequisite for Indianization of Muslims. The crux of Madhok's missionary program for an Indian Islam, similar to Bassam Tibi's Euro-Islam, was that Muslims relinquish their identity and begin to fervently participate in religious-cultural festivals and institutions of Hinduism which he equated with 'nation' and which, contra Islam, was modernity embodied. The resolution of the BJS, passed in 1969, read: 'Indianization – by which we mean the subordination of all narrow loyalties like those of religion, caste, region, language, or dogma to the overriding loyalty to the nation'.[85] That Islam is foreign and Muslims are outsider to India has been imbibed by many Muslims themselves. Salman Khurshid, an important leader of the Congress party and a lawyer, titled his book *At Home in India: A Restatement of Indian Muslims*.[86]

If we compare the condition of Indian Muslims with that of Muslims in the west it becomes apparent that the discourse of integration has serious limits. It thrives regardless of the 'facts' of integration – whatever its indicator; linguistic competence, for instance. The discourse of integration and the related premise of separatism derive their power

---

[80]Pulak Narayan Dhar, 'Bengal Renaissance: A Study in Social Contradiction', *Social Scientist*, 15:1 (1987), p. 30.
[81]Gandhi too seemed to hold such a view; see the 1944 correspondence between Gandhi and Jinnah in K.M. Ashraf, *Hindu–Muslim Question and Our Freedom Struggle*, vol. 2 (Delhi: Sunrise, 2005), appendix 6.
[82]'Ayodhya Judgment New Chapter for National Unity: Advani', *Sify.com*, 2010, http://www.sify.com/news/ayodhya-judgement-new-chapter-for-national-unity-advani-news-national-kj4v4mijdcf.html (accessed on 1 October 2010).
[83]For a representative example, see R. Upadhyay, 'Indian Muslims: Under Siege?', http://www.southasiaanalysis.org/paper1160 (accessed on 12 January 2013).
[84]Balraj Madhok, *Indianization: What, Why and How* (Delhi: S. Chand, 1970).
[85]Cited in Christophe Jaffrelot (ed.), *Hindu Nationalism: A Reader* (Princeton, NJ: Princeton University Press, 2007), p. 170.
[86]Khurshid, *At Home in India: A Restatement of Indian Muslims* (Delhi: Vikas, 1986).

and nourishment from the a priori home which Muslims are invited to/ordered to get integrated into. And this home/nation is enacted, felt and performed, for instance in the media, with the reigning binaries of insider/outsider, autochthonous/immigrants, and internal/external. These binaries are not bare words; they are powerful weapons which at once reproduce and fashion specific histories, emotions, sensibilities, aesthetics, memories, and blueprints for the vistas of future.[87] Muslims are depicted as outsiders not because they don't fit in the pre-designed home but the premise is that howsoever they try they can probably never fit in the home; Muslims' culture/religion sets them apart from 'us' who have unique and superior values. For home to remain home there needs to be a non-home, *foras/foris*, which precisely is the function Muslims in Europe[88] (also the USA), India and elsewhere have been asked to perform in the figure of 'outsiders', 'alien' and so on. Every articulation of Islamophobia is in significant ways at the same time also the declaration of love for home, domophillia.

The fear and anxiety that Muslims, rather than getting integrated into 'our ways of life' remain 'separate' from us and thereby aim to impose 'their' culture on 'ours', historically speaking, is less about the fact of Muslims' integration in the west and more about the past of the westerners themselves who in the vast colonies rarely got integrated into the local cultures and maintained an umbilical link with their respective imperial 'homes'. Seldom did the settler Anglo population in Australia, for instance, integrate into the local Aboriginal moorings. Having unsettled the Aboriginals, the Anglos settled in Australia only to continue to think of England as their 'original' home, mother country. The intense debates over the forms, contents and styles of observing Christmas in the antipodes demonstrate it eloquently. Like in England, during Christmas the settler Anglo community continued to make and serve hot pudding and roasted beef in the torridly hot climate of Australia. Christmas cards with scenes of hills covered in white snow were sold in a fairly warm December of Australia. For the settler Anglo community hot pudding was the link to its imperial home; culture of sentiment triumphed over the environment. Empire and religion fused together so as to institute a separation between the culture of the colonized and that of the colonizers. 'Even on the outskirts of Empire', it was observed in the 1920s, 'someone prepare[s] the dinner for the day which links together the Christian world'.[89] The dinner would but include hot pudding.

Likewise, today when the Dutch complain about the lack of integration by its population of the Moroccan extraction, a historian may hear the echoes from the colonial Dutch settlement in South Africa where the Dutch (called Afrikaners) were the least integrated into the local society and culture. As God's 'chosen people' they loathed the local black

---

[87] My suggestion here is to see 'home' not as an accomplished fact but as a process, what Ahmed et al. call 'homing' and Hage 'making home'; Ahmed et al., 'Introduction' in Sara Ahmed, Claudia Castanda, Anne-Marie Fortier and Mimi Sheller (eds) *Uprootings/Regroundings: Questions of Home and Migration* (Oxford: Berg, 2003); Ghassan Hage, 'At Home in the Entrails of the West: Multiculturalism, Ethnic Food and Migrant Home-Building' in Helen Grace, Ghassan Hage, Lesley Johnson, John Langsworth and Michael Symonds (eds) *Home/World: Space, Community and Marginality in Sydney's West* (Annandale: Pluto, 1997). An analytical advantage of understanding Islamophobia through 'home/homing' is that it also allows exploring the everydayness and micro processes of lives. Bunzl, who I cited above, is concerned more with the discourses of the political and bureaucratic elites.

[88] In Introduction to his book on Muslims in Africa, Robinson writes: 'The conflict began in the seventh century CE, when Muslim armies conquered a great deal of the Mediterranean world that Europe considered *its original cultural home*' (italics added); David Robinson, *Muslim Societies in African History* (Cambridge: Cambridge University Press, 2004), p. xv.

[89] Rhiannon Donaldson, 'Revisiting a "Well-worn Theme": The Duality of the Australian Christmas Pudding 1850–1950', *Eras Journal*, 6 (2004), p. 3.

society.[90] The story of the Dutch settlement during the mid-eighteenth and early nineteenth century in the present-day Kerala (India) is similar. The Dutch and Eurasian populations were rarely integrated into the local society. There were two separate settlements: 'Fort Cochin (*Cochim de Baixa*)' where company officials, free burghers, their associates and dependents lived and 'native Cochin (*Cochim de Cima*)' of mostly local population.[91] The lack of integration into the local society by the British colonial officers in India was evident, *inter alia*, from the notices at their residences: 'natives and dogs not allowed'. J.S. Furnivall theorised such practices in the concept of plural society where different segments of the population met only 'in market places, in buying and selling'.[92]

Many have recognized the violence that the discourse of nation/home routinely enacts. Terms like minority and majority are central to this vocabulary of violence. Connolly thus proposes a shift 'from a majority nation presiding over numerous minorities... to a democratic state of multiple minorities contending and collaborating with a general ethos of forbearance'.[93] Similarly, Talal Asad argues that 'Muslims in Europe... should be able to find representation as a minority in a democratic state that consists only of minorities'.[94] Connolly's and Asad's suggestions seem valuable for they unsettle the notion of majority. In my view, they don't go far enough to adequately question the ubiquity and foundation of the nation. As long as the nation or home remains the pivot of our classification and thinking (should one say, 'unthinking'?), the fear of, violence against and demonization of Muslims – in short, Islamophobia – will likely continue. I thus suggest: let us begin to think of the nation, rather the world at large, as a hotel. A hotel does not usually run along the dark logic of autochthony and belonging. Perhaps because of this, Kafka admired hotels. In a letter, he wrote to his friend Max Brod:

> I like hotel rooms; I am at home at once in hotel rooms, more than at home, really.[95]

Kafka's words are remarkable: in contrast to Germany's Gudrun, India's BJP and Norway's Anders Behring Breivik with whom I began this article, Kafka felt more at home in a hotel than actually at home. As you will recognize, I employ 'hotel' as a working metaphor, not as a sealed territorial entity denuded of solidarity and an ethos of sociability. To readers who still might get this impression, let me alternatively whisper 'hostel'.

---

[90]Howard J. Wiarda, *The Dutch Diaspora: The Netherlands and Its Settlements in Africa, Asia, and the Americas* (Lanham, MD: Lexington Books, 2007), ch. 10.
[91]Anjana Singh, *Fort Cochin in Kerala, 1750–1830: The Social Condition of a Dutch Community in an Indian Milieu* (Ledien: Brill, 2010), ch. 1.
[92]Paul Rich 'Ideology in a Plural Society: The Case of South African Segregation', *Social Dynamics*, 1:2 (1975), p. 168.
[93]William Connolly, 'Pluralism, Multiculturalism and the Nation State: Rethinking the Connections', *Journal of Political Ideologies*, 1:1 (1996), p. 61.
[94]Talal Asad, *Formations of the Secular: Christianity, Islam, Modernity* (Stanford: Stanford University Press, 2003), p. 178.
[95]Franz Kafka, *Letters to Friends, Family, and Editors* (New York: Schocken Books, 1977), p. 44.

Islam and the Quest for a European Secular Identity: From Sovereignty through Solidarity to Immunity

ARMANDO SALVATORE

'L'Orientale' University of Naples

ABSTRACT *This study explores the process of cumulative 'symbolic sublimation' of power within secular formations as it unfolded through the formative phases that saw in Western Europe the rise and consolidation of patterns first of state sovereignty (within early modernity) and then of social solidarity (within late, colonial and postcolonial modernity). It spells out the process of symbolic sublimation through which secular power justifies itself in cultural terms, by effecting the simultaneous mutation and occultation of traditional symbols in order to underwrite sovereignty and solidarity. Finally, it shows that symbolic sublimation, particularly in the current phase that witnesses the erosion of both sovereignty and solidarity, can no longer disguise wider patterns of connectedness within social relations that are irreducible to either modernist formation. This contemporary stage of the 'secular' in the post-colonial era is analysed by reference to political and judicial decisions on issues related to the Islamic headscarf and responses thereto. It reveals the extent to which 'immunity', the obverse more than the antithesis of community, is both the long-term vector and the ultimate outcome of both sovereignty and solidarity as the two historic arrows of the 'secular'.*

Introduction

In this study I explore the entanglements of European identity, conceived as 'secular', with forms of modern collective power related to sovereignty and solidarity, and finally with a social and cultural phenomenon that has been termed *immunitas* ('immunity'), and which underlies both forms. Immunity is not so much the latest stage of a long-drawn-out process of secularization, but a red thread running through different historical phases of the modern construction of socio-political cohesion in Europe.[1] I will argue that sovereignty and solidarity represent two subsequent, yet finally combining dimensions of the 'European secular' regime of power-knowledge, and that both of them, thanks to the mechanism of immunity, are obtained via a demarcation from internal and external otherness, intended as a looming, potentially violent threat to the integrity of the collective body. While one can locate historically specific moments of emergence of discrete secular formations based on sovereignty and solidarity, sociologically they are incorporated in the daily reproduction of the state-society nexus. Secularization, which at a more superficial level can be described as a differentiation of religion from the state and politics and as a corresponding emergence of a space of freedom of belief for the individual citizen, is at

---

[1] Roberto Esposito, *Immunitas. The Protection and Negation of Life* (Cambridge: Polity Press, 2011 [2002]).

a more capillary level an ongoing, never accomplished process of symbolic sublimation, via immunity, of forms of power (those supporting sovereignty and solidarity), into an emerging cultural identity, which is then identified as quintessentially 'secular' and 'European'. This process is necessarily ongoing, so that there can be no 'end of history' for secularization, since it is based on the circularity of a symbolic entanglement (more than engagement) of power with identity.

A further dimension of the process I analyse is the exposure of the secular as a 'post-Christian' regime of power-knowledge; the symbolic sublimation of power typically occurs through the transition from a (medieval and early modern) Christian to a (late modern) post-Christian identity. This argument is not aligned with the increasingly popular propagation of a 'post-secular' age, an idea that is rather enfeebled by new twists in the secularism discourse in the context of migration to Europe, particularly of populations of Muslim cultural and religious background. While arguing along these lines, the study will also show that the 'post' in post-Christian does not entail the wholesale erasure of Christian traditions and identities, but rather their selective reactivation, in a densely symbolic way, within a secular regime of power. The process works through disconnecting such Christian traditions and identities from earlier religious practices and institutions and is supported by the symbolic sublimation of power into identity. It therefore amounts to an overcoming of Christianity rather in the Hegelian sense of *Aufhebung* ('sublation'). This is what justifies the label 'post-Christian' for the late modern regimes of the secular.

I state this work hypothesis through the filter represented by the role that first political philosophers like Hobbes, and later social theorists like Durkheim have played on the edge between arguing as critical public intellectuals and serving as experts acting on behalf of the state and society. They have reflected on ongoing processes that saw the rise and consolidation of modern European states and the modernization and secularization of European societies. The interchange between processes, reflections and policies is mirrored by the fact that in modern and contemporary European societies scholars have been increasingly called to provide 'expertise' to state authorities as representatives of society on issues of crucial relevance for the normative integrity of secular formations – like, in a recent phase, and not only in France, on questions concerning the symbolic relevance of the *hijab* (the 'Islamic veil/headscarf') in state schools (punctually followed, once the symbolic charge of the *hijab* was at least temporarily deflated, by questions concerning the *niqab*, the 'Islamic full/full-face veil'). This demand for expertise somewhat closes the circle, since scholarly reflections are ever more solidly – at least in some strategic constellations –incorporated – in the form of 'expert knowledge' – into the institutionalized mechanisms of symbolic sublimation and practical immunization of secular formations.

Sovereignty and Solidarity: Leviathan vs. Behemoth?

It is important to consider that the type of transformations that accompanied the advent of modernity concern also, if not primarily, the conceptual, institutional and practical space assigned to 'religion'. It was in the course of modern transformations that religion became a clearly circumscribed – optimally, a privatized – sphere, one increasingly differentiated from the realm of politics. This is immediately clear through the emergence of the modern European Westphalian order, but was also partly due to the religious heterodox movements of early modernity, ranging well beyond the doctrinal body and the institutional formation conventionally identified as Reformation. Yet the main rising force setting the conditions of possibility for a drastic separation of religion and politics was the modern Westphalian state. This type of state, consecrated by the peace of Westphalia of 1648, tempered the radicalism of the religious movements and put an end to the unstable medieval balance of spiritual and temporal powers. We can read into the Westphalian outcome a standardization of the notion of 'religion': previously still diffuse, almost inherent in the lifeworld, basically integral to all institutions (not just the bishops and the pope, but also the kings and the emperor), it becomes now a well-delimited 'field', which the sovereign can control, and within which, by time, even non-conformist religious groups will find a degree of protection. Religion is thus in principle separated from the state, yet it contributes to its legitimacy, and is controlled and circumscribed by the sovereign. This shows that the issue of the modern making of 'religion' is not an issue of religion in any 'traditional' sense, but is part and parcel of the modern form of secular power that we call sovereignty.

Yet it is important to stress that sovereignty was not just a political innovation supported by a new regime of international law. It needed to be based on a new and challenging political mythology, which is best expressed by the language and the iconography of Thomas Hobbes's *Leviathan* that not by chance was almost exactly contemporary to the Westphalian outcome. Sovereignty within this emerging modern European order is, philosophically and anthropologically, reflected in Hobbes' argument when he says that the self should fear other and that the only solution to this issue of security is in Leviathan (a biblical monster, also appearing in the Talmud). There is no grace anymore governing the relation between self and other and only the emerging monster, the modern European state, can guarantee the security of subjects, by occupying the space, both symbolic and real, of a Big Other. Leviathan does not replace God, but represents nonetheless, as in the biblical metaphor, a divine agent of God: *Non est potestas super terram quae comparetur ei* is the quote from the book of Job which we read on the famous cover of *Leviathan*, representing the *magnus homo*, the sovereign, whose body (and power) is made of the individual bodies (and powers) of his subjects. Leviathan represented the mutual incorporation of the sovereign and his subjects through the king's acquisition of a second body and a second person much like the Christ. Yet the innovation to the medieval political–theological doctrine of the king as *christomimetés*[2] consisted in the fact that now the sovereign is rather an impersonator of the people, whose longing for security the sovereign now does not just represent, but literally incorporates.

This quite radical intervention on the symbolic fundaments of the *res publica christiana* ushered in a post-Christian political myth, the revised myth of the Leviathan, which inaugurated a radically new type of 'state of grace' under the aegis of sovereign secular power opposed to the 'state of nature' where there is no peace and where *caritas* is powerless. This symbolic entrenchment of the modern state simulates a new type of charisma or rather its sublimation into an impersonal realm of authority pinpointed by the common identity (religious, cultural, linguistic) of the collective body. As much as Leviathan is attributed absolute sovereignty in exchange for providing security to the members of the body-politic, so much the subject affirms a sovereignty over oneself particularly through self-control, so being restrained from harming other at the moment he knows that Leviathan can punish him for that, while also guaranteeing that others will not harm him. Leviathan is actually the Big Other inhabiting each discrete other to the self.

On the other hand, the socio-anthropological engine of early modern transformations was less often an explicit emphasis on the individual than a renewed and radicalized endeavour to build up a kingdom of God on earth. The neutralization of the centrifugal effects of religious radicalism with the centripetal force of state formation altered the social stage,

---

[2] Ibid., p. 83.

whereby also many among the religious radicals favoured an ethic of accumulation and commitment in the framework of the security provided by the modern state. Here solidarity comes in to give a new quality to the collective body and to institute in it a further, complementary form of modern secular power. It is a turn from the body-politic to the social body which brings to more immediate fruition the modern secular power inherent in the social bond. In the cover of Leviathan, the body of bodies is overarched by a crowned head. One can cut the head of the monarch (what indeed happened first in England[3] and then in France), and society can reveal itself as a self-governing body through the division of labour in-built within a modern, differentiated social structure, reflecting a basically democratic model of governance. The resulting form of power was termed organic solidarity by Durkheim, or, if we prefer a Foucauldian idea, we could name it 'governmentality', as other than government or governance, since its engine is nested within mechanisms of subjective discipline, a sort of power machine literally embodied by individuals through their dense (more or less institutionalized) webs of mutual bodily constraints.

The process of complementing sovereignty through solidarity was framed within responses to absolutism. One 'infrastructure' facilitating such responses was a new bourgeois type of public spheres, as famously described by Habermas. Though their roots can be traced back to early modernity and the rise of commercial society, especially from the eighteenth century onwards such public spheres started to provide, in several European countries, the key arenas from which the individuals who were subject to Leviathan's majesty could turn themselves into actively participating subjects of rights. In this way they could politicize the strength of the emerging civil society and devise new responses to the dilemma of how to curb or overcome the mythical power of Leviathan. The ultimate source of legitimation of such claims was the insistence on the fact that the myth of Leviathan did not exhaust the sovereign prerogatives, since the subject was sovereign in his inner forum.[4] An emerging bourgeois intelligentsia succeeded in carving for itself a leadership role as the representative of *demos*, a collective political subjectivity. According to Koselleck, and contra Habermas, we should see in the process less an emancipation from Leviathan than a continuation of Leviathan with other means. This emerging social group was indeed the product of the separation of inwardness and publicness performed by Leviathan, of its creation of a pure realm of subjective belief and morality nurtured by the autonomy gained by religion as a separate field (to this regard, one should not underestimate the Calvinist origin of Locke's thought on the matter).

While Leviathan was still anchored in a symbolic view of the self as the autonomous yet functional cell of the body-politic, one can imagine the passage from the dominance of the modern state to the centrality of civil society as a hegemonic shift from Leviathan to Behemoth, another biblical monster, and indeed one that cannot be as easily tamed as Leviathan. We certainly have a clear idea of Leviathan, the tamed monster of the sea since Hobbes. As to Behemoth, the fat monster of the land, the modern political myth has not imagined it to be as well tamed as Leviathan. It is seldom remembered that Hobbes also wrote *Behemoth*, a work on the English civil war, the event that put in jeopardy the integrity of the crowned Leviathan. Behemoth is therefore latent in modern political myth to the extent it only returns in making sense of the totalitarianism lurking behind the organic solidarity and the division of labour envisioned by the theorists of modern society. As we know,

---

[3] Oliver Cromwell, in the same year of the Peace of Westphalia, famously stated at the trial of King Charles I: 'I tell you we will cut off his head with the crown upon it'.
[4] Klaus Eder, *Geschichte als Lernprozess? Zur Pathogenese politischer Modernität in Deutschland* (Frankfurt: Suhrkamp, 1991); Reinhart Koselleck, *Critique and Crisis: Enlightenment and the Pathogenesis of Modern Society* (Oxford: Berg, 1988 [1959]).

totalitarianism primarily embraces society, rather than the state, and envisions a kind of total self-control by society over itself. Behemoth can thus be seen as the uncivil society hiding behind the ideal of a civil society, a kind of backstage script in sociological theories but also an underlying anthropological dimension perpetually haunting social theory: the return of the internal other to be scapegoated, as the last resort to restore the organic character of the social bond in crisis times.[5] Other than in the myth of Leviathan for which the self (its security, its functional autonomy) occupies the centre stage, with Behemoth the focus is overwhelmingly laid on otherhood. Behemoth is probably the epitome of the regime of the secular, more than Leviathan itself can be. It suggests that the secular is not liberal by default. Illiberal developments do not contradict the regime of the secular but can feed into its cycles of production of power-knowledge, particularly when an explicit focus on otherness is required for warranting the cohesion of the collective body.

Thus, a secular subjectivity emerges within the European modern regime of power (the Westphalian order) via a combination of sovereignty and solidarity, through Leviathan and Behemoth, the two monsters that are sometimes at war, sometimes reconciled, ideally, when the identity and subjectivity of their members are pacified in liberal ways and the self-other tension is subdued by a grammar of individual rights. Yet it would be difficult to overlook that the history of modern Europe has been cyclically affected by upheavals where the internal other has been targeted and discriminated (when not annihilated), up to the current immigration-related identity crises. In this context, however, a more sophisticated European secular strategy to deal with otherhood, built on underlying patterns of *immunitas*, is at play, working not through outright discrimination or threats of annihilation but via a more integrated and sophisticated immunization effort that is to some (or to a large) extent still compatible with the liberal grammar of rights.

Symbolic Demarcation through Immunization from Other?

Let me here analyse two contemporary 'cases' of reconstruction of secular power through a combination of the impetus of both monsters, supported by the immunization measures based on mechanisms of symbolic demarcation from Muslims as the key others in contemporary European secular orders.

A landmark incident has been the work of the so-called Stasi commission, an expert committee formed on the direct initiative of former French president Chirac and that in the Fall and Winter of 2003 first defined and then recommended a ban on all 'conspicuous symbols', first of all the Islamic headscarf, from state schools in France. In a climate of increasingly obsessive media attention that spilled over to other European countries, a commission of male sages, including several social scientists and the leading leftist social theorist Alain Touraine, worked to protect secular republicanism from what they perceived as a kind of political-religious encroachment on the most vital, yet also vulnerable, rings of the chain of transmission of republican authority: the public educational system. This challenge was seen as emanating from 'communitarian' worlds and worldviews blurring the borders between private and public spheres. Through the influence of such worlds, 'religion', intended this time no longer in its normative meaning as a circumscribed field centred on freedom of belief, but rather as an expression of pre-modern patriarchal authority, threatens to infiltrate and mar the modern authority structure of the secular republic. The no longer so recent episode of the Stasi commission is important since it represents a case of an evident convergence, almost without residues, between state policies, scholarly

---

[5]Klaus Eder, 'Leviathan and Behemoth. State and Civil Society'. Unpublished paper, 2010.

expertise and media coverage in providing normative definitions not only of rights, participation and the purportedly correct trade-off between solidarity and freedom, but also of what is a symbol and even more notably what is a dangerous one.[6] The extraordinary visibility of such a convergence has opened up a terrain of public contestability of regimes of the secular by forces that cannot be reduced to 'Muslim subjects', as they are not just resisting an encroachment on Muslim identity rights but attempt to unveil and undo the symbolic demarcation and the immunization mechanisms underlying the new regimes of the 'secular'.

Yet in response to such an exposure, France as well as other European states have sought realignment between political governance, symbolic legitimization/delegitimization and judiciary sanctioning. While the events that surrounded the work of the Stasi commission in France received an exceptional international publicity, a concomitant judgment of the German Constitutional Court (24 September 2003) on the same issue passed almost unnoticed outside of the country. The constitutional organ stated that other than the Christian cross, the *hijab* is *not* in itself a religious symbol. This perplexity was echoed by the words of the former German president Johannes Rau, who in a public speech (22 January 2004) stated: 'the debate on the headscarf would be much simpler if the headscarf were an unambiguous symbol'. A few weeks earlier Iyman Alzayed (29 November 2003), the primary school teacher who wore the headscarf and whose case had triggered the judicial dispute, had similarly declared: 'the evaluation of the headscarf as a symbol is the source of fatal misjudgements. The headscarf… is integral to a religious praxis, to the extent it fulfils the function to cover those body parts that a woman as a responsible human being desires to cover'. The *hijab* appears then as an embodied practice (be it due to 'religion' or to any other moral consideration) – yet undeniably one exposed to an increasing level of administrative monitoring, public scrutiny and judicial decisions.

Far from representing two divergent systems through which a symbolic dimension is incorporated in collective identities and social bodies (notably through authoritatively defining the symbol of the other and a corresponding immunity mechanism to protect society from its purportedly negative influence), the just mentioned French and German moments of simultaneously legal and political construction/deconstruction of *what is a symbol* should be rather considered as two opposite poles of the same spectrum of sovereign interventions. The French moment showed the temptation of an ultimate constitutionalization of the symbolic demarcation. The German moment, which was followed by a variety of judicial and political decisions (most of which fell within the purview of regional organs and had sometimes divergent outcomes), witnessed a fragile, circular and belated reflexivity on the ambiguity and risks of bringing symbolic demarcation straight into the public exteriority of decisions by state organs, instead of letting it work through the exclusionary mechanisms that occur within the social body and in public discourse. In its very crudeness (the outright denial by the judges that the *hijab* is a symbol, also based on purported expert knowledge), the judgment of the German Constitutional Court revealed the ineluctable divorce of authoritatively legal and political decisions from any anthropological insight into the inherent complexity of practices (like the wearing of *hijab*, and even more the wearing of *hijab* in a politically and symbolically overcharged European context) along with their shifting and ambivalent relations both to sovereign power and to the collective power radiating from the organic solidarity of the social body.

---

[6]Talal Asad, *Reflections on Laïcité and the Public Sphere*, Social Science Research Council; Items and Issues, 5 (2005); Armando Salvatore, *The Public Sphere: Liberal Modernity, Catholicism, Islam* (New York: Palgrave Macmillan, 2007).

Situated somewhere between the common sense objection of Johannes Rau and the moral and practical concern expressed by Iyman Alzayed, both of which directed the attention to the meaning of *hijab* as based on the lifeworld of the concerned person, the majority decision of the German constitutional organ made tabula rasa of the possibility that state instances can authoritatively interpret meanings that are far from unambiguous, highly context-dependent and therefore intrinsically tied to the affects they deploy in a world displaying multiple levels (both face-to-face and mediated ones) of connectedness and mutual gaze. Yet this step did not imply any diminishment of the sovereign, 'decisionist' legacy of Leviathan. The democratic state should – so the constitutional judges – intervene *by law* in defining what is a symbol and what it implies: if a parliament (in the German case, a *Landtag*, i.e., the legislative assembly of a *Land* or administrative region) decides so by majority and in a procedurally correct way, there is no space left either for public opinion or expert knowledge to alter or challenge the sovereign decision/definition.

This phenomenon of a public homogenization of the meaning of what is the symbol on the example of the headscarf, taken as a 'negative totem',[7] is a symptom of a symbolic sublimation of the integration mechanisms of European societies, which does not contradict the idea of secularism but rather helps us understand its long-term trajectory, punctuated by recurring crises and new waves of reconstruction and legitimization. Such paradoxes of modern symbolic politics obscure the complexity itself of the anthropological foundation of signs and, with it, the specific case of the headscarf and the genealogy of Islamic veiling as a practice. Here meaning is produced interactively and in a second moment, on overlapping levels, stabilized collectively. It is not, as it cannot be, generated directly on a purely collective level under the protective shadow and the monitoring eye of Leviathan, with the exception of moments where an abundance or excess of meaning is produced: those moments of 'collective effervescence' which cement solidarity. In the routine functioning of modern secular regimes of power, a plurality of differently positioned actors, including government institutions, try to appropriate the meaning of the *hijab*. Yet in everyday practical terms, a centralist, ultimate and definitive collective instituting of meaning remains evanescent, because the variety of social actors involved resist uniformity of meaning and symbolic homogenization. Therefore the authority of judicial or legislative bodies depends decisively on the continual authoritatively public staging of the correct interpretation of what is a symbol, and what is a dangerous one.

An instance of how the normalization of what the secular eye sees as potentially divisive Muslim symbols might run into quandaries punctuated by involuntary humour, is when, around the same time the Stasi commission was at work, in a TV debate Nicolas Sarkozy, who was minister of the interior at the time, asked Tariq Ramadan, identified as a speaker on behalf of European Muslims, to publicly convince Muslim women in France to replace the *hijab* with a bandana. It is easy to comment on this episode ironically, but it cannot be denied that the protagonists of the TV debate were both top media (and political) characters. So the episode is a good example of how the symbolic sublimation of secular power (i.e., the disguising of issues of sovereignty and solidarity in the guise of identity, located at the level of visibility of purported symbols or signs) works within the current post-Christian regimes of Europe: through spectacular media staging. It should be reminded that this type of reasoning cannot be confined to the mere level of an anthropology of culture and symbols, or even to the less lofty level of questionable performances of controversial public personalities, but have become integral to the work of legislating bodies and of judicial

---

[7]Monika Wohlrab-Sahr, 'Politik und Religion. "Diskretes" Kulturchristentum als Fluchtpunkt europäischer Gegenbewegungen gegen einen "ostentativen" Islam' in A. Nassehi and M. Schroer (eds) *Der Begriff des Politischen. Soziale Welt Sonderband*, 14 (2003), pp. 273–297.

instances. Of course there are more contemporary cases, like those involving the *niqab*, which are the object of ongoing investigations, and not only in France. Such incidents are being followed almost on a daily basis in each and every European country by an army of observers and researchers, yet the French and German cases on the *hijab* from 2003 and later probably represent a watershed in the reproduction of regimes of the secular. They are so exactly due to the degree to which they have made shockingly explicit the political dimension of the work on symbols of the self and the other, which within the more classic regime of Leviathan (and Behemoth) were rather well disguised (or, should we say, securely incorporated) within official representations and popular ideologies.

The Regime of the Secular as the Domain of *Immunitas*?

Now we should finally delve on the issue of immunity as the latest implication, at a capillary social level, of both sovereignty and solidarity. What is the condition for the building of the modern European secular subject? It is a restrictive condition: not an advancement but a withdrawal of the self from the empirical other and an aseptic embracement of the general Other (metaphysical, psychoanalytical or otherwise). This condition is an immunitary reaction of self-protection.[8] Elaborating on the notion of *immunitas* as spelled out by the Neapolitan philosopher Roberto Esposito,[9] Luca Mavelli has evidenced how immunity is rooted in Hobbes' notion of sovereignty. Sovereignty entails a reductionist construction of man as a bundle of bodily instincts that requires an abstract dimension of order and protection provided externally by the sovereign.[10] Through the immunization of the individual from a violence that is both internal and external to it (the risk of self to be annihilated by other, but also the intrinsic lack of containment of one's own instinctual aggression towards other), sovereignty is implanted in the fabric of social life itself. The anthropological fundament of the gift (*munus*) as the constitution of the social bond and the sharing of gifts (*communitas*) is transcended through a rupture of the circulation of the *munus* and of the individual constraint to return it. This interruption, aided by a 'transcendental' (quite in the Kantian sense) instance identified with the sovereign, can be termed *immunitas*. Anthropologically speaking, the interruption of the cycle of gift-giving is as much a given as it is its compulsion. In this sense, immunitary mechanisms are intrinsic to social connectedness. The novelty with modern sovereignty lies in devising and inculcating once-for-all mechanisms of immunization from violent encounters and backlashes, supported by a new notion of the law as issued from the sovereign and of rights as conditionally attributed to (or reclaimed from) the subjects.[11] The French republican case reveals that sovereignty is unstable in securing *immunitas* if not complemented by organic solidarity: both working well together through mechanism of symbolic demarcation *and* sublimation.

The process can be interpreted as starting from a self-demarcation of the subject which leads to the erosion of something that was once central to the European political and philosophical tradition, namely *communitas*. Far from being the 'communitarianism' targeted by French *laïcité* and the sages of the Stasi commission (and often identified with Muslim life), *communitas* is nothing else than the exposition of life itself to externalities which is processed and protected through the circulation of the gift, i.e., *munus*. There is in this conception no trace yet of the inherent violence of social life to be redeemed by Leviathan,

---

[8] Luca Mavelli, *Europe's Encounter with Islam. The Secular and Postsecular* (London: Routledge, 2012).
[9] Roberto Esposito, op. cit.; Roberto Esposito, *Bíos: Biopolitics and Philosophy* (Minneapolis: University of Minnesota Press, 2008 [2004]).
[10] Mavelli, op. cit., p. 83.
[11] See Esposito, *Immunitas*.

which only emerges through *immunitas*.[12] Yet we should be aware that *immunitas* is not the result of a degeneration of *communitas* but to some extent represents its necessary dark or flip side, or the outcome of an ever more complex work on *communitas*, as the one incorporated by the sovereign in the theory and the iconography of the modern Leviathan. The original justification of immunitary mechanisms in the social bond is the impossibility of *communitas* to efficiently cover the abundance of human life and social connectedness: ever more so in modern societies built on an abstract division of labour and complex forms of solidarity, which are no longer based on face-to-face interactions and encounters. As a result the social bond is now floating in a rarefied space where ties with the empirical other are episodic and optimally confined to the economy of public representation. The subject can now refer to the generalized, yet absolutely abstracted, Other of universal humanity instead of being exposed to the encounter with a concrete other which always, anthropologically, asks the subject to become other than oneself. Instead of an anthropologically and sociologically risky engagement, what is needed now is a self-projection. The universal abstractness of the other is now a projection of the absolute modern and secular authenticity of the self. To a disembodied idea of the subject corresponds the conceptual erasure of the empirical other as another to engage with.

Muslims and Islam as Other play this negative function (i.e., to stand for an erasure) in today's Europe.[13] Both French-style *laïcité* and multicultural approaches are projections of a European secular collective subjectivity that permanently seeks immunity from empirical others, and that from the vintage point of this immunitary state attempts to embrace and redeem the generalised Other (which, at this purely abstract level, does not exclude, but indeed absorbs Muslims and Islam). In this sense, Islam is less an unwelcome threat in today's Europe than a necessary, and in this sense, welcome, screen that strengthens the immunitary posture and facilitates a redemptive move (namely, 'integration'). Islam plays this role by representing an older stage in the self-identity of Europe, since perceived as 'communitarian' and mired in a 'religious' type of identity. Paradoxically, at first sight (yet less so if we take into account the mutual implications of *communitas* and *immunitas*) Islam in Europe is far from unwelcome since it is like the ghost of community from which immunity sprang up via absolute sovereignty and organic solidarity. In this sense, the presence of Islam fortifies the present cycle of reconstruction of a European secular identity.

Indeed, it was the dynamics inherent in the formation of European secular identity itself, not any intruder, which broke the earlier unstable balance between community and immunity within the social bond. Far from decrying the loss of community, Esposito shows the excessive exposition of the modern European subject to an immunitary protection against *communitas*. The paradigm of self-preservation that underlies Leviathan was still matched, at the time of Hobbes and in the century thereafter, by a difficult yet creative work of balancing the two components (well reflected by Hobbes' contemporary Spinoza). Echoing Bernard Lewis we could then ask the question 'What went wrong?'[14] (yet, this time, not with Islam but with Europe). Is Europe at risk of sinking into a sort of autoimmune disease – i.e., of repulsing its own socio-political body?

Approaching an answer is not easy, since it requires shifting from diagnosis to prognosis. All we can say is that once evoked and put to work, the monster of Leviathan imposes on self and other a regulative dynamics bent on risk reduction and security enhancement. Deviations from the mechanism of individual immunization that might endanger not

---

[12]Mavelli, op. cit., p. 81.
[13]Ibid., pp. 62–84.
[14]Bernard Lewis, *What Went Wrong? Western Impact and Middle Eastern Response* (Oxford and New York: Oxford University Press, 2002).

only the individual body but the body-politic and the social body fall back within the direct purview of the sovereignty of Leviathan and the solidarity of Behemoth, which, as we know, in a Durkheimian fashion, ethically justifies criminal law yet can also, if disengaged from the law of Leviathan, produce the criminalization of the other as such, as the intruder into the body which the immunity system has to repel and if necessary destroy. We are not yet at that stage, but probably at one that reflects a still fragile balance between Leviathan and Behemoth, much like in the 'civilizing process' theorized by Elias. Here the pressure from other is transformed into self-restraint and self-policing, by which violence is not just reduced but incorporated in the armour of individual subjectivity working as a machine of affect control.

Yet the immunity syndrome is more than a dangerous leaning out on *immunitas* unbalanced by *communitas*. On a further twist, the secular subject inoculates himself with 'the same poison which the organism needs to protect itself from'.[15] It is here that we can better see how the constructions of Islam and Muslims as the Other of European secular subjectivity represent the latest stage of the process of reproduction of secular formations. As vividly put by Mavelli:

> Muslims are the necessary pathogens that secular subjects need to incorporate in a limited way in order to develop the antigens which may make them immune from the possibility that life may flourish in its connective and exposed character; immune from the possibility that life may unite all, irrespectively of faith or nationality, in a shared dimension.[16]

This is shown by the passage from discourses on assimilation to approaches to 'integration', representing incorporation not just of the other but of 'the other within', in the framework of a renewed and democratized Leviathan that embraces the generalized Other. This is why multiculturalism is not a radical alternative to French-style *laïcité* but a different articulation of immunitary strategies of universalist redemption and sociopolitical incorporation. In this sense, multiculturalism represents a more sophisticated strategy of reconstruction of community intended as co-immunity: an embracement of generalized, abstract Otherness.[17]

Conclusion: The Post-Christian Twist of Secular Power

In this context the vulnerable presence of Islam in Europe is not merely yet another problem in the historic dealing with religion in the Old Continent, but plays a strategic role in questioning post-Christian tenets of the secular and the related concepts of solidarity and immunity, both pivoting on sovereignty. Islam in Europe can expose the inherent contradictions and weaknesses of European secular models issued of early modern traumas and transformations and the parochial limitations of secular arrangements between churches and states going back to the nineteenth and twentieth century.

The resulting type of secular power, which is simultaneously anthropologically rooted and socio-politically effective, is post-Christian in nature. The post in 'post-Christian' does not mean the erasure of Christian identity, traditions and symbols. It is more a type of overcoming in the Hegelian sense of *Aufhebung* ('sublation'). It is an institutional

---

[15]Mavelli, op. cit., p. 85.
[16]Ibid.
[17]Ibid., p. 92.

disabling of the Christian heritage in ways, however, that preserve and magnify its symbolic power – with the only restriction that the Hegelian dialectics of sublation are rather deluded by a process that is circular and facilitated by a cultural self-immunity. The Hegelian negation of negation does not prevent us from sliding back to a pre-Christian quandary in constructing the relation between self and other, a quandary that was already well reflected in the essentialist and violent anthropology of Thomas Hobbes. Yet this symbolic power is absorbed in the postures and expressivity that the sovereign (or an impersonal civilizing process) expects from the individual bodies. And this is where the case of the Stasi commission still illustrates the point in the most poignant way. But the consequence is that all other forms of body postures, affects and disciplines have to be aligned with this immunitary standard and become moderately expressive, yet inconspicuous, like the small crosses that for the French commission represented a model of non-intrusiveness at the symbolic level. An important symptom that this is a post-*Christian* syndrome is that, while it secularly proposes a Christian symbol as sublimated into a sheer body posture and pure moral choice, is potentially redemptive (in quite Christian way) of Other, at the same time the self can be immunized from contact and 'contagion' with empirical others.

The case of Islam's presence in Europe generates tensions that show ever more clearly how the post of post-Christian regimes does not mean the overcoming of Christian tenets and Westphalian strictures, but their dilution into the presuppositions of life forms themselves, via the entrenchment of a juridical doctrine of the sacredness of individual, and in this sense autonomous, life projects. This discourse is effectively propagated to the detriment of the social and communicative infrastructure of autonomy which lies in lifeworld-rooted notions of justice and solidarity pinpointed by social rights. The notion of a European secular autonomy appears then as the self-indulgent attempt to square the circle.

The only viable alternative to liquidating the internal other is to immunize the social body from it. The liberal secular episteme-*cum*-formation, unlike its illiberal versions, constitutes here a pattern of immunization from all sorts of concrete other through the embracement of the generalized Other, and therefore a protection against the connective and exposed character of the social bond based on the exchange and circulation of gifts and signs. Yet, to conclude, as much as secular *immunitas* crystallized for fear of the exposed character of the social bond, so much today the symbolic demarcation from the Muslim Other and the related public staging of secular identity, which works as a symbolic sublimation of secular power, is becoming exposed to critique. The result is the contestation of this specifically post-Christian type of the social bond, a development that might rehabilitate the exposure of connectedness between ego and alter ungoverned by republican sovereignty and uncovered by organic solidarity. So we might observe the beginnings of an anti-immunitary reaction, which the invocation of a post-secular era or the theorization of a post-secular order are not sufficient to capture, to the extent these are based on a hermeneutic fusion of yet identity-based, secular or religious horizons. To the extent such a post-secular reflex is part of social reality and public discourse nowadays, it seems to work rather as a ruse for the reproduction of a neo-secular order even more tightly entrenched within *immunitas*. Perhaps at the moment when more and more people (actors and observers alike) become consciously critical of the self-referential character of certain rulings (like those revolving around the top-down definition of symbols), they are alerted to the fact that the regime of the European secular modern does not represent a manifest destiny of universalization of human values and of redemption of the uncivilized potential forever coming from other than Europe. This reflexivity does not entail the overcoming of the secular, but equip us to better inhabit it, with irony and circumspection, without falling back into identity traps, which ultimately feed into the reproduction of secular formations. Thus *immunitas* itself shows its own vulnerability and does not herald the end of history.

Islam, Depoliticization and the European Crisis of Democratic Legitimacy

NATALIE J. DOYLE

Monash University

ABSTRACT *A new form of political discourse hostile to Islam has been gaining ground in Europe. Initiated by neo-nationalist parties it appeals to liberal values and is now penetrating mainstream politics. The recent French presidential campaign threw light on the way Centre Right parties vying for government are increasingly instrumentalizing hostility towards Islam to respond to the political crisis triggered by the problem of public debt across the European Union. Critics are approaching this phenomenon through the lens of Foucault's notion of governmentality, questioning the assertion that Muslims cannot integrate in European societies because of their religion and highlighting the failure of European nation states to treat them as citizens and promote their socio-economic inclusion. This perspective yields valuable insights: it shows how the presence of Muslims challenges the belief of European societies in their self-perceived rationality and tolerance, resting on their commitment to secularity as epistemic category. The strident defense of secularism that accompanies Islamophobia is part of the discourse of securitization that characterizes the neo-liberal form of contemporary governmentality and promotes the de-politicization of social problems. The notion of governmentality, however, cannot account fully for the root-cause of Islamophobia: the loss of collective purpose that has triggered a crisis of government and seen the concern for efficient governance to erase the goal of collective self-determination. At heart, Islamophobia constitutes a manifestation of the European states' crisis of democratic legitimacy.*

Introduction

A new form of anti-Muslim discourse has been gaining ground in mainstream European politics purporting to uphold rights supposedly threatened by Islam. The need to defend liberal values is depicted as synonymous with the need to defend 'European identity' which has come to overlap with the Christian identity long invoked by the reactionary Extreme Right. The reference to Christianity still plays a role in this ideology but as a marker of cultural identity, rather than as a source of dogmatic truth. It is thus coupled with an appeal to Enlightenment values within programs that define themselves as a defense of the secularity of western societies and promote a provocative attitude towards Muslim minorities. This fusion of Christian civilizational identity with secularism has been fuelling anti-Islamic activism whose violent potential was demonstrated by the actions of the Norwegian terrorist Anders Breivik.

This new ideology first appeared in the Netherlands and Scandinavia, through the Danish cartoon affair and the pronouncements of such Dutch political figures as Pim Fortyuin, Theo van Gogh, Hirsi Ali and more recently Geert Wilders. The Netherlands and also Scandinavian countries, being smaller countries strongly committed to liberal social mores, gender equality and minority rights, have seen amplified the changes experienced across Western Europe in the last decades of the twentieth century.[1] These are the consolidation of the European Union (EU) and the growing visibility of Muslims as a result of immigration, coinciding with the rising voice of Islamic fundamentalism. In this respect, political developments in these countries have been a stronger expression of a phenomenon also evident in the rest of Western Europe since the late 1990s: the progress of the 'populist' Far Right and its increasing pursuit of a theme acceptable to the main stream, *cultural identity*.

This process has accelerated since the terrorist attacks of 11 September 2001 in contact with the civilizational discourse of American neo-conservatism, which has been used to argue that Muslims cannot integrate successfully in European societies. Since the onset of the European financial crisis, the anti-Islam discourse has become more virulent and influenced the mainstream political debate. It has been utilized by politicians from all parties vying for election. As Ayhan Kaya argues, recent controversies and debates on Muslims have been part of a broader discourse on immigration portrayed as a source of instability and insecurity and used by political elites as part of the neo-liberal form of contemporary governmentality.[2] The recent French presidential elections were a case in point. The prominence of issues to do with Muslim religious customs cannot, however, be attributed exclusively to the French hard-line understanding of secularism, *laïcité*. Behind the apparent idiosyncrasies of French political culture can be identified a common European ideological logic to do with the way European societies define the meaning of their secularity.

As Luca Mavelli argues, this is best understood when it is conceptualized as an epistemic mode of knowledge, rather than a set of institutional arrangements, a mode which transcends the opposition between 'secular Europe' and 'Christian Europe' that plagues all discussions of 'European identity'.[3] Mavelli's analysis is pioneering in the way it highlights the role which the EU has played in promoting a procedural definition of democracy that has empowered claims of European civilizational superiority and perpetuated a logic of cultural exclusion of the Muslim 'Other'. This logic originates in Kant's reformulation of Christian individual subjectivity and runs through nineteenth-century theories of secularization. At the same time, his analysis draws on a conception of modernity inherited from Foucault that cannot account for the crisis that that has allowed the civilizational dimension to acquire such prominence.

Islamophobia as an effect of neo-liberal governmentality is part of a general pattern of de-politicization of the social problems which contemporary European states have failed to address over past decades. This de-politicization covers over a loss of collective purpose, the abandonment of the democratic goal of emancipation and with it, of the concern for the public accountability of government justified by the need for effective governance. The creation of the European Union has aggravated the political disengagement of citizens evident in all western societies and triggered a crisis of democratic legitimacy to

---

[1] Sam Cherribi, *In the House of War: Dutch Islam Observed* (Oxford: Oxford University Press, 2010).
[2] Ayhan Kaya, 'Islamophobia as a Form of Governmentality: Unbearable Weightiness of the Politics of Fear'. Malmö Will Brandt Series of Working Papers in International Migration and Ethnic Relations 1, 2011.
[3] Luca Mavelli, *Europe's Encounter with Islam. The Secular and Post-secular* (London and New York: Routledge, 2012).

which both sides of the political spectrum have contributed. Having abandoned the concern for popular sovereignty in favor of the promotion of social pluralism and defense of disenfranchised minorities, the Left did not question the purely managerial and elitist objectives now pursued through the EU.

In the context of the austerity policies embraced to address the current financial crisis, this failure of the political Left to formulate an alternative project is allowing socio-economic insecurity to feed xenophobia and hostility towards Muslims. This article starts by discussing the context enabling contemporary European Islamophobia: the crisis of European governance. It then examines the circumstances behind the emergence of the neo-nationalist discourse of securitization, its anti-Islam turn and how it has come to penetrate the main stream. Whilst the framework of analysis is Europe, the article focuses on the case of France as the recent presidential elections have vividly highlighted trends also evident in other European countries to do with neo-liberal governmentality and its consolidation by the EU. Drawing on the work of Luca Mavelli, it examines the ambiguities of the EU's definition of contemporary European identity, its ideological re-construction of twentieth century history and the discourse of civilizational superiority that underpins its procedural interpretation of democracy. It then goes on to demonstrate that Islamophobia is not only an effect of de-politicizing governmentality but also the manifestation of a deeper societal loss of political purpose. In this respect, this article also conducts a critique of the epistemological theory of modernity underpinning the Foucauldian notion of governmentality, which limits its heuristic value when it comes to understanding and therefore countering contemporary Islamophobia.

European Governance and the Disempowerment of National Societies

The crisis of political legitimacy which underpins hostility towards Muslims in Europe has its roots in the decline of the party system's hegemony, which characterized political representation from the late 1940s to the 1990s. In that period, the party system successfully structured social demands emanating from the electorate, controlled corporate interests and constituted a political centre that guided policy.[4] From the 1970s, however, it came under stress from the combined effect of internal and external pressures: social changes undermining collective identities and geo-political ones, favouring the appearance of a global economy and worldwide trade competition. The former deprived political parties of their solid ideological bases (the collective identities of class, nation and religion) and reduced their capacity to control the political agenda, whilst the new economic constraints emanating from the latter undermined their effectiveness once in government.[5] In Western Europe, the internal stresses – the rise of so-called 'identity politics', around gender, sexual orientation or regional cultural identity – coincided with the appearance of immigrant settlement, an unexpected consequence of the labour migration of earlier decades, adding to the loss of social homogeneity.[6] This particular historical constellation contributes to explaining the form which the crisis of the party system assumed in Europe: the rise of anti-immigration 'populist' parties. Another factor, however, is to be found in the way European integration was seen as a way out of the crisis.

---

[4]Pierre Rosanvallon, *Democratic Legitimacy: Impartiality, Reflexivity, Proximity* (trans. Arthur Goldhammer) (Princeton: Princeton University Press, 2011).

[5]Stefano Bartolini, 'Political Parties, Ideology and Populism, in the Post-crisis Europe', paper presented at European Seminar organised by the Hellenic Foundation for European and Foreign Policy (ELIAMEP), 1011, July 2011, http://europeanseminars.eliamep.gr/wp-content/uploads/2011/07/Stefano-Bartolini-Paper.pdf.

[6]Stephen Castles, Heather Booth and Tina Wallace, *Here for Good: Western Europe's New Ethnic Minorities* (London: Pluto Press, 1984).

As a response to their loss of steering capacity, parties displaced policy issues from the sphere of political contest towards spheres of state action whose legitimacy is defined exclusively in terms of 'output' competence, that is, to a very large extent, with reference to economic efficiency. The creation of the European Union was part of this strategy of political elites. In Europe, de-politicization was exacerbated by the transfer of a large segment of policy-making to the institutions of the European Union where international agreements are forged that pre-determine the scope of political action at the national level, according to a doubly *functional* logic. Overseen by a supranational legal order the EU constitutes 'a new technology of governance' that creates specialized, autonomous sectors of public power to do with economic activity (competition, free movement, regulatory harmonization etc.), to a large extent insulated from democratic or constitutional scrutiny.[7] Secondly, and at a more fundamental level, the European legal order establishes a purely *instrumental* constitutional framework that entrenches policy choices agreed to by member states and enshrined in treaties, removing them from the national sphere of political contest.[8] To put it differently, the EU pursues pre-decided political ends as opposed to the way national constitutional orders simply establish the procedural and normative framework within which political ends are debated democratically. In this respect, the EU, as 'sectorial state' clearly evolved into a tool of blame avoidance for government political parties and as a result of some degree of collusion between them, allowing political conflict to be eluded.[9]

The creation of the European Union has in fact aggravated the crisis of political representation and its development shadowed by that of 'populist' parties. First approached as a pathology deviating from the democratic norm, Right-wing populism is now understood to be intimately linked to contemporary democracy and its crisis of *legitimacy*.[10] Contemporary democracies have two dimensions: popular sovereignty and constitutionalism.[11] The expansion of constitutionalism – associated with the shift from government to governance, a loss of political centre and declining popular influence on the processes of government – has produced dissatisfaction with democracy at the national level in most liberal democratic countries but in Europe, the dissatisfaction has become more acute with constitutionalism gaining ground, both at the national and European levels: the European Union has weak popular input but supports a complex constitutionalism through the creation of a new form of state action legitimated by the quest for greater economic efficiency.[12] This new, purely regulatory centre is but a manifestation of profound transformation of 'the nature, scope and *modus operandi* of market regulation' experienced in others parts of the world as well, but is unique in its lack of direct accountability to the people.[13]

The 2004 enlargement of the EU to the ex-communist East only aggravated the problem with political integration falling even further behind a form of economic integration that from the start failed to inject political and social rights into the European constitutional

---

[7]TürkülerIsiksel, 'On Europe's Functional Constitutionalism. Towards a Constitutional Theory of Specialised International Regimes', *Constellations*, 19:1 (2012), pp. 102–120.

[8]Ibid., p. 112.

[9]John McCormick, *Weber, Habermas, and Transformations of the European State: Constitutional, Social, and Supranational Democracy* (Cambridge: Cambridge University Press, 2007); Bartolini, op. cit.

[10]Cas Mudde, 'The Populist Radical Right: A Pathological Normalcy', *West European Politics*, 33:6 (2010), pp. 1167–1186.

[11]Yves Mény, '*De la démocratie en Europe*: Old Concepts and New Challenges', 41:1 (2002), pp. 1–13.

[12]Giandomenico Majone, 'The Rise of the Regulatory State in Europe', *Journal of Public Policy*, 17:3 (1994), pp. 77–101.

[13]Mény, op. cit.

citizenship.[14] Rather than help national governments secure greater legitimacy, European integration has since then acquired a logic of its own which has alienated citizens in Western Europe. This first translated in rejections of treaties when these were put to a popular vote, as was the case of the constitutional treaty in France and the Netherlands in 2005, then of its reincarnation as the 2007 Lisbon Treaty rejected by the Irish in 2009 but eventually ratified following a forced second Irish referendum. This alienation was the result of the 'quiet revolution' that saw a European political economy develop alongside the development of institutions of European economic governance.[15] In the late 1980s, the choice made by French socialists to use European integration to pursue greater economic efficiency with the view to sustain the welfare state engendered a market building project, appealing to liberal economic principles favored by the *zeitgeist*, around which a European consensus was forged.

To secure agreement across vastly different political and economic cultures, this project was kept rather vague and accommodated different projects of integration. In recent years, however, the EU's competition rules have increasingly aligned with American-style competition economics, a more neo-liberal understanding of market freedom being enshrined in the judgments of the European Court of Justice.[16] These rules seem to have been used to push political change at the level of member states that undermines the 'social market' approach which motivated public policy in Western Europe in the decades that followed World War II.[17] At the same time, the 'economic constitution' of the EU is constraining the extension of social policy at the European level.[18] The political responses to the financial crisis of the Eurozone have confirmed this evolution. Countries most affected have experienced a 'revolution from above' pushed by the leaders of the dominant nations of Northern Europe and the bureaucratic apparatus of the EU in Brussels and Frankfurt.[19]

The technocratic dictatorship of the *Troïka*, ostensibly claiming to be restoring the economic conditions for effective democracy, has provoked deterioration in inter-state relationships.[20] The reactivation of nationalistic prejudices in the form of a morality tale about hardworking German 'ants' and lazy Greek 'cicadas' has revealed the lack of concern for social solidarity across the union.[21] The austerity measures advocated have destabilized national political systems across the EU with governing parties losing elections and struggling to forge workable alliances. Rather than addressing the imbalances, which developed as a result of the straight-jacket imposed by monetary union on nation states, both national leaders and the European Commission have pushed for even more juridification of

---

[14] Stefano Bartolini, *Restructuring Europe. Centre Formation, System Building, and Political Structuring Between the Nation State and the European Union* (Oxford: Oxford University Press, 2005).

[15] Nicholas Jabko, *Playing the Market: A Political Strategy for Uniting Europe, 1985–2005* (Ithaca, NY: Cornell University Press, 2006).

[16] Stephen Wilks, 'Competition Policy. Towards an Economic Constitution?' in Helen Wallace, William Wallace and Mark A. Pollack (eds) *Policy-making in the European Union* (Oxford: Oxford University Press, 2005), pp. 143–155.

[17] Tony Judt, 'The Social Democratic Moment' in *Postwar: A History of Europe Since 1945* (New York: Penguin Press, 2005), pp. 360–389.

[18] Steven Liebfried, 'Social Policy. Left to the Judges and the Market?' in Helen Wallace, William Wallace and Mark A. Pollack (eds.) *Policy-making in the European Union* (Oxford, Oxford University Press, 2005), pp. 253–281.

[19] Etienne Balibar, 'Europe's Revolution From Above', *The Guardian*, 23 November 2011.

[20] The term '*Troïka*' is being used in the media as shorthand for the three agencies involved in the management of the current financial crisis: the European Commission, the European Central Bank and the International Monetary Fund.

[21] Yanis Vaoufakis, *Thoughts for the Post-2008 World Blog*: 'Never Bailed Out: Europe's Ants and Grasshoppers Revisited', 2011, http://yanisvaroufakis.eu/2011/12/15/never-bailed-out-europes-ants-and-grasshoppers-revisited.

economic policy, presented as 'deeper political integration'.[22] The recently proposed 'fiscal treaty' potentially creates the circumstances for the Commission to advance its liberalizing economic agenda and extend its control in areas hitherto defined as national competences (i.e., labour relations, education, health), protected by previous treaties.[23]

As stated by Jürgen Habermas – whose political philosophy paradoxically contributed to the erosion of the ideological foundations of European democracy, as explored in a later section – the current (mis)management of the crisis has brought to a head the issue of the European Union's democratic deficit: to regain the 'confidence' of financial, the integration of citizens is now required to match the integration of states.[24] The credibility of current policies is constantly undermined by the EU's lack of popular endorsement feeding political instability through the degradation of the legitimacy of democratically elected governments, even in the wealthier Northern countries.[25] The rise of anti-government parties has in turn encouraged the radicalization of the Centre Right.[26] Since the onset of the crisis, the theme of immigration, hitherto the preserve of the Extremist Right, has been taken up by mainstream politics, with prominent conservative leaders such as David Cameron, and Angela Merkel recently proclaiming the failure of 'multiculturalism'. These were curiously echoed by Nicolas Sarkozy although France does not have a multicultural immigration policy. This simply shows that Sarkozy understood they were really talking about immigration *per se*.[27]

As noted above, the use of the term 'populist' to describe extremist Right-wing parties conveys the idea of pathology. It is indeed normative: characterized by nativism, populism is contrasted with the cosmopolitanism celebrated by academic discourse and justifying its support for the European Union.[28] The term 'neo-nationalist' (which originates in social anthropology) thus provides a more neutral descriptor for the new extremist parties that gained a foothold in European parliamentary systems from the 1990s onwards and clearly establishes how these constituted a response to new transnational phenomena at the European level and globally.[29] As Gingrich and Banks point out, European neo-nationalism constitutes a puzzle for the social sciences. Part of the explanation for its appearance can be found in the evolution of the classical party system and the loss of relevance of its Left/Right divide.

European economic integration was a strategy generally endorsed by the two sides of the political spectrum, only allowing differentiation at the level of rights claims, with the Left focusing on an agenda of social liberalization and abandoning its traditional cause of social inclusion through full employment. In the 1980s and 1990s it rallied the Right's pursuit of logic of economic liberal modernization but added to it the language of identity-based rights. European legalism became a strong ally in the pursuit of a progressive agenda for

---

[22]Elisabetta Croci Angelina and and Francesco Farina, 'Real Divergence Across Europe and the Limits of EMU Macroeconomic Governance' in Pompeo Della Posta, and Leila Talani (eds) *Europe and the Financial Crisis* (New York: Palgrave MacMillan, 2011), pp. 46–90.

[23]Fritz Scharpf, 'Monetary Union, Fiscal Crisis and the Preemption of Democracy', London School of Economics Europe in Question Series, 2011, pp. 34–37.

[24]Jürgen Habermas, 'Bringing the Integration of Citizens into Line with the Integration of States', *The European Law Journal*, 18:4 (2012), pp. 485–488.

[25]Scharpf, op. cit., pp. 34–37.

[26]'On the March. Populist Anti-immigration Parties are Performing Strongly Across Northern Europe', *The Economist*, 17 March 2011.

[27]'Nicolas Sarkozy Joins David Cameron and Angela Merkel View that Multiculturalism has Failed', *The Daily Mail*, 11 February 2011.

[28]Ulrich Beck and Edgar Grande, *Cosmopolitan Europe* (Cambridge: Polity, 2007).

[29]André Gingrich and Marcus Banks, *Neo-nationalism in Europe and Beyond: Perspectives From Social Anthropology* (New York: Berghahn Books, 2006).

women, for homosexuals and other marginalized minorities. The Left thus embraced European 'post-national' cosmopolitanism which to some extent delegitimized the attachment of citizens to their national states. In the context of the EU's essentially economic constitution and with the absence of a truly European public sphere, the language of national identity, however, was the only through which social concerns could be articulated.[30] From the 1990s the retreat of the Left from big-picture politics allowed neo-nationalist 'populist' parties to capitalize on the feeling of disempowerment produced by the crisis of the party system and the new climate of economic and cultural insecurity associated with globalization.[31] They did so by combining hostility towards immigration with that towards the EU, attacked for promoting cultural rights undermining national identities. Hostility to immigration thus became a new, perverse form of identity-politics.

Neo-nationalism encouraged a political discourse of fear, to which the EU itself contributed in its ambiguous attitude towards globalization and its 'securitization' approach to immigration, the latter having promoted 'unattainable public expectations for effective defense against the perceived existential threats that migration poses'.[32] In the last decade or so, the discourse of counter-jihad has added a new civilizational dimension to these politics of fear by denouncing the existence of a cultural threat, Europe's 'Islamization',[33] portrayed as the result of a presumed demographic transformation induced by immigration belied by net migration figures close to negative in several countries of Western Europe and the convergent declining evolution of the birth rate among immigrants.[34] The appearance of Muslims in European societies is thus interpreted as undermining 'European identity', a notion underpinning that of European citizenship introduced by the EU's founding treaty.[35]

The phenomenon has been designated as 'Islamophobia', a term which Kaya points outs remains to be defined fully by the social sciences but can be used after Semati simply to designate a 'cultural–ideological outlook that seeks to explains ills of the (global) social order by attributing them to Islam'.[36] This article will follow this line of thought which posits that the dramatic rise of Islamophobia in Europe – demonstrated by a number of opinion polls[37] – is the most extreme manifestation of the politics of fear which became prevalent in all Western states in the first decade of the twenty-first century. At the same time, it will try to unravel the complex set of phenomena that explain why it was in Europe that Islamophobia became so active.

---

[30] Hagen Schulz-Forberg and Bo Stråth, *The Political History of European Integration: The Hypocrisy of Democracy-Through-Market* (New York: Routledge, 2010). This is the context within which the 'domophilia' discussed by Ahmad (this issue, pp. 234–252) was reactivated, in tandem with European cosmopolitanism.

[31] Hans-Georg Betz, *Radical Right-wing Populism in Western Europe* (New York: St Martin's Press, 1994).

[32] Georgios Karyoti, 'The Fallacy of Securitizing Migration: Elite Rationality and Unintended Consequences' in G. Lazaridis (ed.) *Security, Insecurity and Migration in Europe* (Farnham: Ashgate Publishing, 2011), p. 24.

[33] The influence of the securitization paradigm over discussions of Muslims in Europe appears clearly in the identification of minarets with rockets by Barbara Steinemann of the Swiss SVP/UDC party as discussed by Douglas Pratt in this issue (pp. 193–207).

[34] Christopher Caldwell, *Reflections on the Revolution in Europe* (New York: Doubleday, 2009); Ayhan Kaya, *Islam, Migration and Integration: The Age of Securitisation* (London: Palgrave, 2009).

[35] Cris Shore, *Building Europe: The Cultural Politics of European Integration* (London: Routledge, 2000). See also Bo Stråth, 'A European Identity: To the Historical Limits of a Concept', *European Journal of Social Theory*, 4:5 (2002), pp. 387–401.

[36] Ayhan Kaya, 'Islamophobia as a Form of Governmentality', p. 6. See the introduction to this issue for an overview of the notion.

[37] Kaya, *Islam, Migration and Integration*, pp. 15–24.

The French Crisis of Political Representation and the Instrumentalization of Anti-Islamic Feelings

Since the 2007–2008 global financial crisis the European neo-nationalist right has been on the rise. The political deterioration associated with the crisis of the euro has seen it entered government coalitions, as in the Netherlands or exercise indirect influence over government discourse, as in France. Anti-Muslim hostility became normalized, particularly in France, which, during the five years of Nicolas Sarkozy's presidency, was a 'leader' in the introduction of legislative measures framed in civilizational terms as defending a French/European identity supposedly under threat from Islam.[38]

France is a particularly instructive case study. It has one of the oldest neo-nationalist parties the *Front National* (FN) and has the biggest and longest-established Muslim population.[39] France has also been a main champion of European integration and its political system particularly destabilized by the European financial crisis with the unpopular choice to align with the austerity politics advocated by the German government. The French socialist party, especially, was closely associated with the EU's creation and with monetary union, establishing a commitment to European governance shared by the right.[40] This consensus on European integration partly explains the strong disaffection with government parties and the steady decline in electoral participation over the previous decades.[41]

The growth of the FN's appeal conditioned the adoption of a first measure targeting Muslims: female school pupils being forbidden to wear Muslim headscarves, which came after consultations, were held in 2003 by the Stasi Commission, a year after the FN's founder successfully defeated the Socialist candidate in the first round of presidential elections. During the 2007 presidential campaign, Nicolas Sarkozy, the new leader of the Centre Right, recaptured voters lost to the FN, by concentrating on the themes of national identity, immigration, law and order.[42] His discourse merged these themes, adopting a new strategy of 'cooptation of policy positions' that borrowed from the FN's discourse, whilst continuing to ostracize the party and rejecting the possibility of a political alliance.[43] One such policy position was the creation of a ministry for national identity, immigration and co-development first headed by Brice Hortefeux who became an extremely controversial figure due to his repressive approach towards immigration and his proposal to introduce DNA testing for family reunion visa applications. The ministry was condemned by Doudou Diène, the United Nations Special Rapporteur on contemporary forms of racism, racial discrimination, xenophobia and related intolerance for promoting 'an ethnic and racial interpretation of political, economic and social problems and an

---

[38] 'French Minister's Controversial Remarks an Election "Stunt"', *France 24 International News*, 6 March 2012, http://www.france24.com/en/20120207-france-muslims-target-unequal-clash-civilisations-elections-islam-gueant.

[39] Official statistics on religious affiliation being unconstitutional, the number of practising Muslims living in France can only be estimated as being between 6 and 8.5 per cent of the population (3.5 to 5 million, 2 possessing citizenship). 'Islam in France', *Euro-Islam Info*, Paris, 18 December 2012, http://www.euro-islam.info/country-profiles/france/.

[40] Rawi Abdelal, *Capital Rules: The Construction of Global Finance* (Cambridge, MA: Harvard University Press, 2007), pp. 58–65.

[41] 'La Participation électorale depuis 1815', Assemblée Nationale, 2012, http://www.assemblee-nationale.fr/histoire/suffrage_universel/suffrage-participation.asp.

[42] European elections database, Norwegian Social Sciences Database, http://www.nsd.uib.no/european_election_database/country/france/.

[43] Florence Haegel, 'Nicolas Sarkozy a-t-il radicalisé la droite française? Changements idéologiques et étiquettages politiques', *French Politics, Culture & Society*, 29:3, pp. 63–77.

ideological and political treatment of immigration portrayed as a security issue and a threat for national identity' (my translation).[44]

In subsequent years, the theme of national identity continued to be used and not only by members of the Sarkozy's party, *Union pour un Mouvement Populaire*. Echoing a speech made by Sarkozy in 2009 in which he had declared that there was no room in France for the wearing of the *burqa*, a parliamentary representative from the communist party thus pushed for an inquiry on the question, presented as a pressing issue from the perspective of security, women's rights, and secularism.[45] The matter was then taken up in 2010 by the minister for justice, Michèle Alliot-Marie, leading to the law banning the public wearing of the *burqa* voted in with overwhelming support.[46] In the lead-up to the presidential elections of 2012 and the campaign itself, the visibility of other signs of traditional Muslim piety was also hotly debated (ranging from the availability of halal meat to street prayers), with the UMP rushing to seize the initiative and the leader of the FN, Marine Le Pen, consistently arguing the incompatibility of Islam with the central values of French national identity, first and foremost, its version of secularism or *laïcité*.

There is much confusion both in France and outside it on the significance of French *laïcité*. It is the product of the specific circumstances of French history which saw the secularization and democratization of society coincide with the construction of a strong Republican state whose legitimacy had to be asserted against a strongly anti-democratic sector of society supported by the Catholic Church. This struggle against the Church led the state to acquire the power to define what religion was and what its place would be in public life. As Olivier Roy has argued, the French understanding of secularism is haunted by the memory of one religion's erstwhile political power. It is, as a result, ambiguous, both liberal in its insistence that the state stay out of all matters to do with religious belief or worship[47] and illiberal in its tendency to use legislation to control religious institutions.

Laïcité has only ever been defined *indirectly* as a principle emerging from the body of laws and jurisprudence that developed after the law of 1905 that banned the expression of religious beliefs from the sphere of public power and created a legal status for communities of worship that dismantled the absolute hierarchical control hitherto exercised by the Catholic Church. This law, proposed by a socialist and supported by Protestant and Jewish deputies, was the outcome of a political settlement between the Catholic majority and the Protestant and Jewish minorities. It did not necessarily entail endorsement of the system of ultra-rationalist norms elaborated by the positivist mindset of the founders of the Third Republic under the label of *laïcité*. In the last three decades of the nineteenth century, *laïcité* had been used to impose elite control over masses to counter the working class push for socio-economic rights. It was, however, increasingly contested in the decades following the law of 1905, which did not even use the term *laïcité*. It nevertheless survived as a particularly influential, philosophical current facilitating the conservative argument that rationalist principles, and not social conflict, had secured French democracy through state secularism.

The appearance on the world stage of Muslim fundamentalism gave new life to this ideology. Its attempt to create a new form of state deriving its authority from the recreation of traditional Muslim values came to be seen through the prism of the historical fear of a

---

[44]'Un expert de l'ONU fustige le ministère de l'éducation', *Le Nouvel Observateur*, 11 June 2007.
[45]'La Burqa, une prison ambulante', *Libération*, 17 June 2009. See also Natalie J. Doyle, 'Lessons from France: Popularist Anxiety and Veiled Fears of Islam', *Islam and Christian–Muslim Relations*, 22:4 (2011), pp. 475–489.
[46]'Burqa Ban Passes French Lower House Overwhelmingly', *CNN*, 13 July 2010, http://edition.cnn.com/2010/WORLD/europe/07/13/france.burqa.ban/index.html. See Gould on this discussion (this issue, pp. 173–192) for a more detailed discussion of the 'Burka ban' and its echoes in other European countries.
[47]Olivier Roy, *Secularism Confronts Islam* (trans. G. Holoch) (Chichester, NY: Columbia University Press, 2007).

Catholic fifth column whose allegiance to the Church undermined the authority of the Republican state. Whilst the other forms of fundamentalism, Jewish or Christian evangelical, could also have been denounced as promoting anti-Republican communitarianism, the link of Muslim fundamentalism to anti-Western terrorism came to focus on Islam the insecurity generated by the challenges which European integration and globalization pose for French republicanism in its assertion of state power. The demographics of immigration also played a role in this. In the process, the assertion that French society is defined by its commitment to *laïcité* was incorporated by Marine Le Pen in the FN's anti-immigration discourse, leaving behind the white and Christian identity upheld by her father.

As we saw above, under the FN's influence, the discussion on French secularism of state elites and intellectual fellow travelers became radicalized. It came to incorporate references to theological principles of Islam presumably incompatible with the acceptance of the state's commitment to religious neutrality, even though these are features of all monotheistic religions. In addition, the discussion became incoherent in so far as the legal framework established by the law of 1905 prohibits the state from engaging with theological dogma. This incoherence was first demonstrated by the Stasi Commission in the rationale used to prevent girls from wearing Muslim headscarves in schools.[48]

As Asad argued, the ban was justified through arguments that purported to uphold the state's neutrality but were, in fact, deeply normative; they upheld a conception of individual autonomy that presumably promotes emancipation but makes it conditional upon the identity of French citizen; that is, on the individual's submission to the nation state.[49] The Stasi Commission signaled the radical re-assertion of the theology of the state constructed in positivistic terms by the founders of the Third Republic. As Asad rightly points out, this theology, however, only reflects a nationalist aspiration, not social reality in its complexity, and one must make a distinction between the feelings that motivate nationalistic fantasies and the *practices* of civic responsibility that define French republicanism, which are the product of a specific history I have outlined. This is true of all forms of secularism and Asad question the fact that issues to do with the presence of Muslims in Europe are approached as a battle between those upholding secularism and those criticizing the notion of civil religion, when what is needed is a *political discussion* of 'what constitutes the best way of supporting some liberties whilst limiting others, so as to minimize harm to both individuals and society as a whole'.[50]

Roy's analysis converges with that of Asad. It similarly argues that the French debate on Islam's presumed incompatibility with French society's commitment to modern freedom does not engage with social reality. In particular, it is deaf to what French Muslims themselves have to say about their civic identity. He relates this triumph of ideology to the crisis of the French state, a crisis that has specific features conditioned by history but also fits within trends evident in other western states. Roy's discussion of French Islamophobia is thus framed within his understanding of Islamic fundamentalism, not as a threat to secular modernity but as a kind of accommodation to its hegemony. In this respect, it relies on Marcel Gauchet's sociology of modernity and its analysis of religious disenchantment that is often presented reductively as an intellectual endorsement of French state theology, whose positivistic mindset saw religious piety as essentially incompatible with individual emancipation.[51]

---

[48] The headscarf ban was the only one of the recommendations by the Stasi Commission not endorsed unanimously. See Natalie J. Doyle, op. cit. As argued there is in fact no clear social consensus on the norms invoked under the banner of *laïcité*.

[49] Talal Asad, 'French Secularism and the "Islamic Veil Affair"', *The Hedgehog Review*, 8:1–2 (2006), pp. 93–106.

[50] Ibid., p. 106.

[51] This view is endorsed by Mayanthi Fernando in 'Reconfiguring Freedom: Muslim Piety and the Limits of Secular Law and Public Discourse in France', *American Ethnologist*, 37:1 (2010), p. 22.

This sociology of modernity cannot be discussed comprehensively within the constraints of this article which pursues a reflection on the links between European Islamophobia and the crisis of democratic legitimacy: the following section defines this crisis as a loss of collective purpose; it argues that this loss has allowed an elitist republican project to triumph over emancipatory democracy and to de-politicize social problems. Once again starting from the French case, this analysis will explore the limitations of Foucault's definition of modernity in terms of governmentality for an understanding of the way Islamophobia is essentially connected to a crisis of democratic legitimacy. It will highlight the fact that it cannot provide a project of political inclusion to counter the disempowerment of all European citizens, and first and foremost Muslims. In the process, however, it will touch upon another aspect of Gauchet's work, its interpretation of the societal change that has caused European societies to lose sight of their political identity,

Islamophobia and Neo-liberal Governmentality

As discussed above, French contemporary discussions of secularity have totally blurred the traditional political divides and produced extreme ideological confusion. On the right, the traditional ultra-Catholic camp now faces Islamic fundamentalism in which it sees an opponent but whose views on the paramount importance of religion, the place of women, homosexuality, etc., are not essentially different from its own.[52] The liberal Left, on the other hand, has been particularly destabilized in its defence of minorities, including sexual minorities. In the 1980s, it defended the rights of immigrants against the National Front, including their rights of worship it approached as cultural. It could promote an anti-racist agenda that matched the demands made by the first French-born offsprings of North African immigrants for integration into French society, demands that did not mention Islam, keeping it confined to the sphere of their private life.

This defense of immigrants was framed by a Universalist discourse of citizenship and individual rights, rather than by any commitment to the value of cultural diversity. Today, however, the second generation has integrated sufficiently for some to want their cultural origins surviving in religious traditions to be acknowledged by the rest of French society along multicultural lines, something which fits within a more general societal trend of greater individualization. This cultural assertion overlaps with another aspect of the Islamic revival in France, also linked to individualization, the growth of Muslim piety, but disconnected from cultural roots, incorporating 'converts' and 'reverts'.[53] This type of Muslim piety is profoundly challenging to the French Left traditionally supportive of republican secularism as an ally against the anti-democratic stance of early twentieth-century Catholic elites.

The matter has been complicated by new class divisions. Whilst the growing visibility of the Muslim faith is associated on the one hand with the integration into the middle class of the second generation of immigrants, on the other hand, Muslim fundamentalism has also made progress among those (grand)children of migrants who were denied social mobility and now form a kind of underclass relegated by state neglect to poorly serviced fringe suburbs of big cities. For these individuals struggling with both racism and socio-economic exclusion and as a result over-represented in crime statistics, fundamentalist Islam

---

[52] Roy, op. cit.
[53] Fernando, op. cit., p. 23.

functions as a source of solidarity, dignity as well as of ethics.[54] Fundamentalism is the symptom of a social problem but it is now perceived as its cause, allowing Islamophobia to deflect attention from the state's failure to address socio-economic marginalization. State failure has been compounded by the splintering of working-class consciousness, solidarity with immigrants now undermined by the ideological discourse of *laïcité* just as much as racism, something facilitated by the radical Left's hostility towards religious faith, historically conditioned by both Marxism and anarcho-syndicalism.

There is a fundamental class dimension in European Islamophobia. As Kaya points out, the specific form of hostility to Islam encountered in Europe is linked to a radically different pattern of immigration from that of the United States and other 'new world' countries, with Muslims having arrived in European as unskilled workers and remaining largely so. As a result, they have been disproportionately affected by the major socio-economic changes experienced by western societies in the last two decades or so: de-industrialization, greater productivity, the retreat of state provided welfare, the progress of social exclusion. In Europe, and not only in France, Muslims form the bulk of the poor and they have become the target of the discourse of securitization that has grown alongside the loss of what used to be the nation state's exclusive prerogatives.

The notion of security has been vastly expanded to incorporate the need to protect society (and not just the state) against all forms of risks as part of the form of government that characterizes liberal democratic societies defined by Foucault as 'governmentality'.[55] In its neo-liberal incarnation, elite governmentality has constructed a discourse of migration that has externalized the structural failures of western societies and reduced new social divisions to cultural difference. European Muslims have been disproportionately affected by unemployment, poverty, and educational disadvantage, problems that feed into crime statistics but in keeping with neo-liberal individualism, they have been perceived as personally responsible for those problems, first because of their culture and now specifically because of their religion.

The discourse of securitization is part of a broad pattern of de-politicization. As Wendy Brown puts it, 'depoliticization involves constructing inequality, subordination, marginalization and social conflict, which all require political analysis and political solutions, as personal and individual, on the one hand, or as natural, religious, cultural on the other'.[56] Its latest incarnation of European Islamophobia is linked to the specific form of de-politicization of European societies characterized by the shift from government to governance and the constitution of a transnational, European layer of a-political policy-making defined only by its presumed expertise and largely unaccountable democratically. It thus overlaps with the question of democratic legitimacy introduced in section 1.

The line of interpretation I am pursuing is, however, slightly different from that formulated by Brown and Kaya, which relies on the Foucauldian concept of governmentality.[57] It sees the erasure of politics associated with Islamophobia as the product of a crisis of

---

[54]See Farhad Khosrokhavar, *L'Islam dans les prisons* (Paris: Balland, 2004); James A. Beckford, Danièle Joly and Farhad Khosrokhavar, *Muslims in Prison: Challenge and Change in Britain and France* (New York: Palgrave Macmillan, 2005). In this issue, see Khosrokhavar (pp. 284–306) and Andre and Shandon-Harris's discussion of the violent radicalization of Mohammed Mera (pp. 307–319).
[55]Kaya, op. cit.
[56]Wendy Brown, *Regulating Aversion: Tolerance in the Age of Identity and Empire* (Princeton: Princeton University Press, 2006).
[57]Brown's discussion of governmentality touches upon some limitations of Foucault's discussion of the modern state but space constraints prevent me from addressing her analysis's nuances. I discuss these limitations briefly in my concluding remarks.

governmentality but apprehends the crisis sociologically, as the product of a transformation of western societies that has seen the state lose its central structural function. This line of interpretation draws inspiration from Gauchet's current work on the predicament of contemporary democracy.[58] This analysis of the crisis of democratic legitimacy is informed by a sociological theory of European modernity which sees in it the creation of a society of individuals pursuing democratic emancipation, a creation that cannot be reduced to the pursuit of rational autonomy but also involves a new symbolic regime of state power (a question I return to in my concluding remarks). For Gauchet the de-politicization of democracy is related to the progress of European modernity to a new stage of modern individualism in the sense it was first formulated by French anthropologist Louis Dumont, that is, as a horizon of common meaning marked by the paradox that it seeks to generate a social order exclusively from the value of individual autonomy presumed natural and universal.[59]

In this new stage of individualism, the state has retreated from the formulation of a collective purpose imposed from above through civil religion. It now only serves as a symbolic infrastructure of social life.[60] Its power supports a different mode of social cohesion from the one defined by the myth of cultural homogeneity that inspired nationalism and its political theology. This mode of social cohesion is still political but at a purely symbolic level. It relies on the imaginary of the political nation that supports society's project of emancipation predicated on collective self-determination, that is, on the ideal of popular sovereignty. This imaginary, however, is now totally stripped of any transcendent authority over individuals: substantial unity has been replaced by a kind of virtual unity, in which factors of dissociation, including the promotion of individual freedoms, are paradoxically made to serve collective cohesion.

The new mode of social cohesion has promoted a new wave of liberalization and given economics a hold on contemporary democratic societies in the form of a new social ideology, that of neo-liberalism. Neo-liberalism sees society as nothing more than a self-regulating aggregate emerging naturally from the interaction of various individual initiatives and demands. It has encouraged citizens to retreat into their particularistic demands and to surrender responsibility for the whole to the 'expertise' of elites. Through this expertise, these elites have forged links across the globe establishing their domination on an international scale outside public accountability.[61] Both globalization and European integration manifest it and have been accompanied by theorizations of cosmopolitanism that have depicted the retreat from the emancipatory understanding of democracy as ethical progress.[62] A new form of elitist republicanism has triumphed throughout the West that is profoundly suspicious of the notion of popular sovereignty and has enabled the oligarchic evolution of contemporary democracy where economic and political elites now dominate common citizens in the name of expertise and efficacy.[63]

---

[58] Unpublished seminars. See introductory reflection in Marcel Gauchet, *La Démocratie: D'une crise à l'autre* (Paris: Cécile Defaut, 2007).

[59] Louis Dumont, *Essays on Individualism: Modern Ideology in Anthropological Perspective* (Chicago: Chicago University Press, 1986).

[60] See Natalie J. Doyle, 'Autonomy and Modern Liberal Democracy: From Castoriadis to Gauchet', *European Journal of Social Theory*, 15:3 (2012), pp. 331–347.

[61] Elise S. Brezis, 'Globalisation and the Emergence of a Transnational Elite', UNU – WIDER Working Paper No. 2010/05, 2010.

[62] See footnote 30 and Daniele Archibugi and David Held (eds.) *Cosmopolitan Democracy. An Agenda for a New World Order* (Cambridge: Polity Press, 1995).

[63] John P. McCormick, *Machiavellian Democracy* (Cambridge: Cambridge University Press, 2012). McCormick advocates a return to a Machiavellian republicanism characterised by a sharp awareness of the problem of domination.

The politics of fear of neo-liberal governmentality have been used by states to counter this loss of collective purpose and designated a presumably hostile 'Other' through which the collective could re-assert itself. In the case of European states, under the influence of European integration, the 'Other' has been defined also as that of the totalitarian past. This has encouraged the belief that European societies have transcended conventional political attachments based on ethnic origin, national culture or religious tradition and attained a superior form of democracy incorporating the Kantian imperative of universalistic ethics: deliberative democracy, as theorized by Jürgen Habermas through the notion of constitutional patriotism. This belief has reactivated the Enlightenment's a-political rationalist utopia and empowered the ideological interpretation of secularism discussed in the previous section.

Mavelli's Critique of the Civilizational Claims Underpinning the EU's Governance

In *Europe's Encounter with Islam* Luca Mavelli provides an analysis of the growth of Islamophobia in Europe that shows how the contemporary European faith in rational intersubjective communication partakes of a logic which, by necessity, situates Muslims outside the realm of modern autonomy and pluralism.[64] It provides insights in the way it is essentially connected to the notion of European identity that has been actively promoted by the European Union. He argues that the construction of the European Union by political elites has been an attempt to universalize the European secular episteme as originally defined by Foucault. This episteme has paradoxically empowered reactionary attempts to re-Christianize Europe and made it impossible for European societies to engage with Muslims in any other way than seeing them as defective projections of autonomous Europeans. This appears clearly in the evolution of attitudes towards Muslim immigrants in France discussed above, conditioned by a self-referential discourse which, as we have seen, does not in fact engage with the real practices of Muslims, characterized by a diversity that resists essentialization. European Islamophobia demonstrates a resistance to alterity that is in fact intrinsic to European modernity. Mavelli argues convincingly that that this resistance becomes apparent when it is approached through Asad's definition of the secular as an epistemic category. This definition transcends dominant approaches focusing on issues of cultural integration of Muslim *vis-à-vis* the different regimes of secularism of European societies and reveals the specifically 'European' dimension of the tensions surrounding Islam in Europe. Grounded in the rationalistic episteme that constructed the secular modern subject, the European understanding of knowledge in fact emerged in Christian theology itself. Developed by philosophy from Descartes to Kant, it defined rational knowledge as entirely contained within the structure of the knowing subject and predicated on the rejection of all that is external to the individual subject's rationality, his own emotions as well as the empirical 'Other'. It required the autonomous subject to transcend his senses and listen only to the voice of reason contained within himself. Following this voice, the subject progressively withdrew from the transcendent 'Other' that functioned as the authority underpinning the social order: he eventually replaced God as the foundation of knowledge and being. This understanding of rational autonomy became the basis of post-Christian ethics as outlined by Kant at the end of his career in his *Religion within the Limits of Reason Alone*.

This withdrawal from the transcendent 'Other' also encompassed a parallel withdrawal from the empirical 'Other'. The idea of a subject knowledgeable by virtue of the structure of

---

[64]Mavelli, op. cit.

his subjectivity and his capacity to escape the influence of others implies that the secular subject is not required to open up to difference in order to be able to know the empirical 'Other'. As a result, the empirical 'Other' is entirely contained within the structure of the knowing subject and exists only as a projection of the European secular self. In the process, the modern rational episteme impoverished human experience by becoming what Mavelli defines as a quest for immunity from alterity, using a concept developed by the Italian philosopher Roberto Esposito.[65] The search for immunity – that is, for a rational purification of the self – constitutes a secular transposition of the Christian quest for otherworldly redemption but it cannot generate positive social bonds, only a *negative* solidarity predicated on the opposition to an absolute 'Other'. Put in another way, secular immunity does not produce community; all it can produce is *co-immunity*. Historically the 'Other' on which this co-immunity has been predicated has been the Muslim subject, as a defective/defensive projection of the rational European subject and this has been central to the consolidation of European secularity.

Mavelli argues that the immune closure of rational subjectivity in its tragic consequences was paradoxically both theorized and consolidated by the leading theorists of classical European sociology, Emile Durkheim and Max Weber, albeit in slightly different ways. Weber's discussion of modern secularism, like Durkheim's, stressed the idea that the idea of secular autonomy contributed to a condition of social fragmentation. At the same time, though, it held on to the belief in the superiority of European civilization's pursuit of modern rational autonomy and constructed his theory of modernity though a hermeneutics of Islam that saw in it a defective projection of Europe's secular civilization. In other words, Weber replaced the dualism God/man that underpinned the pre-secular social space with that between 'European subject' and 'Muslim subject'.[66]

Habermas's political philosophy can be said to manifest similar awareness of the fact that Kant's project of autonomy ultimately rendered individuals powerless in the face of modernity's anomic forces through its critique of the colonization of the life world by instrumental rationalization. It addresses the loss of transcendent normative authority by advocating a shift from the paradigm of consciousness to a paradigm of communicative action that rescues reason through the intersubjectivity of dialogue: a communicative relationship with the 'Other' can presumably lift the Kantian imperative of universality out of the closure of individual conscience. Habermas's discursive ethics have promoted a proceduralist view of democracy that claims to overcome the tension between the universalism of liberalism and the cultural embedded-ness of the republican perspective touched upon above in the discussion of French secularism, with respect to the French assimilationist approach to immigration. This gave birth to the notion of post-national democracy defined by the notion of constitutional patriotism, a form of political attachment to the norms, values and procedures of a liberal democratic constitution, rather than to a culturally substantive definition of community based on ethnicity, national culture or religion.[67] Habermas came to see in the European Union the political form

---

[65] For a most sustained discussion of the concept of immunity, see Salvatore in this issue, pp. 253–264.

[66] Mavelli also discusses Durkheim's belief in the need for a secular transcendence of the state. Relying only on one short text by Durkheim and on secondary literature, this analysis does not account for the complexity of Durkheim's sociology. Suffice it to say that this analysis is derived from the critique of the neo-Kantian postulates of early French elite republicanism, extended by Foucault, which failed to account for Durkheim's insights into the political. See the introduction by Jeffrey C. Alexander and Philip Smith to the *Cambridge Companion to Durkheim* (Cambridge: Cambridge Univesity Press, 2005) and Bernard Lacroix, *Durkheim et le Politique* (Paris: Fondation des Sciences de l'Homme and Montréal: Presses Universitaires de Montréal, 1981).

[67] Jürgen Habermas, 'Three Normative Models of Democracy', *Constellations*, 1:1 (1994), pp. 1–10.

that came closest to this political model, the idea of Europe embodying a cosmopolitan, post-conventional subjectivity, by definition open to the 'Other'.

The definition of European identity in terms of post-national democracy has, however, not overcome the limitations of the paradigms of secularity. It still feeds Weber's hermeneutics of Islam, in the form of a discourse of redemption that argues that Europeans suffered from religious conflicts but freed themselves from the power of religion and successfully democratized Christian ethics in a way that makes the European Union a model for the world. This discourse of redemption is what defines the imaginary of Europe from which the institutions of the European Union derive their meaning and legitimacy. The commitment to procedural democracy is thus accompanied by a fundamental conceit of superiority that conceals its communitarian prejudices behind the promotion of universally rules-based politics which end up placing on the excluded the burden of their exclusion.

This logic underpinned the enlargement of the European Union to the east as a process of assimilation, with post-communist countries vying for EU membership establishing a kind of hierarchy amongst themselves, according to their degree of 'Europeanness'. As part of this, the presumably universal and culturally neutral measures of modernization and democratization established by the Copenhagen criteria of EU membership were overlooked to give precedence to such countries such as Romania or Bulgaria as against the claims of a much older applicant: Muslim Turkey. Ultimately, European proceduralism empowered reactionary Catholic forces, as demonstrated by the retreat of pope Benedict XVI from his Polish predecessor's commitment to interfaith and his re-assertion of the Christian dimension of European identity. The 'unholy alliance' of Left-wing atheistic political thought and conservative Catholicism discussed by Roy with respect to France can thus be said to manifest a broader evolution at the European level, evident in the ambiguities of Habermas's dialogue with the then Cardinal Ratzinger.[68]

Ultimately, these ambiguities are those of the EU's discourse of redemption, which constantly oscillates between two definitions of Europe: Europe as civilizational identity defined by Renaissance humanism, the Enlightenment but also the Christian ethics of love vs. Europe as procedural project. Both serve the same narrative praising Europe for having secured long-lasting peace after its violent past. This violent past, however, excludes colonial violence and focuses exclusively on the devastation for Europe of the two world wars as consequences of nationalism. Drawing on the work of Tony Judt, Mavelli stresses the exculpatory character of this narrative with respect to the collaboration of a substantial number of Europeans with the Nazi regime. It made of Germany the only country bearing culpability for the tragic violations of human rights and in the process established Europeans as victims, promoting a moral double standard that allowed them to ignore their own nationalisms and the forms of violence they went on to perpetrate.

Whilst illuminating, this part of Mavelli's analysis (and of Judt's own discussion) leaves unquestioned one essential aspect of the peace narrative of European integration: the assertion that peace was essentially secured as against the sovereignty of nation states. This foundational myth first expressed in 1950 by the French foreign minister Robert Schuman, the founder of the first European Community, has remained a central aspect of the European memory constructed by the European Union as a form of *post-totalitarian* project.[69] Even if it rested on the existence of nation states and was to a very large extent directed by them, the

---

[68] Pope Benedict XVI, Jürgen Habermas and Forian Schuller, *The Dialectics of Secularisation* (San Francisco: St Ignatius Press, 2006). For a discussion of the persistent role of Christianity in the discourse of European identity in Denmark and Germany, see Sedgwick and Gould in this issue, pp. 208–233 and pp. 173–192.
[69] Jan-Werner Müller, *Constitutional Patriotism* (Princeton: Princeton University Press, 2007).

project of integration sought to demarcate itself from classical political concepts implicated in the genesis of totalitarianism. On an ideological plane only, it sought to transcend the nation state (or at least its passions). It did so through the creation of a new form of state inspired by the idea of subsidiarity, which facilitated the later shift to neo-liberal governance implicated in the contemporary crisis of democratic legitimacy.[70]

Conclusion: European Integration, Islamophobia and the Limitations of the Critique of Govermentality

The foundational myth of European integration posits that peace and cooperation won over the bellicose impulses of the European nation states despite the fact that it was the pacification of European nation states post-45 that facilitated the European project, not the reverse.[71] The ideological construction of a mythical European memory analyzed by Mavelli has in fact been characterized by a statophobia derived from a specific interpretation of the historical experience of totalitarianism that equates it with statism: the modern state is by definition always potentially totalitarian and Nazism revealed its true nature. The European Union thus defines itself as the rejection of the world presumed to have engendered totalitarian violence, that of the nation state's exclusive sovereignty. This statophobia has its distant origins in what Reinhard Koselleck first analyzed as the a-political 'critical' mindset of the Enlightenment and in the deep mistrust of the people that underpinned its project or rationalization.[72] It has today empowered a reductive interpretation of democracy predicated on a limited interpretation of modern freedom and the re-activation of an old tradition of elite republicanism associated with rationalism.[73] The regression of democracy to elective oligarchy it has encouraged has obfuscated another tradition, that of emancipation from domination through active democratic self-determination.

A variety of thinkers have critiqued the Enlightenment's project and its ambition to generate a general hermeneutic from reason, stressing its conceit and its historical embeddedness in a specifically European experience.[74] The Foucauldian strand of this critique has yielded substantial insights into the new form of domination generated by the liberal state, an analysis developed more recently by such critics as Wendy Brown as a critique of *neo-liberal* de-politicization. This critique however remains limited by the partial understanding the tensions of modern democracy encouraged by Foucault's primarily epistemological perspective on modernity, which discouraged him from taking an interest in the democratic aspirations that developed alongside the Enlightenment's project and in the revolutions of the eighteenth century.

As Brian Singer and Lorna Weir argue, Foucault's work was marked by the neglect of the question of sovereignty which surfaced so vividly in the French Revolution. It privileged the study of governmentality through a study of Machiavelli even though the work of

---

[70]Julien Barroche, *État, libéralisme et christianisme. Critique de la subsidiarité européenne* (Paris, Dalloz, 2012).
[71]Marcel Gauchet, 'La nouvelle Europe' in *La Condition politique* (Paris: Gallimard, 2005), pp. 494–504. As already noted, it goes without saying that this pacification was only intra-European.
[72]Reinhardt Koselleck, *Critique and Crisis. Enlightenment and the Pathogenesis of Modern Society* (Oxford: Berg, 1988).
[73]Like Koselleck, John P. McCormick (op. cit.) sees this tradition as originating in the struggle of the French Enlightenment with monarchical absolutism.
[74]Michel Foucault, 'What is Enlightenment?' in Michel Foucault and Paul Rabinow, *The Foucault Reader* (Harmondsworth: Penguin, 1984), pp. 32–50; Talal Asad, *Genealogies of Religion: Disciplines and Reason of Power in Christianity and Islam* (Baltimore: John Hopkins University Press, 1993). See also Zygmunt Bauman, *Legislators and Interpreters* (Ithaca: Cornell University Press, 1991).

Machiavelli was characterized by the *simultaneous* problematization of ruler and ruled.[75] Early modern political philosophy elaborated new understandings of both sovereignty and governance, the two notions addressing the fundamental question of society's division between elites and masses, that is, the problem of political legitimacy. Foucault showed how this problem was addressed but not resolved by the displacement of *raison d'état* by the liberal 'security' state and a shift of concern for public opinion. As Singer and Weir stress, historically, the division was also countered at a symbolic level, that of sovereignty, starting with monarchical absolutism. Foucault, however, dismissed it. Sovereignty drew on the symbolic resources of an earlier period: the notion of deity which conferred on the monarch a demiurgic role, that of pacifying what became known as the nation, a notion also inherited from the past that saw the ruled as an extension of the king.

The absolutist solution, theorized by Hobbes in contractual terms, was however unstable. It empowered the elites of the two dominant estates to identify themselves as the nation, at the expense of the monarch. The notion of democratic sovereignty then came to offer yet another solution to the problem of legitimacy by shifting it in favour of the perspective of those ruled as they ceased to be the object of power to become perceived its source. The problem became one of *representation*, of the relationship between the two levels of the political: the visible power-holders and the invisible sovereign power they are beholden to. It was, again, not eliminated, as the two terms can never be fused, existing as they do at incommensurable levels. The sovereign is not a determinate entity. The electoral process relies on the fiction that it could be but democracy relies on the maintenance of the division, or as Lefort has argued, on the place of power remaining always empty, only temporarily occupied. It is the place of constant contestation.[76]

The two levels of governmentality and sovereignty must always be kept separate for the dangers associated with modern power to be controlled. Nazism which haunts the self-understanding of contemporary European democracies illustrated it: it erased the distinction by conflating the sovereign people and the governed population and perverted democratic power into the assertion of the majority population's racial superiority. The danger facing contemporary European democracies involves a totally different kind of domination which paradoxically emanates from their very attempt not to repeat the tragedy of Nazism. It has been engendered by the pursuit of a form of universalism untainted by any particularistic attachments which Habermas argues could be secured through democratic deliberation and allegiance to purely procedural norms. As this article has demonstrated, this pursuit has paradoxically engendered a new assertion of superiority but clothed in civilizational terms and invoking liberal principles. This assertion which reactivates the mindset of the Enlightenment facilitates a new form of majority domination: that of those making the choice of religious piety to give meaning to their autonomous individual existence by a majority who does not understand this choice. As we have seen, this tyranny has merged with older forms of racism linked to immigration and has made of Muslims the target of its oppression.

This shift in the definition of democracy has, however, been framed by the appearance of a new logic of democratic legitimacy triggered by societal change across Western societies, societal change marked by decline in visibility of the symbolic level of the political. Across western democracies, legitimacy has been pursued in terms of empirical (largely economic) 'outputs' that have overshadowed democracy's emancipatory objectives. The politics of fear

---

[75]Brian C. J. Singer and Lorna Weir, 'Sovereignty, Governance and the Political: The Problematic of Foucault', *Thesis Eleven*, 94 (2008), pp. 49–71.

[76]Claude Lefort, 'The Permanence of the Theologico-political?' in David Macey (ed. and trans.) *Democracy and Political Theory* (Cambridge and Oxford: Polity Press in association with Basil Blackwell, 1988), pp. 213–255.

analyzed by Foucauldian studies of neo-liberal governmentality constitute a pervert attempt to address this loss of symbolic legitimacy. In Europe, this managerial legitimacy was given an institutional embodiment in the EU, contributing to an even greater erosion of the symbolic dimension of legitimacy. European Islamophobia has been greatly encouraged by this disempowerment of citizens.

If, as this article argues, European Islamophobia manifests a crisis of democracy, then there lies perhaps also the way to counter it, a task that encompasses the one advocated by critics such as Asad, Mavelli, and Salvatore in this issue: giving democracy a post-secular form.[77] The idea of constituent power that underpins liberal democracy sees popular sovereignty as being expressed through the law.[78] At the same time, it stipulates that all who are subject to the constitutional order must have the power to co-institute it. In this sense, the notion of equality is central to democratic legitimacy and a society is only truly democratic if it guarantees conditions of equal political participation for all its citizens. As we have seen, Muslims in Europe by and large belong to the working class and have been the most affected by the changes associated with the global spread of capitalism. Addressing their socio-economic exclusion, if coupled with an overall strategy to combat the greater wealth divide associated with the financial crisis, would strengthen democratic legitimacy empirically and symbolically, by demonstrating commitment to an ideal of democratic sovereignty inclusive also of Muslims.

---

[77] Mavelli, op. cit.
[78] Andreas Kalyvas, 'Popular Sovereignty, Democracy, and the Constituent Power', *Constellations*, 12:2 (2005), pp. 223–244.

Radicalization in Prison: The French Case

FARHAD KHOSROKHAVAR

Ecole des Hautes Etudes en Sciences Sociales

ABSTRACT   *This article purports to show the change in the pattern of radicalization in French prisons over the last decade. Contrary to the extrovert model of radicalization in place up to the beginning years of the twenty-first century where a dozen people could be involved, the new one is introverted, based on very few individuals (mostly two or three people), and in contrast to the previous network in which people with psychological troubles were marginalized, psychopaths or psychically disturbed people can now play a major role. Whereas the extrovert model was easy to detect according to a profiling based on features like long beards, overt proselytizing, aggressive attitudes towards authorities and fundamentalist behaviour models, the new attitude avoids all those features and people exposed to radicalization have internalized the non-visible conduct pattern in order not to attract the attention of the authorities. The article explores some new attitudes resulting in radicalization and the major stumbling-blocks encountered by prison authorities in their attempts to unearth them.*

This article aims at providing an answer to three interconnected questions:

- Is radicalization in French prisons progressing or receding, and what are its predominant features?
- Has there been any change within radicalization patterns – and, if so, what are their new major characteristics?
- How do institutional and organizational factors in prison influence radicalization? Through what mechanisms do they operate and what is their impact on the prisoners with respect to their radicalization?

The answer to the second question conditions the first. There has been a major change within the radicalization paradigm in French prisons (and most probably in French society more broadly, as well as in other European societies). This makes irrelevant its evaluation according to the old paradigm. Due to its sheer size, radicalization is most probably regressing quantitatively. *Qualitatively*, it is espousing a new pattern with new types of action in store, largely unpredictable in their consequences if undetected by authorities. The circumstances contributing to radicalization are studied in relation to the third issue: the institutional, organizational factors fostering radicalization within prison. Among them, three major items are singled out: overcrowding, understaffing and the high turnover of personnel and prisoners.

The Methodology and Choice of Prisons

The method is based on semi-structured long interviews with prisoners regarding their biography, in conjunction with interviews with prison guards, psychologists, psychiatrists, rehabilitation personnel, sport instructors, ministers of religion (imams, but also those of other faiths: priests, pastors and rabbis), prison directors and deputy directors, and other people involved in prison life (unpaid volunteers visiting those prisoners feeling lonely and in need of social assistance). A perusal of the judiciary and penitentiary files of the prisoners balanced the prisoners' accounts, in many cases self-congratulatory or self-exonerating with respect to the interviewer. Those prisons studied were (and are still) visited by the author on a weekly or monthly basis, in some cases daily.

The interviews give an overview of the prison and its inmates; they sometimes give more information about the prison than the prisoner himself. Interviews conducted alone with the prisoners offer a distorted picture of the individuals concerned, but not necessarily of others. Interactions and immersion in the prison give insights into radicalization patterns, through observation of the participants, in particular through an understanding of their grievances regarding daily life in prison and discrimination.

Documents, when declassified, were consulted in the prison archives where the prison directors gave their agreement.

The prisons were chosen according to their importance. (With attention focused on those with a high number of inmates, a high number of Muslims, and a high number of those detained under the judicial heading of 'criminal conspiracy acting in preparation of a terrorist act' [*Association de malfaiteurs en vue d'une action terroriste*]).[1] Fleury-Mérogis, the largest prison in Western Europe, with some 4200 prisoners; and Fresnes, with some 2400 prisoners, make up around 10 per cent of all prison inmates in France. Both are located on the outskirts of Paris. Among the other prisons visited, some were chosen due to the fact that they were jails for prisoners serving long sentences known as *Maison centrale* – like Saint-Maur in central France, one of a number of high-security prisons – and others, because they were home to a large palette of detainees like Lilles-Séquedin in the city of Lille, where a small long-term prison used to coexist with a short-term facility closed down in 2012. Three groups were targeted for interviews:

- Those who were sentenced for terrorist activities (mainly Jihadists, but also Basques and Corsicans sentenced on terrorist charges, and a few neo-Nazi skinheads with extremist tendencies).
- Those who seemed inclined towards radicalization through their grievances towards French or European society and stated a desire for revenge. The prison personnel provided names but the choice of interviewees was ultimately mine. Many believed that Muslims are repressed in France and more generally, in the west, with some inclined towards violent action and others deeming violence inappropriate. Some believed that I was part of the French intelligence agency (the *Renseignements Généraux*, RG) – and therefore, refused to talk about some topics relating to their views on radical Islam.
- Those who explicitly rejected violence and refused to come into contact with those sentenced for terrorist acts, shying away from any ideology that might end up in violence. Their major goal was release, or simply the possibility of living according to their chosen lifestyle. These avoided the complications associated with mingling with 'terrorists' (sometimes referred to as 'the bearded ones' – '*Les Barbus*').

---

[1] This judicial category was created in 1996 by an act of the French parliament and defined as equivalent to an actual terrorist act. It allows provisional detention of suspects.

Women are a tiny minority in prison (with less than 4 per cent in French jails). (There was no female terrorist incarcerated at the time of my inquiry.) I interviewed several female prisoners to ascertain their views on the second and third groups defined above. This was also to understand the female prisoners' connections to the male prisoners falling within the second and third groups. In some cases, relationships were established by male prisoners for the purpose of future marriage, these men being prone to radicalization from my viewpoint. As discussed below, radicalization in prison is finding new ways of building up small, introvert networks of men, largely invisible to the detection strategies set up by the prison authorities. One should bear in mind that in France, for cultural as well as political reasons, studies of radicalization within jails are rare as opposed to other western countries. (French secularism or *laïcité* systematically undervalues the religious dimension of Jihadist radicalization, attributing it to almost exclusively 'social' or 'political' problems, whilst researchers with leftist leanings are, generally speaking, dismissive of 'radicalization' as a valid notion for social sciences.)

Radicalization Theories

The literature on radicalization greatly expanded after the US attacks of September 11, 2001. Radicalization does not only apply to Islamic extremism. It encompasses other phenomena: the neo-Nazi movement, radical anti-abortion activism or so-called 'eco-terrorism'. According to its general definition, radicalization is a process by which an individual or a group adopts a violent form of action as a consequence of extreme political, social or religious ideologies questioning the prevailing social, cultural and political order.[2] The dominant approach towards radicalization consists in distinguishing different steps in its progress (pre-radicalization, self-identification with radical movements, indoctrination as impregnation with extremist doctrines, and direct involvement in violent acts).[3]

Radicalization theories investigate a wide range of social and political factors. There are those which stress as its major causes: psychosocial factors, cultural determinants, international relations, the role of media and the Internet as well as the breakdown of social bonds[4] and political factors.[5] Others stress the intent and purpose of small groups and their representation of reality, in which organizational dynamics play a significant role.[6] In particular, with respect to radicalization among Muslims, network theories feature prominently in empirical studies.[7] Among them, one can single out those insisting on the fact that networks diminish the role of personalities, giving birth to 'leaderless' radical

---

[2] See Randy Borum, 'Radicalization into Violent Extremism I: A Review of Social Science Theories', *Journal of Strategic Security*, 4:4. (2011), pp. 7–35. Alexandre Wilner and Claire-Jehanne Dubouloz, 'Homegrown Terrorism and Transformative Learning: An Interdisciplinary Approach to Understanding Radicalization', *Global Change, Peace, and Security*, 22:1 (2010), pp. 1–26.
[3] See, 'Radicalization in the West: The Homegrown Threat', The New York Police Department Intelligence Division, 2007, in relation to the Islamic extremist radicalization; Clark McCauley and Sophia Mosalenko, 'Mechanisms of Political Radicalization: Pathways Towards Terrorism', *Terrorism and Political Violence*, 20:3 (2008), pp. 425–433.
[4] See for a summary of radicalization theories, regarding especially Islamic extremism, Farhad Khosrokhavar, *Inside Jihadism* (London and Boulder: Paradigm Publishers, 2009), especially ch. 1 'Explanatory Approaches to Jihadism'.
[5] See Martin Crenshaw, 'Political Explanations', in *Addressing the Causes of Terrorism*, Madrid, The Club of Madrid Series on Democracy and Terrorism, Vol. 1, 2005, pp. 13–18.
[6] See Donatella Della Porta, 'Research Design and Methodological Considerations' in Donatella Della Porta and Claudius Wagemann (ed.) *Patterns of Radicalization in Political Activism: Research Design* (Veto Project Report, Florence: EUI, 2005).
[7] See Marc Sageman, *Understanding Terror Networks* (Philadelphia: University of Pennsylvania Press, 2004); Robert Leiken and Steven Brooke, 'The Quantitative Analysis of Terrorism and Immigration: An Initial Exploration', *Terrorism and Political Violence*, 18:4 (2006) pp. 479–494.

groups.[8] This study puts into question this notion of 'leaderless' Jihad by insisting on the new patterns of radicalization in prison and showing the major role played by charismatic personalities.

Some scholars also propose analytical models in which terrorist radicalization is explained through the interaction between the terrorist elites' decision-making processes, the militants' individual motivations and the organizational process of recruitment and socialization.[9] Others refer to decisive cultural factors within specific contexts marked by globalization. The cultural approach includes the typology of 'cultures of violence' established by some scholars.[10] Yet another variety of radicalization studies stresses the specificity of religious ideologies.[11] One should also mention rational choice theories. From their viewpoint, extremist action is a conscious, calculated decision to adopt such action as the optimal strategy to accomplish certain socio-political goals, particularly when the adversary is by far superior militarily, leaving no chance in terms of winning a classical war.[12] For some scholars, radicalization motives can be group-based, individually motivated or be caused by the interaction of some group members when isolated from others, as a result of the groups' concealment strategies.[13]

Radicalization in Prison

Radicalization in prison has been studied in different societies and countries mostly from above, not by concretely engaging in empirical studies of penitentiaries,[14] radical Islam being the primary target of most recent studies.[15] This article, based on an ongoing two-year project on some major prisons in France (2011–2013) intends to present 'radicalization from below',[16] that is, in the *specific* context of prisons rather than through a

---

[8] See Marc Sageman, *Leaderless Jihad: Terror Networks in the Twenty-first Century* (Philadelphia: University of Pennsylvania Press, 2008).

[9] See Ami Pedahzur who proposes a three-stage model, 'Toward an Analytical Model of Suicide Terrorism – A Comment', *Terrorism and Political Violence*, 16:4 (October/December 2004), pp. 841–844.

[10] See Mark Juergensmeyer, *Terror in the Mind of God: The Global Rise of Religious Violence* (Berkeley and London, University of California Press, 2003).

[11] Rick Coolsaet finds that within immigrant Muslim communities in Europe rigid interpretations of Islam (mainly by the organizations like Tabligh and Salafists) gives a clue to their sympathy for radical interpretations of Islam. See R. Coolsaet, *Radicalisation and Europe's Counter-terrorism Strategy*, Royal Institute for International Relations (Brussels) and Ghent University, The Transatlantic Dialogue on Terrorism CSIS/Clingendael The Hague, 2005.

[12] See Diego Gambetta (ed.), *Making Sense of Suicide Missions* (Oxford: Oxford University Press, 2005).

[13] See Clark McCauley and Sofia Mosalenko, *Friction: How Radicalization Happens to Them and Us* (Oxford: Oxford University Press, 2009). The authors define pathways of radicalization in relation to the personal grievances, group grievance and what they call the 'slippery slope', namely the gradual radicalization through activities restricting the individual's social relations, and factors as love, heroism through high risk, conferring a high status on those who are reckless.

[14] See *Prisons and Terrorism, Radicalisation and De-radicalisation in 15 Countries*, The International Centre for the Study of Radicalisation, 19 August 2010, http://icsr.info/2010/08/prisons-and-terrorism-radicalisation-and-de-radicalisation-in-15-countries/.

[15] See Jean-Luc Marret, *Radicalisations et recrutements de l'islam radical dans l'Union européenne: L'exemple des prison*, Fondation pour la Recherche Stratégique, 14 January 2006, http://www.frstrategie.org/barreFRS/publications/notes/20060114.pdf. James Brandon, 'The Danger of Prison Radicalization in the West', *CTC Sentinel*, 2:12 (December 2009), pp.1–4.

[16] In my earlier writings I tried to understand radicalization from below in the sense of personal, individual indoctrination in economically secluded areas (France's poor suburbs) or through identity problems in hyper-secular European societies. See Farhad Khosrokhavar, *L'islam en prison* (Paris: Editions Balland, 2004); *Quand Al Qaeda parle: Témoignage derrière les barreaux* (Paris: Editions Grasset, 2005). In this article, 'radicalization from below' refers to radicalization within the specific context of prisons.

macro-level view of the phenomenon.[17] It differs also from those studies based on the biography of individual cases focusing on their prison trajectory,[18] on the influence of terrorists in jail,[19] or on the ways prisons deal with radicals through different types of imprisonment (total segregation, partial segregation and dispersal).[20] I am more inclined towards mobilization theories of radicalization, rather than of social movements. The study of the subjectivity of those involved, their intention, their aims, and their social interactions are at the core of this perspective with a phenomenological bent.

From a historical perspective, it is worth remembering that violent radicalization first occurred in Europe in the 1970s motivated by a leftist ideology among middle-class people, mainly in Italy (*Brigate Rosse*), France (*Action Directe*) and Germany (*Fraktion Rote Armee*). By contrast, in the 1990s, the main source of radicalization was Islamic extremism. This continued more than a decade and the phenomenon has been mutating, with signs of progressive decline, at least as a phenomenon attracting large numbers of people (not only in the west, but also in parts of the Muslim world, touched by the Arab Spring). In other words, the global process of change within radicalized groups tends to make Jihadism even more of a marginal phenomenon in the west than it has been over the two last decades.

Nowadays in the west, radicalization occurs in prison on a small scale. The notion of small group mobilization, in particular since the September 11, 2001 terrorist attacks, seems more appropriate than the reference to large-scale social movement theories. For clarity's sake, I propose using the notions of 'radicalizer' for the individual playing the active role, through charisma or a capacity for manipulation, and 'radicalized' for another, who, influenced by the former, becomes his disciple. This type of cell encompasses two, rarely three or even more rarely, four people. When the groups extend beyond a couple of people, the penitentiary authorities notice and dismantle them by sending their members to different sections of the prison or transferring them to other prisons. The 'micro-networks' therefore find salience in incarceration, in contrast to the meso- or macro-groups outside prison.

From this perspective it becomes clear how deep frustrations among prisoners in France bringing about radicalization are caused by international politics, a radical version of Islam as the 'religion of the oppressed', the rigid application of *laïcité* in some prisons, the overcrowding, and the lack of acceptable means for inmates to practice their religion.[21] From the end of the twentieth century onwards the neutralization by authorities of large radical networks forming in prison induced changes within that process, in both prison itself and society at large. The theory of the steps of radicalization mentioned above can be verified among some of the prison inmates: those susceptible to influence through their frustration and feeling of humiliation and are enrolled by 'charismatic' 'radicalizers' in a

---

[17] John Fighel, 'The Radicalization Process in Prisons', International Institute for Counterterrorism, presented at NATO workshop, Eliat, 25 December 2007.

[18] Pascale Combelles Siegel, 'Radical Islam and the French Muslim Prison Population', *Terrorism Monitor*, The Jamestown Foundation, 4:15, 27 July 2006; Peter King, 'The Threat of Muslim Radicalization in US Prisons', 15 June 2011, http://thehill.com/blogs/congress-blog/homeland-security/16.

[19] 'Prison Radicalization and How It Happens: An Analysis into Root Causes of Terrorism', *Noor Huda Ismail*, Jakarta, Opinion, 27 August 2010, www.thejakartapost.com/news/2010/08/27/prison-radica...; Mark S. Hamm, 'Prisoner Radicalization: Assessing the Threat in US Correctional Institutions', *NIJ Journal*, 261, pp. 14–19. National Institute of Justice (Washington, DC) 2008 [the case of Kevin Lamar], http://www.ncjrs.gov/pdffiles1/nij/224085.pdf.

[20] Mark S. Hamm, 'Locking Up Terrorists: Three Models for Controlling Prisoner Radicalization', 2011, www.indstate.edu/.../July%20Cornerston...

[21] For a discussion of the specificities and tensions of French secularism, please see Doyle pp. 265–283 and André and Harris-Hogan pp. 307–319 (both this issue).

dissymmetrical relationship. When it comes to prisons, theories of radicalization have to be adapted to reflect the closed environment. Here the capacity of individuals to organize their activities is limited by the institutional framework, an environment in which there is a high concentration of some ethnic, religious or criminal groups in forced cohabitation circumstances. (In prisons close to the large urban centres in France, the rate of Muslim prisoners is higher than 50 per cent, sometimes reaching 70 per cent).[22] Another difference with the external world is the fact that French prison inmates are legally denied access to the Internet. (They can have a computer, but cannot use it to surf the Web). Some succeed in connecting illegally, but radicalized people sentenced under the judicial heading of 'criminal conspiracy in preparation of a terrorist act' are closely watched by authorities and cannot do so for any length of time. (For a short time they might, with the assistance of accomplices, but this is risky for them, and can lead to more restrictions being imposed on them or even transfer to another prison). Internet-based radicalization is therefore unlikely, if not impossible.

The radicalization process in prison puts particularly into question 'rational choice theory', at least on the side of the 'radicalized': more and more, psychologically fragile people take refuge in radicalization. This goes against the dominant view that most radical people are 'normal' and act from their own rational perspective.[23] The view of the 'normalcy' of radicalized people was correct in the case of Al Qaeda-type networks, in which the search for efficiency excluded individuals with mental issues. In the new paradigm, charismatic leaders (the 'radicalizers' in our idiom) look specifically for mentally fragile people with whom they establish a strong emotional relationship (the 'duo' in our jargon) and sometimes succeed in changing their mindset. Less often, this relationship is between a strong psychopath (the radicalizer) and a submissive, normal radicalized person.

Currently, the radicalization process in prison is mainly based on the capacity for concealment of some strongly motivated individuals who communicate with a single person – or more rarely two persons – often mentally disturbed or showing some psychological deficiencies. Radicalization (particularly of the Jihadist type) occurs in confrontation with jail authorities, the confrontation coloured by a perception encouraged by the TV news prisoners watch of the specific predicament of Muslims globally. Prisoners are keen TV spectators. They access a wide variety of channels for eight euros a month – much cheaper than a few years ago, making television an indispensable ingredient of prison leisure time. As will be shown, the rules of the prison, especially in regards to Islam, make radicalization probable during jail times, due to the frustration that is heightened by the ban on the expression of Islamic identity enforced in French prisons in keeping with *laïcité*, a ban not to be found elsewhere. Still, frustration cannot motivate Jihadist radicalization – not unless it is transcribed ideologically, by the prisoner, into an Islamist idiom. The 'ideologization of frustration' is an additional step that has to be taken in order for the frustration to become the keystone of radicalization.

Radicalization is also caused by the conditions prevailing in prison, its organization and specific architecture.[24] Since prison is a place where people are compelled to live together, the conditions within, the way relations are established with the outside (through the visiting room where family and friends come), the relationship between

---

[22]See Khosrokhavar, *L'islam en prison*.

[23]The literature on Islamic radicals is replete with the observation about the 'normalcy' of the overwhelming majority of Islamic radicals. See the works of Diego Gambetta, Marc Sageman, and Robert Leiken, among others.

[24]Due to space constraints, this paper cannot deal with those features promoting or furthering radicalization to do with the specific architecture of the prison.

different sections of the prison (how hermetically closed they are from one another) and the way prisoners can socialize (the degree of freedom they have to move from one cell to another on the same level) are important for an understanding of the radicalization process. In other words, radicalization, when it occurs in prison changes in scale and nature, general theories of radicalization only being partially apt to account for its specificity when the spatial circumstances of involuntary confinement are not taken into account. The number of radicalized people is of a different magnitude outside prison. Escaping close observation, larger numbers of individuals can build up networks that can be regarded as meso- or even macro-groups. In prison, at least since 2005, one can speak of micro-networks being prevalent in French prisons, to the exclusion of macro- or even meso-networks.

The Question of Frustration

Frustration alone does not result in radicalization, but it can lead to it, if given an ideological content. Frustration can be of two different types. One type is endured by prisoners, independently of their faith or creed (e.g., restrictions on bathing in some French prisons where cells have no showers); the second type is directly related to one's faith or ethnicity and is much more easily likely to result in radicalization, because it affects core sacred feelings. Within the first type of frustration, those related to overcrowding stand out, in particular when it forces inmates to share a cell (most often only nine square metres) with one, two, or sometimes three other inmates. With multiple inmates, it is difficult for everyone to stand up at the same time, one or two having to lie down on the bed to leave space for the others.

Frustration can also be engendered by the prison guards' inability to satisfy needs, since they often ignore the legitimate demands of prisoners because of their heavy workload (this stemming from prison overcrowding). Sports practice is often requested by prisoners. But in overcrowded prisons, the opportunities for it are rare. Inmate access to facilities is not only contingent upon a formal waiting-list process, it also depends on the goodwill of the guards who in exchange expect the prisoners to be cooperative. Another point of frustration is access to showering. In those prisons devoid of individual in-cell bathing facilities, and also overcrowded, showering can become a problem. In Fresnes, for instance, prisoners have the right to take a shower three times a week. Many, however, seek the opportunity daily and put pressure on the guards through their requests to be given access to the bathing facilities.

Frustration related to Islam can be ideologized more easily. One contributing factor is the paucity of Islamic ministers. Because of it Muslim prisoners are constantly reminded that they cannot perform their religious duties (first and foremost, the collective Friday prayer). Since Christians and Jews have no such problem, and can perform their rituals respectively on Sunday and Saturday, Muslim inmates argue that their predicament is due to the authorities' contempt for Muslims. Around half of prison inmates in France are Muslims;[25] the lack of Muslim ministers in many prisons makes individual visits and more generally pastoral care of prisoners almost impossible, not to mention the observance of Friday collective

---

[25]There are in France no official statistics of Muslims in prison because it is illegal to officially register someone's religion. As my own research and other estimates (like Jean-Marie Delarue, 'Islam en Prison', *Journal officiel*, 17 April 2012) have shown, around half of some 64,787 prisoners in France (www.justice.gouv.fr/prison-et-reinsertion-10036/les-chiffres-clefs-10041/) are Muslims (not necessarily practising Muslims, but those who consider themselves as such) (see 'Les chiffres clés de l'administration pénitentiaire', January 2012). According to Delarue, those who fast during the month of Ramadan are around 40 per cent of the prisoners. Many Muslims in prison do not state their dietary preferences or even take the meals provided by the jail because they cook for themselves.

prayers.[26] Lacking individual or group access to Muslim chaplains in many prisons, disgruntled Muslims may become easy prey for the radicals in jail exercising influence through their own religious views.[27]

Because of the large proportion of Muslims and lack of Imams, the rejection of Allah's religion by prison authorities appears systematic. Prisoners complain that this rejection ('Islamophobia' as it is described by those who read the media) can also be observed in many other respects, for instance through prayer rugs being prohibited in many prisons. Hardcopy books are banned as well (one can hide forbidden items in the cover) and are torn apart by the authorities to see what is inside them. This is denounced by those prisoners whose Korans had their covers torn for this reason. Less frequently, non-religious causes of frustration can acquire a religious connotation. For instance, some prisoners don't want to be in the same cell as non-Muslims due to their daily prayers (the earliest one begins before dawn and can wake up the other cellmates) but the lack of space means that they sometimes have to endure being with non-religious prisoners – these complaining about the former's religious habits disrupting their sleep or their attitude regarding what is licit or illicit. (For instance eating or touching pork is impure for orthodox Muslims.) Usually, as a solution, prison authorities move prisoners with deep incompatibilities and match them with those sharing the same religion, especially when it comes to short-term detention facilities The fact that prison authorities do not from the start try and match Muslim prisoners with fellow Muslims is perceived by fundamentalist Salafis of being a sign of disrespect for their religious creed. In their eyes, this constitutes 'Islam bashing' on the part of the authorities. But the Salafis are puritanical and they also sometimes upset other Muslims, who find them too intolerant. Another religiously related frustration concerns the holy month of Ramadan and fasting. In the last few years, prisons have started taking this situation into account. They provide Muslims with a small bag containing dates, a bottle of orange juice and milk in addition to the normal dinner. (Lunch is skipped.)

There remains the problem of *halal* food, as there is no systematic policy on this question. Some French prisons make available a range of *halal* food including chicken, sausages and minced meat for private purchase in a kind of shop or *cantine*. In a few prisons this facility exclusively sells kosher meat. Some Muslims find this acceptable, others object to it and are upset by the fact that whilst kosher food is provided for so few Jews, there is no *halal* food for so many Muslims. Even when *halal* meat is provided by the *cantine*, some Muslims find fault with it, believing the *halal* food provided in jails not to be genuine. To support their claim, they mention some TV reports that cast doubts over the Islamic credentials of chicken slaughter. Due to French *laïcité*, even when *halal* food is available, it can only be on a private basis, the prisoners having to buy it rather than it being served as part of their daily meals.

All in all, the food issue has been somewhat ameliorated in the last few years and Muslims in prison are less concerned about it than before,[28] but the issues associated with Ramadan are still far from being resolved everywhere. Discrimination towards Muslims has actually been officially recognized in a report on prisons in France.[29]

---

[26] In 2012 there were 655 Catholic, 70 Jewish and only 151 Muslim chaplains in French prisons (see 'Les chiffres clés de l'administration pénitentiaire au 1er janvier 2012', Direction de l'administration pénitentiaire, at the website given in note 25 above). Since the number of Muslims is most probably at least as high as that of Catholics, the disproportion is blatant: less than one Muslim for four Catholic ministers.

[27] See James Beckford, Danièle Joly and Farhad Khosrokhavar, *Muslims in Prison: Challenge and Change in Britain and France* (London: Palgrave Macmillan, 2006).

[28] In my inquiry into the conditions of Muslims in French prisons between the years 2000 and 2003, I found that in many prisons halal food was simply not available, even at the private '*cantine*'. See my *Islam en prison*, op. cit.

[29] See Delarue, 'Islam en Prison'.

On the whole, long-term prisons (*Maisons centrales*) are more congenial to the prisoners' religious needs than the short-term ones (*Maisons d'arrêt*), where overcrowding and the paucity of Muslim chaplains prevent their specific needs from being recognized. In prison, radical Islamists take advantage of these religious frustrations to accuse authorities of Islamophobia and also to sensitize fellow Muslims to their radical interpretation of Islam.

Organizational Causes of Radicalization: Overcrowding, Understaffing, High Staff and Inmate Turnover

Radicalization in prison can be caused or furthered by organizational factors. Lack of supervision combined with deep frustrations (for instance, a lack of minimal religious provisions) promotes radicalization. Three major items can be singled out: overcrowding, understaffing and high turnover of both staff and prisoners. On July 2012, there were 67,373 prisoners in France and 57,408 available places. Since the long-term prisons are usually not overcrowded, it is the short-term prisons that suffer most from overcrowding. The rate of overpopulation is around 140 per cent, 63 per cent of these prisons suffering from overcrowding and 7 per cent among them reaching an overpopulation of around 200 per cent. (The overall rate is 114 per cent compared with a European mean of 102 per cent on 1 December 2012.)[30] Among the inmates, 86.4 per cent were sentenced for misdemeanour (*peine correctionnelle*) in 2011, 13.6 per cent for felony (*peine criminelle*), which means that an absolute majority of prisoners find themselves in overcrowded short-term prisons. According to official numbers, in 2011 the number of suicides in jail was 116, out of 1932 attempts (against 109 in 2010, out of 2246 attempts).[31] The suicide attempts were thus around three per day, one out of nine being successful – that is, around one every three days. In short-term prisons, there are between 90 and 120 prisoners for each prison guard attending the prisoners, against some 20 to 40 in the long-term prisons. This means that the short-term jails are not only overcrowded, but also chronically understaffed. The guards not only have a duty to supervise inmates and impose restrictions; they must also lend an attentive ear to their complaints (although guards are not legally entitled to it). Some guards perform this 'compassionate' part of their daily tasks despite their heavy workload. They ease the situation for prisoners and humanize the repressive norms that govern their relationship to the penitentiary institution. Overburdened, guards become insensitive to the suffering of the inmates and this, in turn, saps their own feeling of humanity. During the interviews, many voiced the same complaints: their inability to listen to the prisoners and the necessity for them to develop a 'harsh' attitude in order to disregard their own wish to help fragile prisoners.

For the prisoners, this means a denial of their dignity, sometimes at the most elementary levels. For the guards, this means dealing with sometimes explosive situations in which they are just as much victims as the prisoners, albeit in a different way. The rate of suicide among the prison wardens is 31 per cent higher than the overall French.[32] In response to the question asking what was most painful for them in their work in short-term prisons, more than two-thirds of the 31 guards interviewed invariably mentioned insult and disrespect on the part of prisoners (most originating from poor suburbs, where hostile attitudes to the French state have become rife). These factors were put ahead of other problems, like poor salaries and being far from home (more than half of the guards in Paris suburbs

---

[30]See http://prisons.free.fr/.
[31]See 'Les chiffres clés de l'administration pénitentiaire au 1er janvier 2012', op. cit.
[32]See Enquête INSERM sur la période 2005-2010.

are from the overseas departments and territories, and thus live thousands of kilometres from home). In other words, the dire conditions of prisoners have direct repercussions on the state of mind of guards, who have to work under constant stress. Overcrowding has direct consequences for radicalization. Firstly, in cells with two (and up to three and rarely, even four) prisoners, relationships are difficult to observe if they are skilfully hidden. In short-term prisons where there is one guard for over 100 prisoners, the interaction with prisoners is at best superficial, at worst marred by constant tension and mutual distrust. Overcrowding combined with understaffing makes small groups with no external peculiar characteristics (such as long beards or the wearing of *djellabas* in their cells) almost undetectable. In long-term prisons, where one guard supervises around 30 prisoners who can be observed much more closely, the relationships between inmates and guards, based on mutual avoidance of tension, makes radicalization less likely, at least as a result of the prison's organizational shortcomings.

In overcrowded prisons tension is not temporary, but almost constant. The guards describe this by saying that their relationships with most inmates are shaped by an exhausting tug of war. In the confrontation that develops between the prisoner and the institution, the guards play the role of communication channel. In Fresnes and Fleury-Merogis, wardens are occupied with thankless and unattractive tasks that induce tension with the prisoners, not by accident, but almost through a harsh necessity. Radicalization is one of the undesirable consequences of this predicament. One example illustrates this scenario. In Fresnes, depending on the section (there are three major sections, each with some 800 prisoners), Tuesday, Wednesday or Thursday from 10 to 11 o'clock is devoted to Muslim worship. The Muslim chaplain gathers the voluntary prisoners in a sinister room below the ground floor, to hold a discussion on topics of concern to them (how to perform the daily prayers, what is religiously licit and illicit during Ramadan, how to make the ablutions, how to perform the pilgrimage or what to do if one misses a day of fasting, and so on). The prisoners are supposed to register their names the week before, so as to be called by the guards a quarter of an hour before the meeting. An average of 30 people register for this religious gathering, but as a rule, no more than a dozen actually attend it on the day. When asked about this discrepancy, most prisoners express the belief that the guards intentionally avoid calling them, through laziness (it requires more work), out of malice or ill-will towards those prisoners they resent because of some misbehaviour, or simply out of neglect. When asked about it, the guards claim that many prisoners register but when the day of the religious meeting comes, some prefer to rest, engage in other occupations, or are unwell; this explains why prisoners do not answer when called half an hour before. They are supposed to be led from different floors towards the waiting room (there are four, including the ground floor) and from there, collectively guided to the prayer room. I attended some of these sessions for a year. The worship always began 15 or 20 minutes past schedule. Instead of one hour with some 30 people, the meeting generally began belatedly, around 10.20 am, with 10 or 12 prisoners. The Muslim minister grumbled about the guards' attitude, prisoners accused the administration of wilful neglect, and the guards felt unjustly targeted by the latter.

Some of the harshest remarks uttered about prison were probably heard during these meetings (and also about collective showers, the guards refusing to let prisoners shower more than the legally required three times a week). At the end of the religious meeting, prisoners have to wait, usually for 10 to 30 minutes, before being accompanied by the guards back towards their cells. The latter work under strained conditions, with prisoners who sometimes scorn them for their belatedness. They respond that they have to accompany other prisoners – to the sports facilities, to the clinic, to the library, some to their lawyers or other destinations like the SPIP (Penitentiary Service of Probation and Insertion). Against this background of tension some wardens react by making life even more miserable for the most aggressive prisoners by not acceding to their demands for a supplementary shower, or by refusing to hand over some sort of product (tea, coffee, cigarettes and so on) from one cell to the other (it is legally forbidden, but largely tolerated, and guards usually render this service to the 'kind' prisoners). This type of 'civility request' by prisoners is more important than normally accounted for, and serves to appease the prisoners and to humanize their relations with the guards who assume a serving rather than simply a coercive role.

Overcrowding, combined with understaffed services and the dire paucity of Muslim ministers provides a favourable psychological ground for radicalization, the more so as prisoners compare their situation with that of Jews and Christians, who usually are provided with better religious services (if only because of the higher number of Chaplains, and the lower number of their coreligionists). (In Fresnes, there are only two Muslim chaplains, one of them suffering from ill-health, whereas Christian prisoners have access to more than a dozen.)[33] Another cause of dysfunction in large short-term prisons, especially in the large prisons in the Parisian region, is the high turnover of staff. Due to the difficult conditions, which cause exhaustion, guards jump at the first opportunity to move to other prisons in regional areas, where they can enjoy a higher quality of life and much less hectic working conditions. In order to be able to observe the radicalization process among prisoners with a minimum of efficiency, the personnel should be familiar with the prison and its inmates for some time. The high personnel turnover makes this goal more difficult to achieve. In Fresnes, the young graduates of the school for wardens are hastily supervised by more experienced guards (for two weeks). There is a 'prison shock' for them as much as for the prisoners in their first week of detention who are given special supervision so as to prevent them from committing suicide or other desperate acts. The interviews with the young guards revealed their difficulties in coping with stressful situations in front of prisoners, who are only too aware of their fragility as novice trainees (French guards have to work for one year with an unstable status before acquiring the status of civil servants) and sometimes take advantage of the situation. Guards become either too 'soft' or too 'rigid', before adjusting after many months to the inmates and the prison hierarchy. The newcomers are also unable to satisfy in a balanced manner the 'civility requests' of the prisoners. As already mentioned, the latter are not legally provisioned for, but are nevertheless traditionally met by experienced guards, to soothe the prisoners' conditions, to establish confidence building relationships with them and soften the repressive side of the prison. The newcomers are 'clumsy' in this respect. They do too much or not enough for the prisoners, becoming themselves psychologically fragile in front of manipulative prisoners. They frustrate those inmates who ask for minor favours but do not find the appropriate way of relating to the apprentice wardens, unfamiliar with their mores and ways.

Another factor making it less efficient to tackle the radicalization processes in prison is the low number of officers assigned to the task of monitoring this phenomenon. Many prisons are noticeably understaffed in that respect. In some large prisons, they are not only performing the task of monitoring radicalization, but also carry out other duties, which cripples their ability to concentrate on their central task.[34] The Arabic language

---

[33]There are 655 Catholic, 70 Jewish, 151 Muslim, 24 Orthodox, 317 Protestant and 32 other ministers in French prisons. With a rate commensurable with that for other religions, there would be somewhere between four to five times more Muslim chaplains than currently. See 'Les chiffres clés', op. cit.

[34]For obvious reasons, exact figures cannot be provided for intelligence officers in prisons. The fact remains that many on the spot complain about understaffing. In some prisons, although legally able to move from one section to the other, they are restricted in their intelligence gathering by some deputy directors who hold on fiercely to their privileges (for instance by asking the local intelligence gathering officer in their units to submit their findings only to give back to the intelligence officers only the parts deemed deliverable).

plays an important role in the prison radicalization process, particularly among those who strive to radicalize other inmates by showing off their knowledge of the Koran in Arabic in order to impress them. Many officers as well as those who cooperate with them lack knowledge of this language. Seeing Arabic writing or detecting Arabic script on the inmates' computers make them assume the worst and suspect radicalization. In those cases where I was granted access to the documents, what I found was simply ritualistic literature with no radical undertones. A lot of energy is spent on benign texts like the reproduction of some of the numerous Hadith literatures (the sayings of the Prophet), the 99 names of Allah according to tradition, or the preaching of some traditionalist sheikhs speaking of paradise and hell and the torments of the soul among non-pious Muslims. The time wasted is not spent adequately to search for concealed radicals, neglected because of a shortage of manpower. The turnover not only of prison staff but also of prisoners is a matter for concern. In the large short-term prisons, it is very high for prisoners. In the last two decades, more than 200,000 people went through Fleury-Mérogis (the 400,000-prisoner mark was reached in the last quarter of 2012).[35] The turnover makes it difficult to identify those undergoing a process of radicalization, although it makes it more difficult for the already radicalized ones to build up local networks, their transfer to another prison forcing them to begin their network building anew.

Radicalization as a Skewed Trajectory

From the 1990s, with the first Jihadist attacks in France,[36] French authorities developed a plan to monitor prisons, in particular with respect to Islamic radicalism.[37] Up to the present, in each prison an officer has been collecting data, intelligence being centralized nationally through the intelligence services. This started at least a decade before other major western countries adopted the practice. Up to the beginning of the year 2000, the dominant model of radicalization in French prisons (and European prisons more generally) was the 'fundamentalist-radical' model. Consistent with this, many prisoners who showed signs of radicalization were in unison with the fundamentalists: they showed the same attitudes and exhibited similar religious feelings in addition to their Jihadist tenets, based on the holy war against the Infidels. One can summarize these common features:

(1) Growing a beard to distinguish oneself from the shaven people who were supposed to be non-Muslims or 'unfaithful Muslims'.
(2) Taking part in unauthorized collective prayers on Friday in the prison's playground or courtyard, the 'Imam' (prayer leader) being among the fundamentalist–Jihadists rather than the official Islamic chaplain, designated by the prison authorities.
(3) Showing aggressive behaviour towards the guards in an ostentatious manner, so as to encourage other Muslims to act likewise, particularly in matters related to their faith.

---

[35] These numbers were collected during the interviews with the prison staff and not all of them are publicly available.
[36] Jihadists are sometimes called Jihadi Salafists in distinction to the Sheikhi Salafists. The latter are discussed below.
[37] The Algerian FIS (*Front Islamique de Salut*) was outlawed in Algeria in 1992 and was transformed into the GIA (*Groupe Islamique Armé*). In July 1995, Sheikh Abdelbaki Sahraoui was killed in Paris as well as one of his close collaborators in the Myrha Mosque in Paris. The attacks of the Paris underground on 25 July 1995, at the Saint-Michel Station, claimed eight dead and 117 wounded. Since then, up until Mohamed Merah's attacks of March 2012 (he was killed by security forces on 22 March 2012) French security forces had successfully prevented all terrorist attacks in France.

(4) Contesting the legitimacy of the Muslim chaplains in the name of their 'better' knowledge of Islam, denouncing the latter for having 'sold out' to the authorities, for being their 'lackeys' or 'spies'.
(5) Claiming the sartorial characteristics of the so-called Salafis who believe that they dress in the Prophet's likeness: wearing *djellabas* (long dresses), *qamis* (short trousers), using the *siwak* (wooden toothbrush) instead of modern paraphernalia.
(6) In the case of converts, exhibiting an attitude of ultra-orthodoxy, developing an aggressive behaviour towards prison staff and other Muslim prisoners whom they accuse of not being genuine believers, thus publicly marking a break from their past.
(7) Proselytizing, not only towards the 'non-practising' Muslims but also towards other prisoners, in a fashion that made them identifiable by wardens;
(8) Attempting to build up groups of five or six people, sometimes even more, in order to promote their view of Islam in prison ostentatiously, in defiance of authorities. In so doing, they set up groups protecting their members against other prisoners or gangs.
(9) Promoting religious activity in a 'showy' manner during Ramadan and endeavouring to push the other Muslims to follow Ramadan by fasting and more particularly, performing the five daily prayers.
(10) Advocating an 'indoctrination pattern' based on teaching a few prominent topics like Jihad, disbelief (*Kufr*, heresy, miscreance), *Jahiliya* (ignorance, Muslims ignoring their own faith and submitting to rulers governing in contempt of Islamic commandments), idolatry (*taqut*) and political regimes tied to it, different types of commandments relating to Jihad (*fardh ul ayn*, the necessary duty of the individual to take part in Jihad), but also the ritualistic dimensions of faith.
(11) Among the promoters of radical Islam, developing a type of 'charisma' that had to incorporate efficacy. The attraction exercised by the 'leader' could not be exclusively based on pure charisma in the sense of sheer fascination. The leader of the group had to be 'superior' to the other members in terms not only of group dynamics but also of their capacity to deal with problems and propose effective solutions to them.

These characteristics made it easier for the authorities to identify such prisoners and to follow them closely during their stay in prison.

In the traditional model (which still largely prevails in the mind of the prison authorities), the significant factor was the closeness between Islamic radicalism and Islamic fundamentalism, sometimes taken to be identical.[38] This view assumes that Islamic fundamentalism is the anteroom to radicalism and by detecting Islamic fundamentalists, one can identify Islamic radicals. It is true that from the 1980s up to the first half of the first decade of the twenty-first century, radicals looked for religious orthodoxy and often combined fundamentalist views with violent action. Fundamentalism went hand-in-hand with Jihadism, barring few exceptions. One could be a fundamentalist without being a Jihadist, but most Jihadists had a behaviour pattern that was close to fundamentalism in its external outlook. This identification was in accordance with *laïcité*, fundamentalists transgressed norms much more in France than they did in the case of British or American secularism, where tolerance towards 'ostentatious religious signs' is greater. The tracking down of fundamentalists in prison prevented Islamic radicals from acting

---

[38]The definition of Islamic fundamentalism by French authorities (sometimes called *intégrisme musulman*), is mainly based on external signs: long beard, donning of *djellabas*, wearing of short trousers, and for women, of the *hijab*. Statements and all those behaviour patterns putting into question the notion of *laïcité* are taken as signs of fundamentalism. The Salafis (and outside prison, members of the Tablighi Jamaat and sometimes even those who refuse to tightly separate faith as private and public life), are thus characterized as fundamentalists.

in so far as Jihadists brandished the same ritualistic attitudes towards religious practice (daily prayers, fasting in Ramadan, prohibiting the consumption of pork and so on): both groups ostentatiously rejected secular values and subscribed to an ultra-orthodox religious creed.

Radicalization and Prison Activities

The new style of Islamist radicalization is based on introversion and the 'silent expression' of one's religiosity, in contrast to the extrovert, 'talkative' model dominant less than a decade ago. At that time radicals ostensibly showed their faith in fundamentalist prescriptions in order to attract support in prison from a maximum number of people of Muslim faith. This ostentatious characteristic was identified by the authorities as one of the main features allowing them to track Islamic radicals. In today's new strategy, Islamic radicals choose not to display their creed and to act in a covert manner. Nevertheless, the need to find sympathizers and build up concealed groups push them to develop a new type of relationship with other prisoners, less through collective prayers or religious gatherings in prison[39] than in secular activities like sport or apprenticeship classes or else in the daily contact offered by recreation in the prison yard and, of course, in the cells where two to three (and exceptionally, four) inmates live together. During these activities, they surreptitiously establish ties with one or two inmates who they regard as capable of becoming one of 'theirs'. To do so they need to show their radical faith without raising the authorities' suspicions.

They target two different types of prisoners:

- Those who are psychologically fragile and whom they find in sporting facilities (e.g., bodybuilding sessions) or in the professional classes of diverse programmes designed to impart new skills to facilitate socio-economic reinsertion, in collective sporting activities (e.g., football, basketball, volleyball), even during gatherings in prison courts. In the long-term prisons which grant freedom of movement between cells in contrast to the short-term prisons where it is denied, 'radicals' indoctrinate their consenting 'victims' extremely discreetly. In a high-security prison, an Islamic radical thus seduced into adopting a Jihadist interpretation of Islam a young delinquent who was psychologically unstable. He became a staunch follower of this charismatic radical. The authorities became aware of it too late. They chose to transfer the 'radicalizer' to another prison but the 'radicalized' young man remained so. He espoused an extremist ideology that was not his before encountering the other. He became radicalized without any prior knowledge of Islam, the radicalizer having thus achieved multiple aims: converting the person, suffusing him with an extremist view and detaching him from the non-ideological, purely criminal frame of mind that was previously his.
- The second type of individual who can be influenced is one that had some acquaintance with Islam, who finds physical protection and subjective solace by rekindling the religious flame. Here instrumentalization and mental disposition towards faith interact, making attractive the appeal of radical Islam. Prison, a place where one is exposed to mistreatment by other criminals, makes these people designated prey for Islamic radicalism. This involves a strong radicalizer able to protect his 'protégé' and provide him, at the same time, with ideological instruction. Sometimes, those who are sentenced for

---

[39]In some prisons there are no collective Friday prayers; instead, only weekly religious groups under the guidance of the official Muslim chaplain and not necessarily on Fridays.

crimes related to the rape or murder of women and children become Muslims and find protection with a 'radicalizer' or Salafist Muslims (who protect them through a fundamentalist version of Islam that is non-Jihadist, as shown below). Rapists are morally regarded in prison as the worst category. They are put in specific aisles in order to protect them from others who might attack them. Becoming a Muslim automatically provides them with the protection of community members, particularly if they adhere (as they do in a majority of cases) to the Salafist or radical tenet of Islam. In this case, they assume a new identity and the guilty feelings for their past acts disappear. Islamic radicals keep a watch on them, sometimes seducing them into the new religious faith by exercising *da'wa* (a call to adhere to the religion of Allah).

The two cases are different in their nature: in the first, the psychologically deficient individual is exposed to the view of the radicalizer, does not resist him, and becomes more or less manipulated by him, his mental weakness being a trump-card in the former's hands. In the second case, there is something more 'rational' involved, the 'radicalized' receiving the radicalizer's teachings and his protection, if it is needed. The latter has to deploy his knowledge of the Koran and argue with the 'disciple' in order to convince him, at the same time gaining his trust by giving him protection against other prison inmates who might intimidate or mistreat him. Psychological fragility is not a requisite.

The New Paradigm of Radicalization

For a few years now a new awareness has developed among Jihadists about their being targeted by the security forces due to their appearance. Al Qaeda raised its members' attention to this and even boasted that their western members, including converts, were indistinguishable from others; shaven, blond, hiding their religious identity. Abu Mus'ab al Suri, the Jihadist thinker most versed in the social sciences, proposed a new type of Jihadist action, based on decentralized, small, non-hierarchical groups, operating in a totally autonomous manner.[40] In prison, it is most probably not his thoughts that gave birth to small hidden cells, but the experience of repression by the judicial and prison systems. Nevertheless, this mindset had not yet spread widely among those who radicalized in an autonomous manner, within or without the prison up to the beginning of 2000. It was marginal, even among those who belonged to the close circle of Jihadists, for a few years after the 11 September 2001 attacks. In prison, they conspicuously showed their allegiance to the rigorist version of Islam and combined fundamentalism and Jihadism. This allowed the prison authorities to identify them rather easily.

In the last few years, a new line of conduct has developed among radicalized people in prison, which consists in hiding their Jihadist identity.

One can summarize their attitude and the manifestations thereof as follows:

(1) Short beard or a total lack of any beard instead of the bushy beard of the fundamentalist–Jihadists of the past.
(2) The lack of networking of any large group engaging in attempts at building identifiable Jihadist groups. Within the large groups, there were always some 'spies' ('*balance*', snitch, stool pigeon) reporting to the administration. In spite of that, attracting new

---

[40]See Abu Mus'ab al Suri, *Da'wa al muqawama al alamiya* [Call for a Worldwide Islamic Resistance], Minbar al Tawhid wal Jihad, probably around 2002–2003. For a discussion of this aspect of his thought, see my *Inside Jihadism*, op. cit., p. 245, and passim.

members was generally seen as more important than the administration's awareness of their stance. In the new pattern, the refusal to gather in large numbers ostentatiously deprives the prison personnel of any information on the new Jihadists derived from their group visibility. Instead, very small groups (mainly 'duos' or at best, three people, usually in one overcrowded cell in the short term prisons) are being built up that make identification by the authorities much more complicated.

(3) The lack of contact with the Muslim chaplain, the avoidance of collective prayers, in contrast to the former model characterized by illegal collective prayers in the courtyard, which served as a marker of the group and open defiance of authorities.

(4) The introvert attitude, in particular in interaction with others (e.g., concealing one's identity, avoiding proselytizing) as the new marker of radicalized groups. The principle of concealment is paramount and the small group does not look for outside legitimacy from Muslims in prison. It sacrifices the vindication of its righteousness to the safety of a hidden small cell.

(5) The advent of a new type of relationship between one strong personality (the radicalizer) and a weak one, in many cases the mentally disturbed or 'psychologically fragile' prisoners or a psychopathic strong personality and a subservient one looking for protection, or simply in quest of a father figurehead, is another feature of the new paradigm.

(6) The lack of explicit aggressiveness towards guards and attempt at invisibility regarding religion.

(7) The avoidance of any 'markers' during Ramadan, in order to camouflage one's Islamic identity, especially among converts, making their classification as fundamentalist almost impossible for wardens.

(8) The involvement of psychologically fragile inmates in the new groups: this makes possible a new type of cell that we call a 'duo', which has become much more significant than bigger groups, the 'duo' (or more rarely 'trio') formed by the 'self-radicalizer' and the 'rebellious', as explored below.[41]

These features point to a new type of radicalization pattern based on an 'introverted', 'invisible' role model among prison inmates.

The Duo or the Trio

By the 'duo' we mean the close and hidden association between a 'strong' or 'charismatic' personality and a psychologically fragile individual. One can distinguish between two types of duos. The first is the more general one, as we found it in prison, namely a strong, 'normal' personality associated with a psychologically unstable individual under his spell. The second type is made of a psychopath who insidiously captivates a rather subservient but 'normal' person. Illustrating the second type a kind of bogeyman is an inmate who had dominated and terrorized his wife, and sentenced long-term for having tortured a 15-year-old child. In prison he became an Islamist and exerted a strong influence on another prisoner who had not shown any sign of psychological weakness but, nonetheless, had become his disciple. In the first type, a strong personality (the radicalizer) meets a psychologically deficient individual and 'bewitches' him (the radicalized). In the second one, the radicalizer is psychopath-like and the radicalized, a normal but 'meek' personality.[42]

---

[41]The duo, trio, self-radicalized and rebellious are conceptualizations based on my observations in prisons.

[42]In this study we lack adequate psychological concepts to define these two types. It remains that the two types are dissimilar as to the personalities involved. In the first case the radicalizer is 'normal' and the radicalized,

The duo has many 'introverted', 'hidden' characteristics that are in sharp contrast to the extravert models of those 'manifold' groups of the years 2000 to 2005. Within the duo, affective relations are more significant than ideological ones. In contrast to the old model where ideology was on par with charisma, in the new type of duo cell, the strong personality of an ideologically motivated individual prevails over a weak (fragile) personality who does not seek ideological justification so much as a sheer surrender of his 'Self' to the ringleader. Ideology becomes marginal on his side, the charismatic, strong individual having that type of motivation much more than him. The dissymmetrical relationship between the radicalizer and the radicalized is dissimilar to that of the Islamist cells of the late 1990s and the early 2000s. In them, relationships were tightened ideologically, all members sharing the same type of radical mindset and being more or less aware of radical Islamist notions like Jihad, *Kafir* (heretic, disbeliever), *Fitnah* (dissent within the Islamic community) and the like. In the new relationship, these dimensions are less significant than the need for the weak individual (the 'radicalized') to find psychological support in the strong personality of the 'radicalizer'.

The duo can become a trio. The few cases identified point to the fact that the third person seems to be more marginal, or becomes involved in a way that is marked by his attachment to the 'charismatic' leader, reproducing the type of attachment of the 'radicalized'. The 'impersonal', 'leaderless' Jihadist group pointed out by some researchers here is not what shapes the group.[43] In a way, the group is not 'leaderless' but rather, marked by a 'hyper-leadership'. In the former extrovert pattern of radicalization, those who were psychologically fragile were more or less marginalized, even excluded, because they were not regarded as efficient enough. They were perceived as not being trustworthy.[44] In the new model, psychologically fragile individuals are sought after because they can follow through an 'indoctrination' pattern that leaves little room to reasoning and a lot to feelings of dependency and blind trust towards the charismatic 'radicalizer'. The earlier model was by far more 'rational' and 'theologically grounded', whereas in the new model, this dimension changes deeply. It becomes less 'ideological' and more 'feeling-oriented'. There is a change in charisma as well: the 'radicalizer' does not need to be very efficient or capable of performing any type of strong leadership to be fascinating to the single person destined to be enrolled in the radicalization process through close interaction with him.

In all the prisons studied we found duos, many of them unnoticed by the prison authorities. In one long-term prison, where the wardens had the opportunity to observe prison inmates closely, a duo of charismatic radicalizer and psychologically fragile follower was detected, but belatedly. The latter had already fallen under the former's charm. The radicalizer was transferred to another prison, but the radicalized showed signs of radicalization through his utterings and his antagonistic attitude towards prison staff, once their secret story had been uncovered and the person upon whom he was dependant had left the prison. Many duos, according to our observations, were spotted after the radicalized had accomplished his task. In one of the short-term prisons visited, a convert, largely unnoticed due to a lack of external signs, had played the active role of radicalizer, fascinating a fragile Muslim individual, the duo remaining unnoticed.[45]

---

psychologically disturbed. In the second, the radicalizer is psychologically disturbed (a type of 'perverse' psychopath) and the radicalized, 'normal', but rather passive or docile.

[43]See Marc Sageman, *Leaderless Jihad*, op. cit.

[44]One could interpret the case of Zacaria Moussaoui, the French citizen of Moroccan origin, sentenced to life imprisonment in 2006, in this light. He was supposed to be part of the September 11, 2001 attacks against the US but was not perhaps taken seriously enough by the group, in spite of the fact that he was alleged to have been a replacement for the 'first' twentieth hijacker. See for his role in the 9/11 attacks *The 9/11 Commission Report: Final Report of the National Commission on Terrorist Attacks upon the United States* (New York: W.W. Norton and Company, 2004).

[45]Due to our sociological ethics, we did not mention them specifically, by their names, to the authorities.

The Self-radicalizer

Besides the 'duo', the 'lonely self-radicalizer' is also appearing, with no immediate connection to any inmate within the prison but entertaining ties to prisoners in other penitentiaries or people outside the prison like a family member or an association. The latter avoids talking about Jihad, but makes references to the Muslims' dignity being jeopardized by secular governments. In contrast to the duo, the self-radicalizer's connections are not necessarily fragile in psychological terms. This self-radicalizer is largely unknown to prison authorities because he does not express his views publicly in prison. All those markers that might help authorities uncover radical people are ineffective in his case. In many respects, the model of the self-radicalizer corresponds to the profile of Mohammad Merah who, in March 2012, killed seven people and injured five others, in the cities of Toulouse and Montauban.[46] He was in touch with an association, *Forsane alizza*, but during his stay in prison apparently did not develop any network there.

The self-radicalizer is not a lone wolf strictly speaking. He is influenced by a group, but when it comes to perpetrating a terrorist act, he does it alone. In prison, some of the putative self-radicalizers refused to express their feelings but indirectly pointed to the fact that there is no need for a group in order to act, that group action is hampered by the authorities. In other words, the self-radicalizer is indoctrinated by a group in a more or less explicit manner, but he does not envisage acting collectively, his perception of the radical action being highly individualized and based on logic of self-exhibition through media channels. Mohammad Merah's case was admired by some young prisoners who in the interviews expressed their views enigmatically, but did not hide their pride in his 'heroic' actions. Some objected to his killing children, but found it natural for him to declare war on soldiers who fought against Muslims in Afghanistan or elsewhere. There is an 'exhibitionist' dimension to the self-radicalizer that did not exist to the same extent in the Al Qaeda type of extremist, in so far as the group logic prevailed over the individual's Self, whereas in this case, the Ego is paramount and his stay in prison gives him the opportunity to imagine his future actions without being jostled by life in the outside world. Prison becomes the ideal place for the radical attitude to be embodied in a single individual ready to act, once outside the prison's walls.

In short-term prisons, self-radicalizers find favourable conditions since they are lost in the masses and no warden can watch them closely, as discussed above. Some other prisoners do notice them, however (and revealed their existence to us, giving some hints of their radical views). On the whole, they have a hard time hiding their identity, and since they are obsessively focused on their Jihadist vision, they become 'unsocial' in prison, look lonely and forsaken. This introversion is a burden to them, but they have no other choice. Their success in remaining unnoticed depends on their steadfastness to remain aloof, lest some informers detect their radicalism and inform authorities. Still, if they find a soulmate in prison that is not a 'snitch', the small group thus formed might evolve into a duo.

The Rebellious

In prison, one finds individuals regarded by others (be they wardens or prisoners) as in constant revolt against the rules. The prison authorities respond by sending them into solitary confinement (*quartier disciplinaire*, '*mitard*') and denying them benefits of probationary detention. But once these strategies reveal their inadequacy, the only way to preserve the prison's peace is to send them to another prison, with stricter norms and regulations.

---

[46]See André and Harris-Hogan's case study, pp. 307–319 (this issue).

We met prisoners who, in a decade, had been moved to as many as 30 prisons! Some of them develop anti-establishment views that can be transcribed in the jargon of Jihad or other types of extremism, usually, anti-Islamic.

In one case, a prisoner of North African origin who had been to more than 17 prisons described how there was a conspiracy against him and explained that this was down to his not being as meek as others. Lately, he had made inroads into Islamic activism. He attempted to grow a thick beard reminiscent of Islamic fundamentalists or other types of anti-establishment protesters, without much success as other prisoners did not trust him on those issues. In this sense the rebellious are different from the simple fundamentalists who ask that the rules of *laïcité* governing religious behaviour in prison be infringed.

Another type of rebellious inmate was identified: a skinhead with racist feelings who expressed ideas about a presumed Islamic domination of the country, which required violent action in order to prevent French society's Islamization. He had already changed prison many times. In prison, this type of individual is forced to hide his feelings, due to the numerical presence of Muslims. But in some prisons, their numbers seem to grow (in the eastern and south-eastern regions, in Paca in particular). They might, in the future, build up self-assertive groups within prisons. As lonely individuals in prison, some of them are in a state of revolt against the 'Muslims' and society in general. Their proneness to violent action is coterminous with their desire to build a 'supremacist' ideology justifying the use of violence against both Muslims and society at large, deemed 'passive' towards the presumed Muslim threat.[47]

Yet another case was that of a prisoner of North African origin who had been sent to a high-security prison, although originally he had not been sentenced to a long-term prison. Since no short-term prison could cope with him, he was sent to a long-term penitentiary with strict rules. But there too, he was unruly and threatened the 'peace' of the prison. In the meantime, he had developed an ideology close to the Jihadist one and told us, in scarcely covert words, of his intention to take revenge as a Muslim, once outside the walls of the prison.[48]

The rebellious are marked by an internal rage. Many of them are from North African immigrant families. They combine the embittered feeling of being victims of racism with a sense that prisons are reminiscent of the colonial past known by their parents. They refuse prison regulations in the same way they deny legitimacy to a society that exploited their parents and gave them, from their viewpoint, no chance to succeed. They are victimized and inhabited by an embittered sense of helplessness. Their revolt justifies violence against society. Once espousing radical ideologies, they can become relentless Jihadists. Some of them, during the interviews, demonstrated a real propensity towards radicalization through their rejection of society's norms and the way this rejection refers to Islam, a rejection susceptible of promoting radical action.

---

[47] Anders Behring Breivik, the Norwegian terrorist, can be said to have embodied this type of individual. He killed a total of 77 people and maimed 151. He did not spend any time in prison before his crime but some individuals with neo-Nazi credentials in prison show signs of similar readiness to engage in violent action in the name of white supremacy.

[48] Among his declarations during the interview: 'Once out, I'll show them how capable I am! [*de quel bois je me chauffe!*]. Some people like Merah [the French terrorist of Algerian origin who killed seven people and injured six others before being put to death by the security forces] might find me good enough for their company! I could teach them a violent lesson, they are suppressing the Muslims and as some people say, Jihad might be an appropriate response'. I assured him that his name would not be revealed to anyone (I kept the quotes anonymous in keeping with the ethics of scholarly research). His statements might be interpreted as an expression of anger, but they might also be understood as a resolve that might be followed by violent action.

In French prisons, alongside those prisoners of North African background and some white skinheads, the rebellious include Antillais (French Black people from the West Indies). Some of them embrace Islam in prison. This induces a major change in their attitude towards the other French West Indians, be they prisoners or prison guards. They designate them as *fils d'esclaves* (sons of slaves) to distinguish themselves: reborn individuals with Islamic credentials, who have rejected the colonial past and any subjective ties to French society by repudiating Catholicism and embracing Islam, from their viewpoint the religion of the oppressed. One should mention the fact that in the large prisons of the Paris suburbs, Antillais prison guards are sometimes in the majority (up to 60 per cent). They constitute a distinct subculture within the warden body. They sometimes speak Creole (a mixture of French and local African languages) with the prisoners originating from their region (overseas territories that are the residues of French colonization, now part of French society with full French citizenship). Once they embrace Islam, many of the West Indians refuse to talk Creole with the guards and their former sympathy with fellow Western Indians among guards mutates into a scarcely disguised contempt for them. What gives them pride is the anti-colonial, anti-hegemonic dimension of their religiosity. Islam also gives them the opportunity to reject French society, as well as those Blacks from overseas territories who 'cooperate' with the French, namely the guards from the West Indies.[49] The West Indian rebellious individuals espouse radical Islam or radical ideologies that vindicate their revolt against white society. They construct their mindset on their own, without assistance from a large group. In the cases observed, a 'Salafi' or a former Jihadist sometimes taught them the rudiments of religious revolt.

The Advent of the Salafis as a Force Countering Islamist Radicalization

In radicalization, the question of generations is paramount. In the 1980s, thousands of young people from Europe and the Arab world joined the Jihadist movement, went to Afghanistan to fight against the 'godless' Russian invaders (a few thousand from Europe being a fair estimate). Many of them returned home and brought turmoil. Today, their numbers have probably dwindled to a few hundred. The main emerging trend in Europe is the Salafi movement, puritanical, with sectarian features, but not extolling holy war. The neo-sectarian Salafi movement attracts thousands of young people in Europe (especially in France) and the Jihadists, in this sense, can be more and more characterized as dropouts from this movement rather than associated with the building-up of autonomous movements. This new trend attracts many young reborn Muslims or converts and Jihadism is receding as a mass phenomenon. The Salafi phenomenon has a strong capacity to take root in Europe and build up a strong sense of hyper-fundamentalist Islamic identity, close to the Wahabi tenet. In the late 1980s and in the 1990s, the lack of Salafi ideologues and authorities made radicalization by far easier, for want of any established group claiming legitimacy in fundamentalist Islam. Salafism nowadays provides many young Muslims with this identity.[50] It advocates non-violent rupture with society and its depraved mores, not Jihad. It dissociates *da'wa* (the calling to join Allah's religion) from *Jihad*, contrary to the Islamic extremists of a decade ago who closely associated them. One can summarize their characteristics as follows:

---

[49]One finds some examples of this type of radicalized Black people in my book *Quand Al Qaeda parle*, op. cit.
[50]See Samir Amghar, *Le Salafisme aujourd'hui* (Paris: Michalon Publishers, 2011); Patrick Haenni, *L'islam de marché: L'autre révolution conservatrice* (Paris: Seuil Publishers, 2008); Natalie J. Doyle, 'Lessons from France: Popularist Anxiety and Veiled Fears of Islam', *Islam and Christian–Muslim Relations*, 22:4 (2011), pp. 475–489.

- They are mostly sectarian and non-violent, their closure to themselves and their rejection of the 'lukewarm' Muslims making them a 'cultish' circle in prison. They reject the idea of 'non-practising Muslims' (those who do not perform five daily prayers), declaring them 'heretics' (*kuffar*).
- They espouse a strong sartorial and ritualistic identity as already mentioned above, long daily prayers, particularly the supererogatory ones, giving absolute privilege to the reported traditions of the Prophet mentioned by the few major authorized Hadith-compilers (Al-Bukhari and five or six authorized others).
- They have been able to marginalize another trend of fundamentalists in prison, namely the Tablighi, members of Tabliq wal Da'wa, whom they accuse of heretical tendencies.
- They are marked by a flexible attitude and great adaptability to situations: they can be devout Muslims solely dedicated to the ritualistic Islam, they can also be trafficking inmates, working in small groups (a group of five were sometimes followed in this study), selling mobile phones and hashish to others, justifying their illicit commerce by mentioning the country of 'miscreants' (France) where what is illicit in a Muslim country becomes licit.
- They have developed an erudite capacity for the understanding of the *fiqh* (Islamic jurisprudence) and *Sunna* (traditions inspired by the Prophet and attributed to him) that is missing from many other groups. Among the converts to this brand of Islam, a systematic study of Arabic gives them a legitimacy that most of the former Jihadists now in jail lack.
- They have their roots in the poor French suburbs, so young jailed Frenchmen of North African origin can relate them to their own districts and relatives.
- Their puritanical outlook and their sectarian ideology give them an identity in rupture with the hedonistic and secular French people, vindicating their claim to a radical difference from the major trends of French society, which pleases many young people looking for a specific identity in opposition to the strict secular identity dominant in France.

The comparison of the new generation of radicalized Muslims in prison with the former ones, particularly those sentenced for Jihadist action, gives some insight into the changes that have occurred within radical Islam. Among the prisoners who show inclination towards radical religiosity, the new generations are mainly attracted to those who surreptitiously bring them Islamic knowledge. They are much more fascinated by them than by the older generation of Jihadist elders who have committed violent acts and (in consequence) given long-term prison sentences. Even when they do meet them, they do not show any great interest in them. The Jihadists are admired, but mostly not followed by the new generation. Those who really inspire them are mostly the Salafis, belonging to their own generation rather than the Jihadist forefathers in jail, with the exception of the 'duo' (see above). Salafism, in prison, is the most potent obstacle towards radicalization in the sense that it absorbs many young people's need for a new identity in rupture with society and transforms it into a non-violent sectarian attitude. Salafism as such has been institutionalized and even in prison, there are people identifiable as such (long beard and sometimes, short trousers, supposedly akin to the Prophet's dress). They have a real knowledge of fundamentalist Islam through their learning of Islamic jurisprudence and some fluency in Arabic. Among converts, learning Arabic has become a real trend that can absorb long hours each day. During the heyday of radical Islam in France, there was no institutionalization of fundamentalist Islam. Now, even in a country as secular as France and ideologically non-religious through *laïcité*, and in its prisons, one finds institutionalized Salafi indoctrination, to the despair of many secular French people and administrative authorities.

The paradox is that the very same people who are regarded by prison authorities as acting against the major tenet of the French Republic (its *laïcité*) are becoming the bulwarks against radical Islam for the many young people from the poor suburbs now in prison. In that respect, Salafists, nowadays present in every prison close to the large cities, distract many potential Jihadi sympathizers from the violent version of Islam. Their neo-fundamentalist tenet fascinates the new generation more than the destructive creed of the Jihadists, and proposes a solution to the identity problems of the young people of the poor suburbs (the '*beur*' from the so-called '*banlieues*'), mostly of North African origin, overrepresented in French prisons. Since they transgress the tenets of French *laïcité* (they are sectarian, act in community rather than individually, proselytize and publicly brandish their religious identity in defiance of society's secular norms), Salafists are unpalatable to the prison authorities who see them as embodying values that are counter to their own view of citizenship. The guards show their distaste for them and mock them, as do some other prisoners, by referring them as the 'Bearded Ones' (*les Barbus*). Among the Black inmates from the '*DomTom*' who convert to Islam, many become Salafists and are considered as betraying the French West Indian identity in which Christianity plays a major role. Salafists are now omnipresent in the major French prisons, in contrast to a decade ago, when they were barely beginning to surface. They are becoming a major strand of the Muslim population in prison, as in French society at large. They are regarded as a threat by the penitentiary system, yet they represent an alternative to radical Islam that also challenges *laïcité*.

Conclusion

In French prisons, the combination of close scrutiny by authorities of the different obstacles to communication among prisoners set up by the prison system (e.g., by isolating people from one another), makes the development of large networks highly difficult. The model for combating radical Islamic networks in prison was set up in the first half of the 1990s and has since then shown signs of at least partial success. On the other hand, intense frustration due to the lack of facilities for prisoners causes a high level of resentment, in particular in regards to religion. This favours radicalization when combined with a radical ideology (mainly Islamic radicalism but also new types of ideology, namely neo-Nazi, white supremacist, etc, which turn against Islam and promote extremism in a different way).

The scarcity of services caused by prison overpopulation (the lack of adequate sports facilities, showers in some prisons, the restrictions on religious celebrations due to too few Muslim ministers) and the repression of what is perceived by authorities as Islamic fundamentalism have induced an atmosphere of heavy suspicion that pushes a minority of the Muslim population towards radicalization. At the same time, the established policy of supervision has been successful in preventing radical Muslims from building up large and durable networks within prison.

Another factor now curbs the radicalization process in prison: the arrival of the Salafists. They are more or less established, their identity clearly asserted and their capacity to attract young people, undeniable. They also appeal to new converts who find that their version of Islam tallies with their own identity problems, proposing peaceful, sectarian solutions rather than violent perspectives with uncontrollable consequences. Most of these young people ask for alternative ways of life. They do not intend fighting a violent war against the west. A decade or two ago, this group did not exist and Jihadism was in part a reaction to the uprooted situation of many young second and third-generation Muslims of North African origin in France. Today, Salafism proposes an alternative to Jihad and is largely present in the French prisons, in spite of the authorities' disapproval and an effort to limit its influence. This sectarian version of Islam dissuades many young Muslims from being tempted by the Jihadist ideology.

All in all, the last decade's repression of the large networks by French authorities has noticeably reduced the scope for large Jihadist cells in French prisons. A new type of Islamic radical has appeared who acts alone or in very small, introvert groups escaping the authorities' attention. But they are quantitatively less important than the former large groups. With all the required caveats in mind, one can claim that the Jihadist tenet in French prisons is on the wane, the new emerging radicalization process touching a much smaller number of prison inmates than in the late 1990s, with authorities preventing extensive groups from taking root in prison and the Salafists now luring many aspirant Muslims towards a purely puritanical, ultraorthodox version of Islam.

Mohamed Merah: From Petty Criminal to Neojihadist

VIRGINIE ANDRE and SHANDON HARRIS-HOGAN

Global Terrorism Research Centre, Monash University

ABSTRACT   *The 2012 killing of three French soldiers and four Jewish civilians by a 23-year-old petty criminal turned neojihadist simultaneously manifested some of contemporary French society's worst fears, namely the radicalisation of its youth and home-grown terrorism. The attacks were the final step in Mohamed Merah's radicalisation, a process influenced during his family, accelerated during his time in prison and nurtured by divides within French society. This article aims to shed light on his radicalisation by examining the social and familial milieux he grew up in and the impact incarceration had on his identity and beliefs. More broadly, this article will demonstrate how in a country where the ultra-Right's hijacking of the Republican notion of secularity or* laïcité *is leading to an increasingly divided society, neojihadism is providing some Muslim youth with an alternative source of identity.*

During the mid 1990s France experienced a string of deadly bomb attacks perpetrated across the mainland by jihadist militants.[1] These acts of politically motivated violence were carried out by members of the Algerian GIA (Armed Islamic Group), which had only minimal contact with the Islamist community in France.[2] During the period from 1996 until 2012, France was able to prevent any successful neojihadist[3] attacks emerging from within its own community.[4] However, this dramatically changed when, over a period of 10 days in March 2012, a French national of Algerian origin carried out multiple acts of political violence in the name of neojihadist ideology. Mohamed Merah, then aged just twenty-three, shot seven unarmed people in the head at point blank range. His first three victims, killed in two separate incidents four days apart, were French paratroopers of North African descent who had recently returned from Afghanistan. The third attack killed, at a Jewish school, a rabbi, his two young sons and an eight year-old girl. Police eventually tracked the perpetrator back to his apartment via his mother's computer IP address, which was used to respond to an ad posted

---

[1] Alison Pargeter, *The New Frontiers of Jihad: Radical Islam in Europe* (United States: University of Pennsylvania Press, 2008).
[2] Gilles Kepel, *The War for Muslim Minds* (United States: Harvard University Press, 2006), p. 243.
[3] Neojihadism can be defined as 'simultaneously a religious, political, paramilitary and terrorist global movement, a subculture, a counterculture, and an ideology that seeks to establish states governed by laws according to the dictates of selectively literal interpretations of the Qur'an and the traditions of the Prophet Muhammad (normally) through enacting violence'. See P. Lentini, 'Antipodal Terrorists? Accounting for Differences in Australian and "Global" Neojihadists' in Richard Devetak and Christopher Hughes (eds) *The Globalisation of Political Violence: Globalisations Shadow* (Australia; Routledge, 2008), p. 181.
[4] In 2000, French and German police prevented a major Al Qaeda bombing plot at the feet of Strasbourg Cathedral during the popular Strasbourg Christmas market.

by the first victim.[5] In preparation for his capture Merah had turned his apartment into a virtual fortress complete with barricades, stockpiled at least eight guns, including three Colt 45 pistols, a Sten submachine gun and a shotgun (most likely bought illegally on the street) and purchased large amounts of ammunition and ingredients to make petrol bombs.[6] He was eventually killed jumping from a window after a 30-hour stand-off with police.

The March 2012 attacks manifested one of contemporary French society's worst fears: an act of political violence perpetrated by a Muslim youth radicalised at home in those socio-economically disadvantaged suburban areas where the Muslim population has become segregated from the rest of French society. The killing of military personnel in Montauban and Toulouse were initially thought to be the actions of an Extreme Right anti-Muslim activist, akin to the Norwegian Anders Breivik. However, the subsequent shootings of Jewish children in front of their day school revealed a different reality. The murders were the final act in Mohamed Merah's radicalisation, a process, which began during his childhood and accelerated dramatically while he was incarcerated. This article sheds light on Merah's process of radicalisation from petty criminal to neojihadist by examining the social and familial milieux he grew up in, the effect imprisonment had upon his identity and beliefs and how his subsequent adoption of a fundamentalist ideology led him to commit these acts of politically motivated violence. More broadly, this article demonstrates how neojihadism is providing an alternative source of identity to some young Muslims in a divided society. Indeed, Merah's journey into radicalisation is symptomatic of the malaise severely affecting French Muslim youth, a problem exacerbated by the French Ultra Right's hijacking of the Republican notion of *laïcité*.

A Social Familial Milieu of Delinquency, Violence, Racism and Hatred

> In Toulouse, we are all infamously known by the social services and the police. My father, a former drug dealer, did five years of imprisonment; my brothers Kader and Mohamed are thugs, recycled in the most radical Salafism, my sister Souad is a notorious fundamentalist, my mother is a scandalous woman, most of our relatives are delinquents.[7]

This is how Mohamed Merah's eldest brother Abdelghani describes the Merah family.[8] Mohamed Merah himself was born in Toulouse in October 1988 and appears to have had a troubled childhood.[9] Unlike his other siblings who were born in Algeria, Merah was born in 'Izards', a suburb of Toulouse with a predominant gypsy community. His parents divorced when he was around five and his father, who was physically abusive towards his two oldest sons, spent most of his time in Algeria where he was illegally importing French goods. He was also later convicted of dealing drugs in France.[10] At the age of

---

[5]L. Smith-Spark, 'Who was French Gunman Mohammed Merah?', *CNN*, 23 March 2012, http://edition.cnn.com/2012/03/21/world/europe/france-shooting-suspect-profile.
[6]'Mohammed Merah and Abdelkader Merah (Shootings in Toulouse, France)', *The New York Times*, 4 April 2012, http://topics.nytimes.com/top/reference/timestopics/people/m/mohammed_merah/index.html.
[7]Abdelghani Merah, *Mohamed Merah, Mon Frere Ce Terroriste* (Paris: Calmon-Levy, 2012).
[8]It is important to note that Abdelghani Merah broke away from his family after marrying a non-Muslim woman with Jewish ancestry. Though his writing gives valuable insight into the life of Mohamed Merah it must be acknowledged that his views would likely be impacted by this event.
[9]Merah, op. cit.
[10]Ibid.

eight Merah was temporarily placed in care due to neglect by his mother.[11] Merah perceived both his parents' separation and his forced placement in State care as parental abandonment, and he expressed his frustrations through violence and delinquency, which resulted in regular suspensions from school.[12] According to a social services' report, Merah had difficulty 'in school. He was however an intelligent child who had capacities to succeed... He had no structured activities, preferring to spend his time in the company of his neighbourhood friends without any adult supervision'.[13] Merah eventually dropped out of school and began living off the proceeds of petty crime. This lifestyle was encouraged by his mother who celebrated the numerous misconducts committed by her children.[14] Abdelghani recalls how his little brother spent most of his time in the street with his gypsy friends:

> It was the city of the Izards that was taking care of his education. He stayed out without anyone caring for him... Mohamed had the same life as the street children. He could manage on his own and based his way of living on the neighbourhood's young gypsies he frequented with morning to evening. Pilferage and mendicancy became his specialisation... Instead of telling him off, my mother would laugh at his mischief.[15]

Mohamed Merah was arrested for the first time at age 17, as part of a group of youths who stoned a bus.[16] He proceeded to earn another 17 convictions for various misdemeanours over the following few years.[17] In 2007 Merah was imprisoned for the violent theft of an elderly woman's handbag[18] and sentenced to 20 months incarceration with no opportunity for early release.[19] Significantly, it was while in jail that Merah turned to Salafism; his sister noting that he 'rediscovered Islam... having largely ignored his family faith as a young man'.[20]

In part due to his heritage, Merah was exposed to radical ideology from a young age. His upbringing coincided with a dramatic upsurge in violence and Salafist ideology in Algeria, which he was exposed to during annual family vacations to a country on the brink of civil war. Merah's relatives in the village of Oued Bezzaz were supporters of the Islamic Salvation Front (FIS), a group which aimed to establish an Islamic state ruled by sharia law. Most were also sympathisers of the Armed Islamic Group of Algeria (GIA) and some relatives joined the militant organisation.[21] Mohamed's father also began adopting an Islamist discourse around 1992. The Merah children were subsequently exposed to violent images. In

---

[11] J. Lichfield, 'Scooter Terrorist Mohamed Merah "Was Not a Lone Wolf"', *The Independent*, 4 September 2012, http://www.independent.co.uk/news/world/europe/scooter-terrorist-mohamed-merah-was-not-a-lonewolf-8102822.html.
[12] Merah, op. cit.
[13] Ibid.
[14] Ibid.
[15] Ibid., English translation by Virginie Andre.
[16] H. Alexander, 'Toulouse Shootings: The Making of a French Jihadi Killer with a Double Life', *The Telegraph*, 24 March 2012.
[17] O. Moore, 'Mohammed Merah: Petty Criminal, Part-time Jihadist, Polite but a Loner', *The Globe and Mail*, 6 September 2012.
[18] *The New York Times*, op. cit.
[19] Merah, op. cit.
[20] Alexander, op. cit.
[21] Merah, op. cit. In 1991, the FIS won a majority of seats in parliament in the first round of elections. The FIS would have won the absolute majority if the military had not cancelled the second round of elections in January 1992. This led to the radicalisation of the FIS, the subsequent creation of the splinter group GIA and the beginning of the Algerian civil war. See Luis Martinez, *La Guerre Civile en Algérie, 1990–1998* (Paris: Karthala, 1999).

1994, Abdelghani and his younger brother Abdelkader witnessed while visiting their relatives during the Algerian civil war:

> ... Islamic terrorists and security forces taking turns exhibiting the bodies of those they had killed during the night or early in the morning in the village square; one day it was a policeman or a decapitated civilian; the next day it was the body of a terrorist.[22]

In addition to being exposed to the extremist discourse of his father, and daily physical abuse, Mohamed was raised in an 'atmosphere of racism and hatred' where the children were taught that 'Arabs are born to hate the Jews'. For instance, when one of the children asked if they could have a Christmas tree, the father forbade it, noting the concept to be 'contrary to Islam'. He went on to explain that his decision was based on the fact that a 'Jew wanting to kill the Prophet hid himself behind a pine tree'.[23] Additionally, during Merah's early childhood his uncle once explained to him that 'Jews should die to the last'.[24] Exposure to such comments appears to have normalised anti-Semitism to Merah and planted the seeds for his later acts of violence. Moreover, in 2003 Mohamed's brother Abdelkader stabbed the eldest brother Abdelghani seven times after he refused to leave a girlfriend with Jewish ancestry.[25] Abdelghani notes that 'Mohamed was immersed in all this' and later 'the Salafists gathered a bomb already wired to explode'.[26]

It has been noted that normative support provided by families plays a significant role in sustaining violence.[27] Abdelghani blames Mohamed's eventual involvement with neojihadism mostly on the influence of his sister, Souad, and brother, Abdelkader.[28] According to a family friend: 'it was progressive in their family. It was Kader [Abdelkader] who was full on in it [radical Salafism]... He then played the role of the man. He indoctrinated [Souad] in this. It was a spiral... All three were radicalised'.[29] Both Souad and Abdelkader actively proselytised their relatives, friends and acquaintances, including Mohamed. Abdelkader also began to reprimand drug dealers and delinquent friends[30] and Souad began to radicalise their mother, who would soon applaud violent attacks conducted in the name of Islam.[31] As early as 2008 Souad Merah was under surveillance as a 'follower of radical Islam' and in June 2011 she was listed as being 'known for her links' to radical Salafists.[32] Significantly, following the Mumbai attacks,[33] Souad publicly claimed that she would one day commit a suicide bombing in the Toulouse underground taking her children with her.[34] Indeed,

---

[22]Ibid.
[23]Ibid.
[24]Ibid.
[25]J. Lichfield, 'How My Hate-filled Family Spawned Merah the Monster, *the Independent*, 12 November 2012, http://www.independent.co.uk/news/world/europe/how-my-hatefilled-family-spawned-merah-the-monster-8307341.html.
[26]'French Interior Minister Slams Toulouse Gunman Merah's Sister For "Religious And Racial Incitement"', *European Jewish Press*, 13 November 2012, http://www.ejpress.org/article/63125.
[27]M. King, H. Noor and D. M. Taylor, 'Normative Support for Terrorism: The Attitudes and Beliefs of Immediate Relatives of Jema'ah Islamiyah Members', *Studies in Conflict and Terrorism* 34:5 (2011), p. 412.
[28]Lichfield, op. cit.
[29]'Mohamed Merah: Itineraire d'un Terroriste', M6 Television Production, 2012.
[30]M6, op. cit.
[31]Merah, op. cit.
[32]Lichfield, op. cit.
[33]In 2008, militants belonging to Pakistani terrorist organisation Lashkar-e-Taiba staged an attack across the Indian city of Mumbai killing 164 people and injuring over 300.
[34]Merah, op. cit.

rather than attending 'the school of the French Republic' which 'corrupts Muslim children', Souad's children have been educated from home. According to Abdelghani they are taught a curriculum that praises the heroism of Salafists and normalises violence.[35] Souad and Abdelkader also attempted to radicalise Abdelghani's son, exposing him to radical literature and telling him that he should commit a suicide bombing in the Toulouse underground.[36] Mohamed also shared a fascination for the morbid with his sister, an interest which developed significantly following his incarceration. He would attend funerals and slip inside morgues to watch dead bodies. Mohamed noted that, to him, 'death was beautiful'.[37]

Even allowing for the influence of previously held ideas, beliefs and grievances, many individuals initially become involved with radical groups of all ideological persuasions through the influence of personal relationships. A study by the Saudi Ministry of the Interior found that 'nearly two-thirds of those in the sample say they joined Jihad through friends and about a quarter through family'.[38] An additional study of more than 500 Guantanamo Bay detainees further concluded that knowing an al Qaeda member was a significantly better predictor of those who may engage in politically motivated violence than belief in ideology.[39] This necessity of social interaction helps to explain why to date, there is very little evidence of lone-wolf neojihadists.[40] Despite initial reports of Merah acting alone it has subsequently become clear that the most significant early influence upon his radicalisation were in fact his social networks, particularly his family.

Mohamed's brother Abdelkader Merah was identified in a 2008 investigation into a Brussels, Belgium-based neojihadist recruitment network. The network was sending Belgian and French militants to Cairo en route to join militants in Iraq, and may also have connected Europeans to neojihadist groups in the Afghanistan–Pakistan border region.[41] Indeed, Mohamed's family and their contacts appear instrumental in facilitating his travels through South Asia.[42] The period Mohamed spent with his brother in Egypt following his imprisonment appears particularly significant in the development of his international neojihadist connections. Mohamed and Abdelkader were also linked to a militant neojihadist network known as the Toulouse group. The group, led by an imam of Syrian descent, was formed in 2006 with the aim of targeting American interests in France and sending recruits to Iraq.[43] The brothers also arranged for their mother to marry the father of Sabri Essid, a member of the group. Essid was detained in Syria while running an al Qaeda safe house with another Frenchman, which facilitated fighters going to Iraq.[44] Though he was convicted in a French court in 2009 Mohamed remained in contact with him while in prison.[45]

---

[35] Ibid.
[36] Ibid.
[37] Ibid. On active fascination with death and jihadism, please see Farhad Khosrokhavar, *Suicide Bombers: Allah's New Martyrs* (London: Pluto Press, 2005).
[38] S. Atran, 'Who Becomes a Terrorist Today?', *Perspectives on Terrorism*, 2:5 (2008), p. 6.
[39] M. Abrahms, 'What Terrorists Really Want: Terrorist Motives and Counterterrorism Strategy', *International Security*, 32:4 (2008), p. 98.
[40] S. Helfstein, 'Edges of Radicalization: Ideas, Individuals and Networks in Violent Extremism', *Combating Terrorism Centre*, 14 February 2012, http://www.ctc.usma.edu/posts/edges-of-radicalization-ideas-individuals-and-networks-in-violent-extremism.
[41] P. Cruickshank and T. Lister, 'How Did Mohammed Merah Become a Jihadist?', *CNN*, 26 March 2012, http://edition.cnn.com/2012/03/26/world/europe/france-shooting-suspect.
[42] J. Klausen, 'France's Jihadist Shooter was No Lone Wolf', *The Wall Street Journal*, 23 March 2012, http://online.wsj.com/article/SB10001424052702304636404577299550343286104.html.
[43] *The New York Times*, op. cit.
[44] Klausen, op. cit.
[45] P.C. Siegel, 'French Counterterrorism Policy in the Wake of Mohammed Merah's Attack', *CTC Sentinel*, 23 April 2012, http://www.ctc.usma.edu/posts/french-counterterrorism-policy-in-the-wake-of-mohammed-merahs-attack.

After Prison: 'Stealing Was No Longer For The Sake Of Stealing But To Please Allah'

> My young brother was in terrible need of recognition. He wanted to exist. I'm convinced that Sabri Essid and his followers have in their own way succeeded to fill the several weaknesses that existed in Mohamed's personality.[46]

According to his elder brother, Mohamed's radicalisation was significantly accelerated in prison. In a similar situation to his brother Abdelkader, Mohamed came under the influence of radical neojihadists while incarcerated. That Merah's radicalisation significantly accelerated in prison is not surprising, given the hundreds of inmates convicted of offenses proscribed under preventative French terrorism laws. Based on figures collected by Europol, between 2006 and 2010 even though France recorded zero neojihadi terrorist attacks (including failed or attacks), the government arrested 439 individuals for 'Islamist' related activity. During the same period other broadly comparable European countries only detained a fraction of that number. For instance, Belgium arrested only 42 individuals for 'Islamist' related activity and Germany and the Netherlands detained just 35 respectively.[47] Additionally, this large number of inmates are also systematically dispersed across French prisons, meaning they are exposed (albeit to a limited degree) to the general prisoner population.[48] Evidence suggests that those who act as 'radicalisers' among this population do take advantage of the countries 'poorly run and overcrowded prisons' and that such conditions 'not only provide the 'breeding ground' for radicalisation but may represent one of its causes'.[49]

According to Philip Jenkins:[50]

> The prison experience has become a distressing normal expectation of the life of the poor. The result is to foster already strong forces alienating Muslims, and especially the young from mainstream society, and to foster new forms of solidarity. Increasingly too, those exposed to criminal and prison subcultures make those values and expectations a normal component of youth culture and of street society. Invisible cities develop their own laws, their own ethics, their own governments.

It can be argued that while in prison neojihadism provided Mohamed with a support network, a moral code, a new language of resistance and an identity. During his incarceration Merah adopted a new rhetoric and began to grow his hair and beard in the Salafist style.[51] To him the Republic had become a Republic of infidels. According to his elder brother, Merah's delinquent behaviour was given new meaning by the Salafi's in prison. Abdelghani noted that Mohamed no longer saw stealing as a behaviour designed to enrich himself, but perceived the behaviour as a way to 'to please Allah and serve the cause by dispossessing the infidels'.[52] From a distorted religious point of view theft become legal if it served the cause of Allah

---

[46]Merah, op. cit.
[47]European Police Office, 'Europol 2011: EU Terrorism Situation and Trend Report', 2011, https://www.europol.europa.eu/sites/default/files/publications/te-sat2011.pdf, p. 18.
[48]The International Centre for the Study of Radicalisation, *Prisons and Terrorism: Radicalisation and De-radicalisation in 15 Countries* (London: Kings College, 2010), p. 18.
[49]Ibid., p. 30.
[50]Philip Jenkins, *God's Continent: Christianity, Islam, and Europe's Religious Crisis* (New York: Oxford University Press, 2007), p. 155.
[51]Merah, op. cit.
[52]Ibid.

or if it was gained as spoils of war and used to help to fight the infidel.[53] From a petty criminal, Mohamed Merah began transforming into a violent neojihadist.

French sociologist Farhad Khosrokhavar notes that within France, Islam is increasingly becoming 'the religion of the repressed'.[54] Olivier Roy takes this argument a step further contending that: 'Islam has replaced Marxism as the ideology of contestation; when the Left collapsed, the Islamists stepped in'.[55] In fact, it has become the ideology of the dispossessed. Merah is far from being the only individual within France who turned to this ideology of contestation. In 1995, another French Algerian youth, Khaled Kelkal, turned to Islam to express his rejection of French society.[56] Feeling excluded by what he perceived as French society's stigmatisation and racism he joined the GIA.[57] While acknowledging the country's political deficiencies Gilles Kepel notes that the most serious radicalising influence within French society remains the prison system:

> The traditional networks of Corsican gangs and others, which controlled the penitentiary world... is now marginalised and it is the 'emirs' who now impose their authorities on lost individuals. These are individuals who are decultured. They neither have a French culture nor a North African culture; they are in between. They don't know where they live anymore. Salafism is very restrictive. It tells you how to shape your personality, how to dress... something very strong that gives an immediate identity to youths who are outside of any positive system with which they could identify. They will turn into heroism the stigmatisation they feel they are victims of.[58]

Khosrokhavar notes that such 'emirs' not only play a role in spreading ideology in prison but also provoke feelings of admiration among North African youth as they symbolise courage in the fight against western imperialism.[59] He observed that young North African prisoners draw an immediate parallel between their treatment within French society and the Palestinian plight, and therefore associate closely with incarcerated Muslim radicals.[60] Roy contends these men are part of 'a lost generation, unmoored from traditional societies and cultures, frustrated by a Western society that does not meet their expectations'.[61] According to Neumann, for such individuals joining an Islamic group, rather than the gangs that traditionally operate in prison, gives them a unique sense of strength and superiority; this new-found identity in turn makes them even more vociferous in the defiance of the rules and regulations to which they are subject.[62] Given Merah's upbringing and sympathies, it is easy to understand his attraction to the ideology of such radicals while in prison.

---

[53]Ibid.
[54]Farhad Khosrokhavar, *Quand Al Qaeda Parle: Témoignages Derrière Les Barreaux* (Paris: Grasset et Fasquelle, 2006), pp. 52–53.
[55]Cited in C. Smith, 'Europe's Muslims May Be Headed Where the Marxists Went Before', *The New York Times*, 26 December 2004.
[56]For an understanding of Kelkal's pathway within the French Algerian context, see Martin Evans and John Phillips, *Algeria: Anger of the Dispossessed* (New Haven: Yale University Press, 2007).
[57]James Beckford, Daniele Joly and Farhad Khosrokhavar, *Les Musulmans en Prison en Grande Bretagne et en France*, Atelier de Recherche Sociologique (Louvain-la-Neuve: Presses Universitaires de Louvain, 2005), p. 273.
[58]Interview with Gilles Kepel in special television report 'Mohamed Merah: Itineraire d'un Terroriste', M6, 2012.
[59]James Beckford et al., op. cit., p. 175.
[60]Ibid., p. 175.
[61]O. Roy, 'Islamic Terrorist Radicalisation in Europe', in Samir Amghar, Amir Boubekeur and Michael Emerson (eds) *European Islam: Challenges for Public Policy and Society* (Brussels: CEPS, 2007), p. 55.
[62]Peter Neumann, *Joining Al-Qaeda: Jihadist Recruitment in Europe, Adelphi Papers* (London: Routledge, 2008), pp. 26–27.

Merah emerged from prison in 2009 almost fully radicalised, and openly proclaimed his fascination for violent jihad.[63] A friend of the Merah family recalls that 'he didn't say "I" anymore but "us"'. He thought 'the Muslim brothers... would kill everyone, all the militaries of France and then all the Jews and France would become a country, a Muslim state'.[64] Merah began to repeat that 'Muslims would conquer the world' and French military personnel began to be perceived by him as legitimate targets. Each time he heard of a French soldier being killed in Afghanistan, Merah would cheer and cry 'God is with us'.[65] Merah also attended secret religious classes taught in apartments by self-proclaimed ideologues, and regularly consulted with a French Syrian Salafist who had direct ties to Sabri Essid. He also became increasingly interested in public political and social debates, particularly on issues that dealt with Islam and Muslims.[66]

In Search of the 'Real Brothers'

In the year following his release from prison Merah traveled extensively in search of 'the real Muslims and to learn the real Islam'.[67] Neumann notes that once released some radicalised inmates 'will become "seekers" who will try to establish a connection with the movement on their own' or alternatively others may have established links to facilitators who 'may facilitate the integration into the Islamist militant structures after their release'.[68] Merah's contacts to radicals overseas appear to have been facilitated by the Toulouse group, notably through Abdelkader and Essid. After his release Merah spent time with his brother Abdelkader in Egypt, where he was studying at a Koranic school. He also travelled to Turkey, Syria, Lebanon, Jordan, Iraq and even Israel, where he was briefly detained by police.[69] Significantly, in 2010 Merah entered Afghanistan, via Tajikistan. A short time later he was detained at a roadblock in Kandahar and turned over to American forces. After being placed on a US 'no-fly' list Merah was deported back to France. Despite this setback Merah was able to return to Northwest Pakistan in 2011.[70] He told police later that he was trained by al Qaeda in Waziristan during this period, and that the 'brothers in Pakistan' supplied him with funds for his attacks.[71] Indeed, during his final stand Merah boasted that he was acting under instruction from al Qaeda. However, the only posthumous claim of responsibility for the attacks came from central Asian group Jund al Khilafah (JaK).[72]

Although the Amir of JaK, Moez Garsallaoui, was a contact of Merah[73] an attack in France would be a completely new tactic for the group, which has no known track record of attracting Western operatives. Additionally, being predominantly based in the North Caucasus, JaK's presence in the Afghanistan–Pakistan border region is likely to be small. However, it is possible they have become integrated with a larger group like the IMU (the Islamic Movement of Uzbekistan), which has close ties to al Qaeda and

---

[63]Merah, op. cit.
[64]M6, op. cit.
[65]Merah, op. cit.
[66]Ibid.
[67]M6, op. cit.
[68]Neumann, op. cit. p. 26.
[69]Cruickshank and Lister, op. cit.
[70]Klausen, op. cit.
[71]Cruickshank and Lister, op. cit.
[72]Ibid.
[73]J. Zenn, 'Militants Threaten to Return to Central Asia after NATO's Withdrawal from Afghanistan', *Eurasia Daily Monitor*, 10:6, 14 January 2013.

has been implicated in several plots to attack Europe.[74] Merah's attack does also fit with modern al Qaeda strategy. In June 2011, al Qaeda's media production arm released a video urging sympathisers to attack western targets with firearms and *Inspire* magazine has also repeatedly urged such undertakings. A document found on an alleged Austrian al Qaeda operative (believed to be written by a senior al Qaeda figure), recommended that foreign fighters should be trained quickly and sent back to their home countries to enhance the group's ability to target the west regularly.[75] However, whether Merah was acting under directions from al Qaeda or an affiliated group, or simply in the name of the ideology, remains unclear.

It also appears as though his siblings may have known about Mohamed's specific intentions and actively encouraged his behaviour. Souad provided money, mobile phones and Internet addresses to Mohamed in the months before the attacks[76] and noted afterwards that: 'Mohamed had the courage to act. I am proud, proud, proud... Jews, and all those who massacre Muslims, I detest them'.[77] Abdelkader was also with Mohamed when he stole the scooter used in the drive-by shootings and the two men dined together the night before the attack on the Jewish school.[78] Indeed, Abdelkader has been detained since the attacks and is under investigation for complicity in the murders.[79] Notably, police found explosives in Abdelkader's car when he was arrested.[80] The police also detained Zoulikha Aziri, the mother of Mohamed, and Yamina Mesbah, Abdelkader Merah's wife. However, both women were released without being charged.[81] Interestingly, Merah also divorced his wife just prior to the first attack[82] and though he publicly espoused extremist rhetoric he was witnessed at a *raï*[83] nightclub around the time of the first shooting.[84]

In addition to the time spent in the company of radicals at home and overseas there were a number of indicators of Merah's radicalisation immediately prior to the first attack. He spent significant amounts time on the Internet surfing neojihadist websites, and participating in associated forums. In 2010, he also made a short film praising neojihadist ideology.[85] Merah was also known to have extensively sought out and viewed violent jihadist videos online.[86] Watching such material would likely have increased his desensitisation to violence while simultaneously reinforcing his ideological worldview. Several years prior to the attack Merah had forced a young boy from his local neighbourhood to watch beheading videos with him. Upon discovering that the boy's mother had complained to police, Merah travelled to the family's house in full military clothes and proceeded to wave a sword around while chanting 'Al Qaeda! Al Qaeda!'[87] However, towards the end of 2011 Merah became more discreet in his behaviour. After reading the works of Abu Musab al-Suri online, notably the *Global Islamic Resistance Call*, he

---

[74] Cruickshank and Lister, op. cit.
[75] Ibid.
[76] Lichfield, op. cit.
[77] Ibid.
[78] Alexander, op. cit.
[79] Lichfield, op. cit.
[80] D. Gardham, 'British Links to Toulouse Terrorist', *The Telegraph*, 23 March 2012, http://www.telegraph.co.uk/news/worldnews/europe/france/9163544/British-links-to-Toulouse-terrorist.html.
[81] *The New York Times*, op. cit.
[82] *The New York Times*, op. cit.
[83] *Raï* is a type of contemporary Algerian music mixing traditional Arab vocals and popular western music.
[84] Moore, op. cit.
[85] Merah, op. cit.
[86] Smith-Spark, op. cit.
[87] Alexander, op. cit.

began to employ counter-surveillance strategies such as shaving his beard and avoiding Islamic dress.[88] He also became conscious of possible phone surveillance and tried to avoid public spaces where he may have been monitored.[89] Instructions were also found on his brother's portable hard-drive including 'how to dress for the jihad', 'what to do when you're being followed' and 'how to deceive people in order to integrate their community'.[90] This shift in behaviour demonstrates Merah's killings to have been carefully and consciously thought out, planned and executed actions.

Paul Wilkinson noted that 'it is intrinsic to the very activity of terrorism that a form of media, however crude, is utilised as an instrument to disseminate the messages of threat and intimidation'.[91] Mohamed Merah went to significant lengths to gain notoriety and publicity for his attacks. Video footage of the killings, filmed by Mohamed himself, was sent to *Al-Jazeera* on the day before he was killed. The video had been edited and manipulated with religious songs and recitations of Koranic verses laid over the footage.[92] Kepel contends that neojihadists such as Merah who advocate a method not an organisation, act out individually against proximity targets and then post the images on the Internet in an attempt to create emulators.[93] Merah was also an active user of Twitter and YouTube and his last tweets, sent during the siege, were signed 'Mohamed Merah-Forsane Alizza'.[94] Forsane Alizza or 'Knights of Glory' is a radical Salafist group established in France in 2010. It appears to be part of a loosely connected network of European Islamists and according to the group's website its main objective is to support the Mujahideen throughout the world.[95] The group has no formal structure yet counts between 30 and 100 official members and likely many more sympathisers.[96] Both Mohamed and his brother were known to the French DCRI, the domestic intelligence agency, as members of Forsane Alizza.[97] Significantly, the group lists its principal targets as, 'the French military, which is portrayed as destroying Muslim lands as part of a Western conspiracy to destroy Islam' and 'Jews, Jewish institutions, and Israel, which are blamed for the global persecution of Muslims'.[98] Considering the targets chosen by Merah it would appear that the group's ideology had a significant influence on his actions.

Mohamed Merah: A Backlash to *Laïcité*?

> The Salafist's know how to recuperate the youths who are fragile, channel their anger and give a meaning to the lives of a few lost souls like Mohamed, who are in search of adventure and adrenaline.[99]

---

[88]For a discussion on the Abu Musab al-Suri's works and ideology, see B. Lia, *Architect of Global Jihad: The Life of Al-Qaida Strategist Abu Mus?ab al-Suri* (New York: Columbia University Press, 2008).
[89]M6, op. cit.
[90]Ibid.
[91]P. Wilkinson, 'Media and Terrorism: A Reassessment', *Terrorism and Political Violence*, 9:2 (2007), p. 53.
[92]*The New York Times*, op. cit.
[93]Gilles Kepel, *Terreur et Martyre* (Paris: Flammarion, 2008), pp. 189–190.
[94]Klausen, op. cit.
[95]International Institute for Counter-Terrorism, 'Forsane Alizza: Background Brief', http://www.ict.org.il/LinkClick.aspx?fileticket=99fFLwpcQLQ%3D&tabid=320.
[96]P. Neumann et al., 'ICSR Insight: Toulouse Gunman's Link to UK Extremists', *Insights*, 21 March 2012.
[97]Gardham, op. cit.
[98]P. Neumann et al., op. cit.
[99]Merah, op. cit.

While the case of Mohamed Merah clearly demonstrates the impact of social networks and prison on the radicalisation process, the killings in Montauban and Toulouse also expose larger issues which exist within French society. This is clearly illustrated in the question of French *laïcité* and how its hard interpretation is pushing a minority of Muslims towards extremism. In the years prior to Merah's attacks, there was continual public debate around issues such as the *hijab*, the *burqa* and street prayers as well as *laïcité*, contributing to a stigmatisation of Islam and Muslims within French politics and society.[100] Merah was particularly sensitive to this atmosphere, his brother noting that the anti-Muslim discourse of Marine Le Pen and debates regarding street prayers infuriated Merah.[101] Controversial policies regarding the behaviour and dress of Muslims in French society, and the stigmatisation of the community as a whole, likely accelerated Merah's radicalisation and commitment to violent action.

According to French sociologist Jean Baubérot, the historical *laïcité* established by the law of 1905 initiated an emancipation movement, determined to free the state from the dominion of religion and its institution, and to better establish equality, liberty and ultimately religious freedom and freedom of conscience, especially with respect to protestant and Jewish minorities.[102] The consequence of the movement was the expulsion of religion from the political sphere into civil society. However, the concept of French *laïcité*, 'whereby the state expels the religious life beyond a border that the state itself had defined by law', differs from the concept of secularisation where 'a society emancipates itself from a sense of the sacred that it does not necessarily deny'.[103] In other words, *laïcité* should be viewed 'as the common principle of all laws that have regulated the place of religion in the French public sphere since the assertion of the principle of the separation of the church and state'.[104] Religion, consequently, became confined to the private sphere, in ways that did not accord fully with the spirit of the law of 1905, which aimed to increase freedom of conscience, freedom of religion and the possibility of its external expressions in the public sphere.[105] Paradoxically, this resulted in the increased empowering of the state over the individual. Over the last 20 years, an ideological interpretation of *laïcité* has become predominant in France, which sees a shift in the original meaning towards a hard *laïcité*. This interpretation started with the debate around the wearing of *hijab* in schools, which brought to the forefront the question of Islam and its place in French society. Baubérot calls this interpretation of *laïcité* by the political Right and the Front national '*lepenised laïcité*',[106] a concept instrumentalised as a weapon to fight Islamic communitarianism. French sociologist Valentine Zuber notes the increasing multicultural transformation of French society through the influx of non-Christian immigrants who remain attached to their religious rites are in conflict with the customs of the Republic life, and often do not feel at home in the *laïcité*'s radical separation between private and public spheres.[107] As result, Khosrokhavar contends that:

---

[100]See Natalie Doyle, this issue.
[101]Merah, op. cit.
[102]Jean Baubérot, *La Laïcité Falsifiée* (La Découverte: Paris, 2012).
[103]O. Roy, *Laïcité Face a l'Islam* (Paris: Stock, 2005); translation – Georges Holoch, *Secularism Confronts Islam* (New York: Columbia University Press, 2009), p. 13.
[104]Ibid.
[105]Baubérot, op. cit.
[106]Ibid.
[107]V. Zuber, 'La Commission Stasi et Les Paradoxes de la Laïcité Française' in Jean Baubérot (ed.) *La Laïcité a l'Epreuve: Religions et Libertés Dans Le Monde* (Paris: Universalis, 2004).

The refusal of intermediate communities and the will to replicate the hard version of *laïcité* in the world of the twenty-first century, very different to that of the nineteenth, has meant that we are helpless in the face of ultra fundamentalist Islam. Even if it only concerns a few thousand people (with a few tens of thousands of sympathisers), no other version of Islam is able to thwart the attraction that it exerts over the socially excluded.[108]

Ultimately, this contemporary manifestation leaves the socially excluded within French society vulnerable to extremist interpretations of religion, particularly the stigmatised Muslim community.

Recent research has revealed suburbs within French cities where law, and the republican social pact, no longer function as intended.[109] The study determined that within these communities many individuals could no longer find work, did not feel represented politically and blamed a racist and xenophobic French State and society for their situation.[110] Kepel observes that these individuals fall into a communitarian logic whereby individuals shut off from society at large, live among themselves in their own community and their identity becomes centred on religion.[111] Merah was raised in just such a community. In some instances, these closed societies can foster extreme identities and interpretations of religion. Consequently:

> 'Islamisation' in disadvantaged French suburbs operates as much as a religion substituting for non-existent communities, and that is why this process is most widespread in the *banlieues*.[112] By becoming active Muslims, these socially disaffected people are seeking some form of community that could compensate for the lack of any social group capable of giving them a sense of dignity and identity within a society where they count for very little.[113]

In France, there is an Islam of the youth, predicated on a complex generational rupture, a quest for authenticity and affirmation of identity and protestation.[114] Perceived attacks on the religion or identity of the community, such as the recent ideological debate regarding Muslims and *laïcité*, only serves to strengthen the youths' sense of disaffection and radicalise their views. In Merah's case, anti-Muslim attacks in the disguise of *laïcité* certainly reaffirmed his ideology of contestation and led to its violent expression. Roy notes that the hard *laïcité* 'reinforces religious identities rather than allowing them to dissolve in more diversified practices and identities'.[115] As *laïcité* relays the religious to the private sphere, the state has no control over a deterritorialised, decultured and global fundamentalist interpretation of Islam.[116] By reconstructing the division between the public and private spheres, hard

---

[108]F. Khosrokhavar, 'Ce Que La Loi Sur La Burqa Nous Voile', *Le Monde*, 1 August 2009, http://www.lemonde.fr/idees/article/2009/07/31/ce-que-la-loi-sur-la-burqa-nous-voile-par-farhadkhosrokhavar_1224664_3232.html.
[109]Gilles Kepel, *Quatre Vingt Treize* (Paris: Gallimard, 2012). See also Gilles Kepel, *Les Banlieues de l'Islam* (Paris: Seuil, 1991).
[110]Ibid.
[111]Ibid.
[112]The term 'banlieue' refers to the housing complexes built by government on the outskirts of the major cities, in the surburbs.
[113]James Beckford et al., op. cit. p. 116.
[114]Farhad Khosrokhavar, *L'Islam Des Jeunes* (Paris: Flammarion, 1997).
[115]Roy, 'Secularism Confronts Islam', op. cit., p. 99.
[116]Olivier Roy, *L'Islam Mondialisé* (Paris: Seuil, 2004).

laïcité is allowing extremism to flourish among vulnerable youth who find their identity marker in Islam.

The radicalisation of Mohamed Merah is symptomatic of a wider French identity crisis, if not a European crisis of illiberalism.[117] The backlash of hard *laïcité* means that individuals, such as Merah, see the field of their individual religious freedom considerably reduced under the increasing pressure of illiberal French laws (e.g., the laws restricting the wearing of the *hijab* and the *burqa*). This results in individuals identifying with narrow identities and fundamentalist interpretations of religion that supersede the French national identity. Hard *laïcité* perversely encourages communitarian identities that can sustain extremists such as Merah. The difficult challenge now facing France is to realise the changing face of French society, and to promote a genuinely liberal understanding of its neutrality with respect to religious diversity. We can only hope that Merah's murderous path will not serve as a model for French youths looking for ways to express their discontentment with a society they feel in conflict with.[118]

---

[117]See N. Doyle, 'Lessons From France: Popularist Anxiety And Veiled Fears of Islam', *Islam and Christian-Muslim Relations*, 22:4 (2011), pp. 475–489.

[118]One example of this risk was demonstrated during a BBC interview in April 2013. Medecins Sans Frontieres' co-founder Jacques Beres recounts how he met and treated in Syria two young French Muslim brothers who had been injured during the conflict. One of the two brothers told him he had been inspired by Mohamed Merah: 'He told me that the real hero is Mohammed Merah, that he was an example to follow'. Cited in D. Crawford, 'From Belgian School to Syrian Battleground', *BBC*, 24 April 2013, http://www.bbc.co.uk/news/magazine-22277462 (accessed 7 May 2013).

Index

Note: Page numbers in **bold** type refer to figures
Page numbers in *italic* type refer to tables
Page numbers followed by 'n' refer to notes

Aborigine people 83
absolutism 88
accountability 100, 109
Action Directe 120
activism, anti-abortion 118
Adenauer, K. 9
Advani, L.K. 82
Afghanistan 14, 24, 33, 47, 135; and Pakistan border 143, 146
Ahmad, I. 3, 67–84; and Doyle, N. 1–5
Air France 77
Air India 77
Air Italy 77
Akhtar, J.N. 75
Al-Jazeera 148
Al-Qaida 33, 81, 130, 133, 143, 146; media and videos 147; networks 121
Albania 67
Algeria 4, 140; Armed Islamic Group (GIA) 139–41, 145; *Front Islamique de Salut* (FIS) 127n37, 141
Ali, H. 98
Allen, P. 74–5
Alliot-Marie, M. 6, 15–16, 105
Alzayed, I. 90–1
Ameline, N. 17–18
American Journal of Sociology 73
American Public Policy Alliance 62–3
Amir-Moazami, S. 14
Amiraux, V. 16n46
anarcho-syndicalism 108
Andre, V., and Harris-Hogan, S. 4–5, 139–51
anti-abortion activism 118
anti-Semitism 71, 142
Arab Spring 120
Arabization, of Europe 57
Arafat, Y. 57
Arendt, H. 70, 80
Asad, T. 106, 115
At Home in India (Khurshid) 82
atom bomb threat 80

Auge, M. 79
austerity measures 101
Australia 70–1, 83; swimming pool dress code 78
Australian Journal of Political Science 73
Austria 10, 73
autonomy 8, 110
Aziri, Z. 147

Badinter, E. 18
Bahners, P. 9–10
Balkans 28
Banks, M., and Gingrich, A. 41–4, 51, 102
Barth, K. 71
Baubérot, J. 14, 22, 25
Bayly, C. 81
Behrendt, L. 75
Belgium 3, 6–25, 144; civil servants 19–20; *Conseil d'État* 22; headscarf debates and legislation 9, 19–25; House of Representatives 19; religious neutrality 19; Senate 21; social cohesion goal 21; *Vlaams Belang* party 19–20, 23–4
Belien, P. 61
Benedict XVI, Pope 112
Benveniste, E. 76
Berghahn, S., *et al.* 9
Berlin, Turks in 68–70, 84
Berlingske Tidende 56, 63
Bernhardt, R. 38
Besant, Dr A. 74
Bin Laden, O. 80–1
blame avoidance 100
blogs, anti-Islamic 61–3
Blum, R., and Prinzig, M. 34
Both, H. 32
Bougarel, X. 78
Bowen, J. 14, 71
Bramadat, P. 7–8, 23
Breivik, Anders Behring 72, 84, 97, 134n47, 140
Brigate Rosse 120

INDEX

Brim, C. 62
British Airways (BA) 77
British Broadcasting Company (BBC), Radio 4/ Home Program 74
British Journal of Sociology 73
British National Party (BNP) 50
Brix, E. 38
Brix, H. 58, 61–3; and Hansen, T. 57
Brod, M. 84
Brown, W. 108, 113
Bruce, S. 80
Buffet, F.-N. 16n50
Bulgaria 112
Bultmann, R. 54
Bunzl, M. 71–3
burqa 10, 16n47, 17–23, 34, 105, 149; ban 14; or Republic 15
Busse, D. 12

Calvinism 88
Cameron, D. 102
caritas 87
Catherine the Great, Queen of Russia 81
Catholicism 3, 19, 24, 68; 105–7, 135; empowered forces 112; Swiss churches 28, 36, 40
Cato Institute 62
Center for American Progress (CAP) 42, 62–3
Center for Security Policy (CSP) 61–2, 65; *Shariah: The Threat to America* 62
Central Intelligence Agency (CIA) 61
Cesari, J. 78
chador 10
Chirac, J. 89
Christian Democratic Union (CDU) 12, 23–4
Christian Social Union (CSU) 12, 23–4
Christianity 2–9, 31–2, 43, 53–4, 97, 112; and cross 90, 95; heritage 95; and Occidental values 9, 13, 17
Citizens' Initiative (Switzerland) 26–40; argument analysis and reactions 30–3; background and motivation 29–30; consequences and counter-policy prospects 37–9; issues and responses 34–7; post-vote 33–4; values comparison (Swiss/Islamic) 32; vote 30
citizenship 23, 107
civilization 110–13
Clinton, W. (Bill) 61
co-immunity 111
Cold War 73, 81
colonialism 72, 75, 83–4
Committee against the Refugee Law 54
Committee on the Present Danger 61, 65
communitarianism 15, 92, 149; anti-Republican 106
communitas 92–4
constitutionalism 100
Contributions to Indian Sociology 73
Coolsaet, R. 119n11
Cromwell, O. 88n3

Daily Mail 60
Dalrymple, T. 58
Danish Association, The 52–6, 64
d'Appolonia, A.C. 72
David Horowitz Freedom Centre 61–2
dehumanization 16
deindustrialization 108
democracy 30, 34, 73, 112–14; Swiss challenge 32
Democratic Humanist Centre Party 21
Denmark 2, 9; anti-immigration laws 43–4n10; anti-Islamic activism 41–4, 53–4, 65; between elections (2001–11) 43–66; Cartoon Crisis 44, 49, 60, 98; Commission for Ethnic Equality 44; Commission on Welfare (Ministry of Finance) 47; Common Foreign and Security Policy (CFSP) 45; Constitution 45; crisis of representation 44, 49; islamophobia 41–66; krone and euro 45–6; Law on Foreigners (1983) 54; Liberals 46, 49–50, 65; National Socialist Movement 52–3, 66; National Socialist Workers' Party 52–3; People's Party (DPP) 41–6, 49–51, 56–8, 63–5; Progress Party (PP) 45–6; referendum campaigns 45–6; Social Democrats (SDP) 44n11, 46, 49, 65; Socialist People's party (SF) 45; Stop Islamization (SIAD) movement 41, 52–4, 62–6; street-level thuggery 41–3, 51–3; *Tidehverv* movement (National Church) 41, 54–61, 65; and unemployment benefit (*kontanthjaelp*) 47; voter sentiment and proportional representation 46–51, **47, 48, 50, 51**; welfare benefits and lower taxation 43–4n10, 45–7, 51, *see also* neo-nationalism
dependence 16
depoliticization 98–100, 108
Derrida, J. 3, 77
Descartes, R. 110
Diène, D. 104
dignity 16, 108
Dinet, E., and Ibrahim, S. 2
discrimination 38, 104
diversity 39–40
djellabas 125
domophilia 3, 67, 70–3, 83; Indo-European linguistic equivalent (home/territory) 76–7; nation-state as home 67, 73–81, 84; non-indigenous sense of belonging 75
Doyle, N. 3–5, 19, 26, 44, 49, 53, 97–115; and Ahmad, I. 1–5
dualism 72; God/man 111
Dumont, L. 109
Durkheim, E. 86–8, 94, 111
Dutch (Afrikaners) 83–4

eco-terrorism 118
Eder, K. 89n5
Edict of Nantes (1598) 39
egalitarianism 34
Ekstra Bladet 56
elites 109–10

INDEX

emancipation 106–9, 114
emirs 145–6
English Civil War 88
Enlightenment 11n24, 15, 31, 81, 97, 110, 113–14
equality 10; gender 7, 16, 21
Esposito, J., and Kalin, I. 1
Esposito, R. 92–3, 111
Essid, S. 143–6
ethics 108–9, 112
Eurabia narrative 56–8, 61, 65
Europe: financial crisis 97–8, 101, 104; and national societies disempowerment 99–103
European Commission 101–2
European Constitutional Treaty (2004) 9, 15
European Convention on Human Rights (ECHR) 22, 40
European Counter Jihad Conference 63–5
European Court of Human Rights (ECtHR) 18, 25
European Court of Justice (ECJ) 25, 101
European Economic Community (EEC) 45
European Union (EU) 18, 39, 44–5, 49, 55–7, 98–103, 110–13; Charter of Fundamental Rights 18; citizenship 14–15; Copenhagen membership criteria 112; creation 100; Danish opposition 52; Turkish membership 80
Europe's Encounter with Islam (Mavelli) 110
evangelism 5
exclusion 10, 17; socio-economic 107

face veils 7, 23, 91; bans 19–20; terminology 10
Fairbrook Foundation 62
fanaticism 4, *see also* radicalization
Faroe Islands 45–6
Fascism Past and Present 42n7
Fearmongers: German Fear of Islam (Bahners) 9
female circumcision 60
Fernando, M. 106n51
Fichte, J.G. 75
financial crisis, European 97–8, 101, 104
Fischer, D. 38
Flemish Liberals and Democrats 21
Fokas, E. 78
Fonck, C. 21
foris/foras (outsider/stranger) 67, 76, 80, 83
Forsanne Alizza (Knights of Glory) 133, 148
Fortyuin, P. 98
Foucault, M. 98–9, 107–8, 113–15
Fraktion Rote Armee 120
France 2–25, 57, 72, 78, 101–11, 120; anti-Islamic feelings and political representation 104–8, 148–51; DCRI intelligence agency 148; *Front National* (FN) 104–7; headscarf debates and legislation 9, 14–25, 86, 89, 92, 104; International News 2n9; islamophobia 106–10; and Mohamed Merah 139–51; National Assembly 14–18, 24; political representation crisis 104–7; post-colonialism 14; presidential campaign 97–8; prison case study 116–38; public social order preservation 16–17; *Rapport d'information* (2010) 15–18, 23–4; and religion 2–3; religious beliefs expression law (1905) 105; Republicanism 2, 14–17, 106, 109; Revolution 113; Senate 14–17; tryptich of Liberty, Equality and Fraternity 2, 15–17, 20, 23; *Union pour un Mouvement Populaire* 104–5
Frederick the Great, King of Prussia 81
Free Press Society (FPS) 41, 59–65; impact in Denmark 63; *Sappho* magazine 60–3
freedom 34; of religion 32–4
Freedom Party of Austria 73
fundamentalism 24, 27, 106, 140; behaviour models and French prison case study 116–38; common features 127–8; Islamic 98, 105–7

Gaffney, F.J. 62
Gandhi, Mohandas 74, 82n81
Garsallaoui, M. 146
Gates of Vienna (blog) 61
Gauchet, M. 107–9
Gaza 33
gendering 14
Germany 3, 6–25, 28, 57, 67, 120, 144; *Bundestag* 9; CDU/CSU 12, 23–4; Christian religious affiliation 13, 17; Federal Constitution 12–13, 24; Federal Constitutional Court 6–8, 11–12, 20, 90; headscarf cases, debates and legislation 6–13, 17, 20, 23–5, 92; Hessian Supreme Court 9; *Leitkultur* (foundation culture) 17; Nazi regime 112–14; Turks in Berlin 68–70, 84
Germany's Road to Ruin (Sarrazin) 9
Gingrich, A. 71; and Banks, M. 41–4, 51, 102
Giordano Bruno Society 58, 63
Global Islamic Resistance Call (Suri) 147
globalization 3, 36, 44, 72, 106; impacts 7
Gottschalk, P., and Greenberg, G. 1
Gould, R. 3, 13n31, 17n51
governance 99–103, 114; and civilization claims critique 110–13; economic 101; European and national societies disempowerment 99–103; French political representation crisis 104–7
Governance of Islam in Western Europe (Maussen) 7
governmentality 4, 88, 97–9, 107–9; neo-liberal 98, 107–10, 115
Gravers, A. 52–4, 62–4
Gray, J. 5
Greenberg, G., and Gottschalk, P. 1
Greenland 45–6
Guantanamo Bay 143

Habchi, S. 15
Habermas, J. 88, 102, 110, 114
Hage, G. 83n87
Haider, J. 77
halal meat 60, 105, 123
Hamas 33
Hansen, T., and Brix, H. 57
Harris-Hogan, S., and Andre, V. 4–5, 139–51

INDEX

Hasselbach, O. 64
Hassemer, Justice W. 6–8
headscarf debates and legislation 6–25, 90–1, 104; Christianity-based arguments 13; reasonings and court decisions 7–25; school ban 16, 86, 89, 106n48; terminology 10
Hedegaard, L. 53, 56–66; and Eurabia 56–8, 61, 65; and hate speech 63
Hegel, G.W. 86, 94–5
Hervik, P. 56
hijab 86, 92, 149; as symbol 90–1
Hinduism 69, 81–2; and original inhabitants 81; Right and Babri Masjid 82
Hizbollah 33
Hobbes, T. 86–7, 93–5, 114
Hoffman-Rispal, D. 15
Hollande, F. 2
Holy Jihad Denmark (fatwa) 58
Home (Behrendt) 75
homogeneity 39, 99, 109
Hoover Institution 62
Horowitz, D. 57
Hortefeux, B. 104
hostility 11, 99, 103, 108–10
human rights 6, 9, 14, 30, 34
humanism 112
humiliation 16, 81, 120
Hunt, M. 79

I Still Call Australia Home (Allen) 74–5
Ibn Warraq 58–60
Ibrahim, S., and Dinet, E. 2
identity 6, 10, 16, 90; Christian 97, 106; cultural 98; defence 80, 97; European 73, 77, 97–9, 103, 112; French 14, 17; German shift 11–13; Muslim 78, 90; national 14, 22, 103–5; politics 99; Swiss Muslims 28–9, 35
identity-based rights 102–3
illiberalism 3, 151
immigration 28, 103; Danish opposition 45–6, 52; French proposals 104; North African 107
immunitas (immunization) 85–6, 92–6
imprisonment 16
In the House of War (Hedegaard *et al.*) 58, 63
inclusion 10
India 4, 68–71, 81–2; Allahabad High Court 82; anti-Hindu nationalism 68; Bharatiya Janata Party (BJP) 68–70, 82–4; and *Cochim de Cima* 84; Congress and *Samajwadi* 69; Home Rule Movement 74; Partition of 74; Renaissance 81
Indianization (Madhok) 82
India–Pakistan War (1965) 75
individualism 108–9
individuality 23
inferiority 16, 19
Information 56
Inspire magazine 147
integration 3–4, 15, 25, 35, 82, 101, 106–7, 110, 113
International Free Press Society (IFPS) 61–5

internationalization 14, 34
intolerance 104
Iran 24, 33
Iraq 33, 47, 146
Islam: bashing 123; fundamentalism 98, 105–7; Quran 28, 58, 123, 127, 130; Sharia law 19–20, 31, 62, *see also* Muslims
Islam in the West (articles collection) 56–7
Islamic Movement of Uzbekistan (IMU) 146–7
Islamist Watch (blog) 61
isolation 16
Israel 146
Italy 77–8, 120

Jami, E. 61
Jenkins, P. 144
Jihad Watch (blog) 61–4
Jihadism 4, 118–38; counter- 103; indoctrination pattern 128; leaderless 119; neo- and Mohamed Merah 139–51, *see also* radicalization
Jordan 146
Joris, E., and Riederer, K. 34
Journal of Ethnic and Migration Studies 7
Judaism 35, 55, 105–6, 148; Arab hatred 142; and homeland 74
Jund al Khilafah (JaK) 146
Jyllands-Posten 60

Kafka, F. 70, 84
Kalin, I., and Esposito, J. 1
Kant, I. 98, 110
Kaya, A. 98, 103, 108
Kelek, N. 11
Kelkal, K. 145
Kepel, G. 145, 148–50
Khader, N. 59, 63
Khosrokhavar, F. 4–5, 18, 22, 25, 116–38, 145, 149–50
Khurshid, S. 82
Köchler, H. 38–9
Koenig, M. 8
Koningsveld, P., and Shadid, W. 7
Koselleck, R. 80, 88, 113
Krarup, S. 53–9, 64–6; Islam objections 55n63
Kundnani, A. 57
Kuwait 24

laïcité doctrine 2, 9, 14, 19, 23–5, 92–4, 98, 105–8, 139–40; Commission on the Application of the Principle 14; impact on Merah 141–51; in prisons 120, 123, 128, 134–7
Lang, J. 35
Langballe, J. 53, 58–9, 63–5
language 10; divide 20, 23
Le Pen, M. 105–6, 149
Lebanon 33, 67, 146
Lefort, C. 114
legislation *see* headscarf debates and legislation
legitimacy 97–115; political crisis 99–100

INDEX

Lenzin, R. 29, 35
Leviathan (Hobbes) 87
Lewis, B. 93
liberalism 1, 43, 70, 73; Indian 81–2
liberty, personal 7
Libya 33
Lienemann, W. 30–5, 39–40
Life of Muhammad – the Prophet of Allah, The (Dinet and Ibrahim) 2
Lisbon Treaty (2007) 101
Littman, G. 57–8, 61–3
Locke, J. 88
Luca, L. 15
Ludin affair 14
Luther, M. 71
Lynde and Harry Bradley Foundation 62

Maastricht Treaty (1992) 45; rejection by Denmark and opt-outs 45–6
McCormick, J.P. 109n63
Machiavelli 113–14
McKenna, M. 75n37
Madhok, B. 82
Mali 2
Mamdani, M. 2
Manning, E. 73
marginalization 16
Marianne and le voile intégral (Hoffman-Rispal) 15, 21
Marxism 108, 145
Mas, R. 14
Maussen, M. 7
Mavelli, L. 92–4, 98–9, 115; civilizational claims critique 110–13
May, N. 61
media 32–3, 43, 90, 147; and FPS 59–64; staging 91; Swiss image 32, 36
Merah, Abdelghani 140–2
Merah, Abdelkader 142–3, 146–7; scooter theft and complicity 147
Merah, Mohamed 4–5, 127n37, 133, 134n48, 139–51; behaviour shift 147–8; family and upbringing 140–3; French society impact 139, 143–51; March attacks (2012) 139–40; prison and radicalization 140–8; Salafism and *laïcité* 141–51; theft and Allah 144–6; travel and study 146; use of social media 147–8
Merah, Souad 142–3, 147
Merkel, A. 17, 17n51, 102
Mesbah, Y. 147
migration 4, 36; cheap labour 70, 99
minaret building ban (Switzerland) 3, 26–40; consequences and counter-policy prospects 37–9; issues and responses 34–7; threat and power symbolism 29–33; vote outcome shock 35
Minkenberg, M., and Willems, U. 6–7, 25
missionaries 2
modernity 86, 98, 107–10, 113
Moreton-Robinson, A. 75

Mort du multiculturalisme allemand, La (Gould) 17n51
Moussaoui, Z. 132n44
Mühlheim, M. 37
Mujahideen 148
mullahs 33
Müller, A. 23
Muller, F., and Tanner, M. 29–31, 34
multiculturalism 7, 17, 25, 57
Muslims 1–5; anti- activism 3; converts and reverts 107; cultural topics (articles) 58–64, **59**; Egyptian 37; as European identity threat 73, 77; garment prohibitions 6–25; good and bad 2, 71; Islam/Islamism 39, 42; negative global image 33–4; presence as religious freedoms threat 32–4; Shi'a 28; Sufis 28; Sunni 28; in Switzerland 28–9; Turkish Alevites 28
Muslims Go Home (YouTube) 78–9

Narasimha Rao, P.V. 68
national societies, disempowerment 99–103
nationalism 68, 72–4, 77, 109, 112
nativism 102
naturalization 77
Nazi regime 112–14
neo-conservatism 98
neo-jihadism: lone wolf 143; Mohamed Merah support 139–51; zero attacks recorded (France) 144
neo-liberalism 107–10
neo-Marxism 54
neo-nationalism 41–66, 102–3; Danish history 44–6; political impact 49–51; sentiment extent (voter) 46–9, **47, 48, 50, 51**
neo-Nazi movement 118, 137
neologism 2
Netherlands 61, 78, 97, 101, 104, 144
Neumann, P. 145–6
neutrality 34; as Swiss principle 39
Nietzsche, F. 55
niqab 10, 15–21, 86, 92
North Atlantic Treaty Organization (NATO) 39, 80
Norway 61, 72, 84

obloquy 17
Operation Defensive Shield 57
Orientalism (Said) 71
Otherness 4, 71, 74, 82, 95, 98, 110–12; Europe 8; political and cultural 10; symbolic demarcation 89–92

Pakistan 70, 143, 146; –India War (1965) 75
Palestine 145
Parallel Societies (Schiffauer) 11
patriotism 72
Penitentiary Service of Probation and Insertion (SPIP) 125–6
Phillips, M. 60

INDEX

Pind, S. 59, 63
Pipes, D. 60–2
pluralism 110
populism 4, 99, 102–3; right-wing 100
praest 53n47
Pratt, D. 3, 9, 26–40
Prinzig, M., and Blum, R. 34
prisons 4; conditions and officer stress 124–7; facilities 122–4; frustration and ideologization 121–4; headscarf as 20; high turnovers (inmate/staff) 124–7; intelligence officers 126n34; and *Les Barbus* (bearded ones) 117, 137; long-term 123–5, 134; methodology and choice (Fleury-Mérogis/Fresnes) 117–18; Muslims and inmate statistics 121, 122n25, 124; North African and West Indian prisoners 135–7; overcrowding 124–7; radicalization (French case study) 116–38; religious service leaders 122–6; short-term 123–7, 133; system as serious radicalizing influence 145; understaffing 124–7; women 118
Project for the New American Century 62
Protestantism 28, 105; Federation of Swiss Churches 36

Qantas 75
Quebec model 22
Quran 28, 58, 127, 130; torn covers 123

racism 29, 41, 65, 104, 107, 145; biological 52; cultural 44
radicalization 87; attitudes and manifestations 130–1; charismatic (radicalizer) 120, 128–9, 144; common features 127–8; duo and trio associations and characters (strong/fragile) 121, 129–33, 148; and fundamentalism 127–9; internet-based 121; introversion and silent expression 129–31; and Mohamed Merah 139–51; and prison recruitment activities 129–30; prisoner target types 129–30; in prisons (French case study) 116–38; rebellion and solitary confinement 133–5; Salafi advent 123, 135–8; and seekers 146; and self-radicalizer 133; theories 118–21
rai (music) nightclub 147
Rajapaksa, M. 79
Ramadan, T. 91
Rana, J. 1
Raoult, E. 15n39
ratio legis 21
Ratzinger, Cardinal (Pope Benedict XVI) 112
Rau, J. 90–1
Reagan, R. 61
Reformation 86
Rehman, S. 61
rejection 10
religion 2–3, 13, 17, 105; freedom of 32–4; Switzerland 26–8, 35–40
Religion within the Limits of Reason Alone (Kant) 110

religiosity 4, 89, 135; affiliation 104n39; alien 6, 11, 22; notion of 87; and state relationship 7
Richard Mellon Scaife Foundation 62
Riederer, K., and Joris, E. 34
rights: human 6, 9, 14, 30, 34; identity-based 102–3; women's 10, 18–19, 105
Romania 112
Rose, F. 60
Roy, O. 14, 22, 105–6, 112, 145, 150
Roy, R. 81–2
Rudd, K. 71
Ruggie, G. 72
Runnymede Trust report (1997) 2

Sahraoui, Sheikh Abdelbaki 127n37
Said, E. 71
Salafism 5, 123, 130, 137–8, 141–51; characteristics 135–6; as counter-Islamist radicalization force 135–8; heroism 143–5; and *laïcité* 148–51; *Sheikhi* 5
Salvatore, A. 3–4, 85–96, 115
Sanskrit 76
Sarkozy, N. 16n47, 79, 91, 102–5
Sarrazin, T. 9–11n24
Saudi Arabia 24, 33; Ministry of the Interior 143
Sauer, B. 10n19
Scandinavia 97
Schavan, A. 17n52
Schiffauer, W. 11
Schlegel, A.W. 72
Schlegel, F. 72
Schuman, R. 112
secessionism, regional 42n8
secularism 3–4, 8, 34, 73, 80, 85–98, 105, 110, 128, 149; as *immunitas* domain 85–6, 92–6; post-Christian power twist 86, 94–6; republican 107; symbolic demarcation 86, 89–92
securitization 1, 14, 21–3, 87, 99
security 103–5, 108
Sedgewick, M. 2–3, 9, 41–66
self-determination 109
self-preservation 93
separatism 82
Shadid, W., and Koningsveld, P. 7
Sharia law 19–20, 31, 62
Sheikh, J. 52n40
Shooman, Y., and Spielhaus, R. 22
Shultz, G. 61–2
Siegel, P.C. 120n18
Singer, B., and Weir, L. 113–14
Smith-Spark, L. 140
sociability 84
social compact 25
Social Democrats (SPD) 12, 23
solidarity 84, 108; negative 111; and sovereignty 86–95
Somers, B. 21
El-Sonbati, J. 37

INDEX

Soros, G. 42, 63
South Africa 83–4
sovereignty 13, 44, 77, 99–100, 114; decisionist legacy 91; and solidarity (Leviathan *vs.* Behemoth) 86–95
Spectator 57–8
Spencer, R. 61–4
Spielhaus, R. 11; and Shooman, Y. 22
Sri Lanka 68, 71, 79
Stasi Commission 89–92, 104–6
Steinemann, B. 31, 103n33
Steyn, M. 57–61
stigmatization 8, 17, 145, 149
Stoler, A. 75n38
Stop Islamization of America (SIOA) 62–3
sublation 86, 94–5
submission 16, 20
subservience 16
suicide 124
supermodernity 79–80
supremist ideology 134
Suri, Abu Mus'ab 130, 147
Switzerland 3, 9, 26–40; Census (2000) 28; and Citizen's Initiative 26–40; Council of Religions 35–40; Democratic Union of the Centre (SVP/UDC) 29–31; Federal Constitution and matters of religion 26–8, 39–40; Federal Council 30; Federal Democratic Union (EDU/EDF) 29–31; Federation of Protestant Churches (SEK-FEPS) 30; Muslim population and statistics 28–9; state and peace-keeping responsibility 27–8, *see also* minaret building ban (Switzerland)
symbolism 13, 19, 90–5
Syria 146

Taliban 33
Tamil militancy 79
Tanner, M., and Muller, F. 29–31, 34
territorialities rebundling 72
terrorism 1–2, 24, 33, 49, 56–7, 133; Algerian 4; attack arrests 144; in India 69; Islamic 4; Madrid bombing (2005) 81; Mumbai attacks (2008) 142n33; since 9/11 attacks 35, 47, 58, 98, 120; suicide bombing 143; and terrorist influence in jail 120; War on 57
Tibi, B. 78; Euro-Islam 82
Tietze, N. 8, 24
tolerance 34, 39, 81
totalitarianism 89, 113
Touraine, A. 89
Triadafilopoulos, T. 25
Troïka 101
Trumpbour, J. 81
Turkey 28, 80, 112, 146
Turks in Berlin 68–70, 84
Twitter 148

Uganda 71
unification 4; European 4
United Kingdom (UK) 67, 72, 78; Independence Party (UKIP) 50
United Nations (UN) 39; Special Rapporteur 104
United States of America (USA) 77; Constitution 77; Department of Homeland Security 78; Middle East Forum 60

values 6, 9–10, 20, 24; Christian-Occidental 9, 13, 17, 31; Enlightenment 97; Flemish 21; French Republican 14–17, 20–3; irreconcilability 15; Swiss–Islamic comparison 32, 34
Van Gogh, T. 98
vanda matram (anti-Muslim song) 69
Vester, H. 44n11
victimization 4
videos 147
Voile intégral, le 10n20, 14–23; Commission of Enquiry (National Assembly) 18; Fact Finding Mission 15; values invocations and death metaphors 16
Voltaire 81
Von Engelhardt, D. 72n16

Walzer, M. 73
Warsi, Baroness S. 1
Waziristan 146
Weber, M. 111
Weir, L., and Singer, B. 113–14
welfare state 101; Danish 43–4n10, 45–7, 51
Werbner, P. 4
Westergaard, K. 60–1, 65
Western Anatolia 67
Westphalia Treaty (1648), and order 77, 86–9, 95
Why I Am Not A Muslim (Ibn Warraq) 58–60
Wiese, K. 11
Wilders, G. 61, 71, 77, 80, 98
Wilkinson, P. 148
Willems, U., and Minkenberg, M. 6–7, 25
Winter, Y. 33
Wodak, R. 10
Wohlrab-Sahr, M. 91n7
women's rights 10, 18–19, 105
Woolsey, R.J. 61–2
World Council of Churches (WCC) 38
World War II (1939–45) 4
Wren, K. 44

xenophobia 29, 41, 99, 104

Yemen 33
YouTube 148
Yugoslavia 28

Al-Zawahiri, A. 80–1
Zuber, V. 149